Microsoft Access 7.0a for Windows® 95

GW00762333

Timothy J. O'Leary
Linda I. O'Leary

Microsoft Access 7.0a for Windows® 95
International Editions 1996

Exclusive rights by McGraw-Hill Book Co–Singapore for manufacture and export. This book cannot be re-exported from the country to which it is consigned by McGraw-Hill.

1 2 3 4 5 6 7 8 9 0 BJE UPE 9 8 7 6

ISBN 0-07-049106-2

Library of Congress Catalog Card Number 95-82268

Information has been obtained by The McGraw-Hill Companies, Inc. from sources believed to be reliable. However, because of the possibility of human or mechanical error by our sources, The McGraw-Hill Companies, Inc., or others, The McGraw-Hill Companies, Inc. does not guarantee the accuracy, adequacy, or completeness of any information and is not responsible for any errors or omissions or the results obtained from use of such information.

When ordering this title, use ISBN 0-07-114545-1

Printed in Singapore

Contents

Database Overview

A word processor helps you enter and manipulate text. An electronic spreadsheet helps you enter and analyze numerical data. A database program helps you enter and manage information or data electronically.

A database is an organized collection of related data. Before computers, most data was kept on paper. Paper records organized in a filing cabinet by name or department are a database. The information in a telephone book, organized alphabetically, is a database. A school's records of teachers, classes, and students are a database.

With computers, the same data can be entered and stored electronically, typically on a disk. The big difference is that an electronic database can manipulate—sort, analyze, and display—the data quickly and efficiently. What took hours of time to pull from the paper files can be extracted in a matter of seconds using a computerized database.

Relational Database Programs

Most microcomputer database programs are relational. These programs organize data into tables consisting of columns (called fields) and rows (called records). For example, a state's motor vehicle department database may have a table consisting of personal information on each vehicle owner, such as their name and address. Each vehicle owner's personal information forms a record. Each record may consist of the following fields of data: first name, last name, street, city, state, zip code, Social Security number, and license number.

The tables in a relational database are related or linked to one another by a common field. For example, the motor vehicle department may have a second database table containing data for each vehicle owned and a third on outstanding citations. The data in one table can then be linked to the data in another table by using a common field, such as the owner's Social Security number or driver's license number. The ability to link database tables creates a relational database (see example below). Relational databases allow you to create smaller and more manageable database tables, since you can combine and extract data between tables.

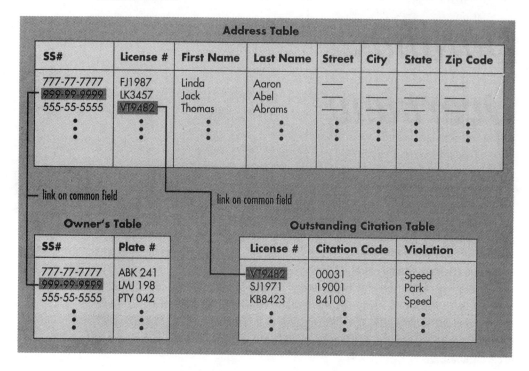

Advantages of Using a Database Program

One of the main advantages of using a computerized database program is the ability to quickly locate specific records. Once you enter data into the database table, you can quickly search the table to locate a specific record based on the data in a field. In a manual system, you can usually locate a record by knowing one key piece of information. For example, if the records are stored in a file cabinet alphabetically by last name, to quickly find a record you must know the last name. In a computerized database, even if the records are sorted or organized by last name, you can still quickly locate a record using information in another field.

A computerized database also makes it easy to add and delete records from the table. Once you locate a record, you can edit the contents of the fields to update the record or delete the record entirely from the table. You can also add new records to a table. When you enter a new record, it is automatically placed in the correct organizational location within the table.

Another advantage of using a computerized database system is its ability to arrange or sort the records in the table according to different fields of data. You can organize records by name, department, pay, class, or any other category you need at a particular time. This ability to produce multiple table arrangements helps provide more meaningful information. The same records can provide information to different departments for different purposes.

A fourth advantage is the ability to analyze the data in a table and perform calculations on different fields of data. Instead of pulling each record from a filing cabinet, recording the piece of data you want to use, and then performing the calculation on the recorded data, you can simply have the database program perform the calculation on all the values in the specified field. Additionally, you can ask questions or query the table to find only certain records that meet specific conditions to be used in the analysis. Information that was once costly and time-consuming to get is now quickly and readily available.

Another advantage of database programs is the ability to quickly produce reports ranging from simple listings to complex, professional-looking reports. You can create a simple report by asking for a listing of specified fields of data and restricting the listing to records meeting designated conditions. You can create a more complex professional report using the same restrictions or conditions as the simple report, but you can display the data in different layout styles, or with titles, headings, subtotals, or totals.

In manual systems, there are often several file cabinets in different departments containing some of the same data. With a computerized database system, more than one department can access the same data. Common updating of the data can be done by any department. The elimination of duplicate information saves both space and time.

Database Terminology

Database: An organized collection of related data that is stored as a table in a file.

Delete: To remove a record from the database file.

Edit: To change or update the data in a field.

Field: The smallest item of information about a record, such as last name.

Query: To ask questions of the database, which then displays only those records meeting specified conditions.

Record: A collection of related fields, such as Social Security number, first name, and last name.

Report: A printed and formatted presentation of specified fields of data for specified records in the file.

Search: To locate a specific record in a file.

Sort: To arrange the records in a file in a specified order.

Table: A collection of data that is organized into columns (fields) and rows (records).

Case Study for Labs 1–5

As a recent college graduate, you have accepted your first job with The Sports Company, a chain of sporting goods stores located throughout the United States. The company has recently purchased Microsoft Access 7.0a for Windows 95, and you have been assigned the job of updating their current recordkeeping system for employee records.

In Lab 1 you will learn how to design and create the structure for a computerized database and how to enter and edit records in the database. You will also print a simple report of the records you enter in the database file.

In Lab 2 you will continue to build, modify, and use the employee database of records. You will learn how to sort the records in a database file to make it easier to locate records. Additionally, you will create a customized form to make it easier to enter and edit data in the database file.

In Lab 3 you will learn how to query the database to locate specific information. You will also learn how to use and link multiple tables and calculated fields.

In Lab 4 you will learn how to use Microsoft Access 7.0 to create weekly and monthly employee status reports. You will use multiple files to create several different reports. The reports will display selected fields of data for the records in the database. It will also include a report title, subgroupings of data, and descriptive text to clarify the meaning of the data in the report.

Lab 5 demonstrates the sharing of data between Access and Word. You will learn to import an Access table into a Word document and to perform a mail merge using an Access table as the data source.

Before You Begin

To the Student

The following assumption has been made:

- Microsoft Access 7.0 or 7.0a for Windows 95 has been properly installed on the hard disk of your computer system.

- The data disk contains the data files needed to complete the series of labs and practice exercises. These files are supplied by your instructor.

- You have completed the Windows 95 lab module or you are already familiar with basic Windows 95 terminology and procedures. You can also refer to the Windows 95 Review at the end of the manual if you need to review these procedures.

To the Instructor

The following assumption has been made:

- Microsoft Access 7.0 or 7.0a has been installed using the default program settings. These settings are in effect each time the program is loaded.

Microsoft Office Shortcut Bar

The Microsoft Office Shortcut Bar (shown below) may be displayed automatically on the Windows 95 desktop. Commonly, it appears in the upper right section of the desktop; however, it may appear in other locations, depending upon your setup. The Shortcut Bar on your screen may display different buttons. This is because the Shortcut Bar can be customized to display other toolbar buttons.

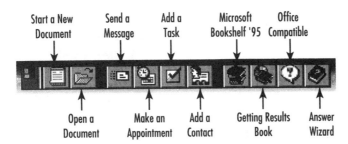

The Office Shortcut Bar makes it easy to open existing documents or to create new documents using one of the Microsoft Office applications. It can also be used to send e-mail, add a task to a to-do list, schedule appointments using Schedule+, or access Office Help.

Instructional Conventions

This text uses the same instructional conventions as described in the Introduction to the Labs at the beginning of the Windows 95 lab module.

In brief, they are:

- Command sequences you are to issue appear following the word "Choose:." Each menu command selection is separated by a /. If the menu command can be selected by typing a letter of the command, the letter will appear underlined.

- Commands that can be initiated using a button and the mouse appear following the word "Click:." The menu equivalent and keyboard shortcut appear in a margin note when the action is first introduced.

- Anything you are to type appears in bold text. Instructions you are to follow appear in blue.

Creating a Database

1

Somewhere at home, or maybe in your office, you probably have a file cabinet or desk drawer filled with information. Perhaps you have organized the information into drawers of related information, and further categorized that information into file folders. This is a database.

As organized as the information in your file may be, it still takes time to manually leaf through the folders to locate the information you need—and imagine how much more time it takes in a large company. Now, however, you can use an electronic database management system to store, organize, access, manipulate, and present information in a variety of ways.

In this lab you will learn how to design and create a computerized database using Access 7.0a for Windows 95, and you will quickly appreciate the many advantages of a computerized database.

Concept Overview

The following concepts will be introduced in this lab:

1. Database
A database is an organized collection of information.

2. Templates
Every Access database is based on a template file that includes pre-defined settings that are used to define the default characteristics of a database.

3. Database Development
The development of a database follows several steps: planning, creating, editing, form design, data analysis, report design, and printing.

4. Objects
A database file is made up of many different types of objects, such as tables, forms, and reports.

5. Views
Access allows you to view objects in your database in several different window formats called views. There are several basic views: Design view, Datasheet view, Form view, Print Preview, and Layout Preview.

6. Field Names
A field name is used to identify the data stored in a field.

7. Data Types
The data type defines the type of data the field will contain. There are nine data types with Text as the default data type.

8. Field Properties
Field properties are a set of characteristics that are associated with each field, such as field size.

9. Primary Key
A primary key is a field that uniquely identifies each record. It is usually the first field in the table.

10. Table Names
Each table in a database must have a unique name and it should be descriptive of the data to be stored in the table.

11. Data Entry Guidelines
The data you enter in a field should be typed exactly as you want it to appear and in a consistent form.

12. Modes
Two modes of operation, Navigation mode and Edit mode, control how you can move through and make changes to the data in a table.

13. Column Width
Column width refers to the size of each column in Datasheet view. It controls the amount of data you can see in the column.

CASE STUDY

As a recent college graduate, you have accepted your first job as a management trainee with The Sports Company. This company consists of a chain of sporting goods stores located in large metropolitan areas across the United States. The stores are warehouse oriented, discounting the retail price of most items 15 percent. They stock sporting goods products for all the major sports; basketball, football, tennis, aerobics, and so on.

Your training program emphasis is on computer applications related to retail management. You have been assigned to the Southwest regional office as an assistant to the Regional Manager. Your primary responsibility is to convert the current database of employee information to an electronic database.

Part 1

Loading Access

The Sports Company plans to use Microsoft Access version 7.0a for Windows 95 to create several different databases of information.

Concept 1: Database

A **database** is an organized collection of information. For example, the information in your address book is a database. Databases are used in a wide variety of professions. Salespeople may use a database to keep track of sales leads, customers, and payments. Real estate agents use property listings that are maintained on a database to find properties that match the needs of their clients. Schools use databases to maintain information about their students, teachers, and employees.

Most microcomputer database programs store information in tables. A **table** contains data about a specific topic that is organized into vertical columns and horizontal rows. A table is made up of records. A **record** is all the information about one person, thing, or place. For example, all the address data on one person is a record. A single record is contained in one row of the table. Each item of related information in a record is called a field. A **field** is the smallest item of information about a record, such as a person's name. For example, the customer table might contain fields such as First Name, Last Name, Street, City, State, and Zip Code. Each field is displayed in a column of the table.

A simple example of a database is shown below. This database consists of two tables of data, a Customer table and an Orders table. The Customer table contains information about the customers, such as their names and addresses. The Orders table contains data about the orders placed by each customer.

Access, like most database programs, is **relational**. This means that you can define a relationship between tables by having common data in the tables. The two tables below both have the customer number as the common data. The common data lets you extract and combine data from multiple tables.

Customer Table

Customer No.	Name	Address	City	State	Zip Code
1250-42	Mid-Atlantic	411 E. Industrial Way	Rockville	MD	20737
1544-55	East Coast	62 51st Ave.	New York	NY	10010
1642-22	North Lakes	42 Lake View Dr.	Chicago	IL	60616
1699-21	South Pacific	123 Monterey Dr.	Redlands	CA	92373
1725-99	South West Ind.	1762 Prickly Pear Dr.	Santa Fe	NM	87501

one record → (pointing to row 1544-55)

common information defines relationship between tables

one field (pointing to City column)

Orders Table

Order No.	Customer No.	Sales Date
C125	1544-55	10/28/99
C126	1725-99	9/14/99
C127	1544-55	11/04/99
C128	1699-21	5/15/99

If necessary, turn on your computer and put your data disk in drive A (or the appropriate drive for your system).

The Windows 95 desktop screen should be displayed. To start Access 7.0 for Windows 95,

Choose: **Start/Programs**

The Programs menu should display the Microsoft Access option.

Choose: Microsoft Access

When you start the program, the Microsoft Access startup dialog box shown in Figure 1-1 is displayed.

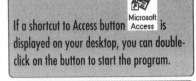

If a shortcut to Access button is displayed on your desktop, you can double-click on the button to start the program.

If the Microsoft Office Suite is on your system and the Office Shortcut Bar is displayed, you can click the Start a New Document button, select Blank Database, and choose OK, to load Access.

Figure 1-1

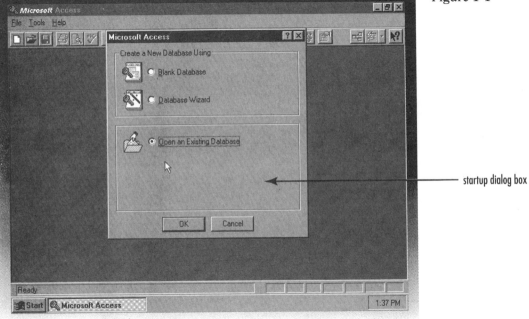

startup dialog box

The startup dialog box allows you to create a new database or open an existing database. You will use this feature in later labs. To close the startup dialog box,

Choose: Cancel

Refer to the Sizing Windows section in the Windows 95 Review for information on this feature.

The Microsoft Access application window is displayed (see Figure 1-2 in the box below).

If necessary, maximize the Access window.

Examining the Access 7.0 Window

As you can see in Figure 1-2, many of the Access window features are common to the Windows 95 environment. Among those features are a title bar, menu bar, toolbar, ▭ Minimize, ▭ Restore, and ▣ Close buttons, icons, and mouse compatibility. You can move and size Access windows, select commands, use Help, and switch between files and programs just like in Windows 95. Your knowledge of how to use Windows 95 makes learning about and using Access 7.0 for Windows 95 much easier. The taskbar at the bottom of the screen displays the button for the open application.

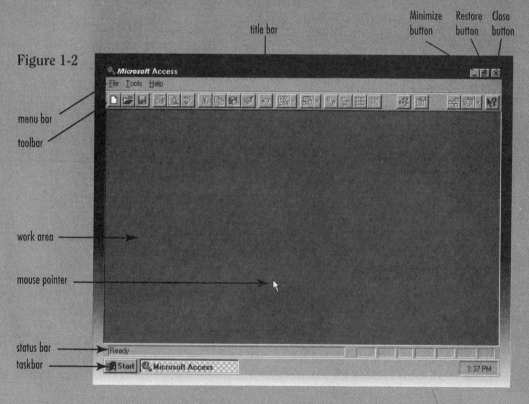

Figure 1-2

The initial Access window that is displayed is called the **startup window**. Its menu bar contains only three menus that are available for this window. If a menu is not appropriate for a given window, it does not appear on the menu bar.

The toolbar contains many of the same buttons as you have seen in toolbars in other Windows 95 applications. Many, however, are specific to Access. Only the first two buttons, ▭ New Database and ▭ Open Database, and the last one, ▭ Help, are currently available for use. All the other buttons are dimmed, indicating they are unavailable. There are 19 toolbars in Access. Most toolbars appear automatically as you perform different tasks and open different windows. The toolbar operates just like Windows 95 toolbars.

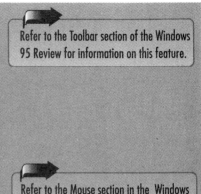

Refer to the Toolbar section of the Windows 95 Review for information on this feature.

The center area of the window is the **work area** where different Access windows display as you are using the program.

Just below the work area the status bar provides information about the task you are working on and the current Access operation. In addition, the status bar displays messages such as button and command descriptions to help you use the program more efficiently. Like the menu bar and toolbar, the information in the status bar changes as you work.

The mouse pointer appears as an arrow ▷ and operates as in Windows. It also changes shape depending on the task you are performing or its location in the window.

Refer to the Mouse section in the Windows 95 Review, for information on this feature.

Learning About Access

Before you create the employee database, you decide to create a simple database using a Database Wizard to learn about many of the Access features. A **Database Wizard** is an automated feature that guides you step by step to create a new database.

Click: ☐ New Database

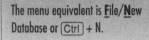

The menu equivalent is <u>F</u>ile/<u>N</u>ew Database or Ctrl + N.

The New tab dialog box displays two tabs, General and Databases. The General tab displays one icon, 📇. Selecting this icon allows you to create your own custom database from scratch without using a Database Wizard.

To use a Database Wizard to create a database, open the Databases tab.

The New dialog box on your screen should be similar to Figure 1-3.

Refer to the Dialog Box section of the Windows 95 Review for information on this feature.

tabs   selection of database templates

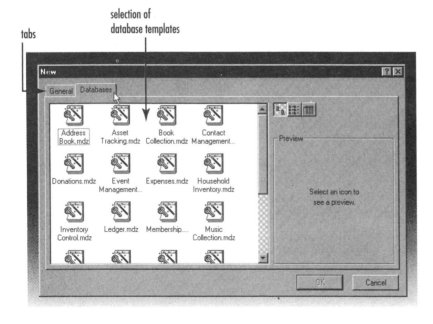

Figure 1-3

This tab displays 22 icons representing many types of databases that can be created using the Database Wizard. These predesigned databases, called templates, give you a head start in creating many different types of databases.

Concept 2: Templates

Every Access database is based on a database template file. A **template** file includes predefined settings that are used to define the default characteristics of a database. The basic settings used to create a database are stored in the Blank Database template. There are 22 other database template files that contain settings and specifications that are designed to help you create the many different types of databases. These templates include settings that guide you step by step to help you create tables, custom entry forms, and professional reports. Once you have created a database using a template, it can be modified to meet your specific needs.

You will use the Database Wizard to create a database to hold name and address information.

Double-click: Address Book.mdz

The File New Database dialog box on your screen should be similar to Figure 1-4.

Figure 1-4

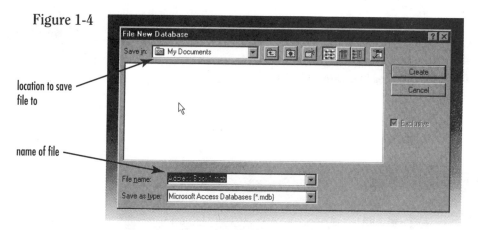

location to save
file to

name of file

Refer to the Saving Files and Naming Files sections of the Windows 95 Review for information on these features.

If the location is already correctly specified, skip this step.

The first step in creating a database is to name the database file. You need to specify in the dialog box the location and name of the database file. By default Access sets the location as the My Documents folder on the C drive. To change this to your data disk in the A drive, from the Save-in drop-down list,

Select: **A: (or the appropriate drive for your system)**

The suggested filename Address Book1 is acceptable. To create the file,

Choose: Create

The Database Wizard has started, and it displays a brief preview window with information about what the Address Book database will store. To continue,

Choose: Next >

The Database Wizard dialog box on your screen should be similar to Figure 1-5.

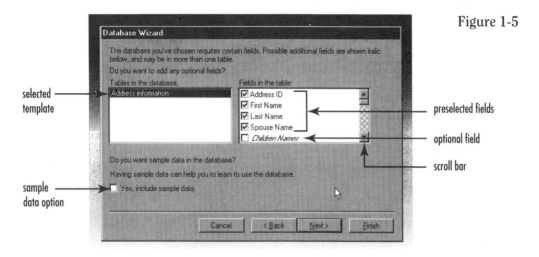

Figure 1-5

This and the next several Database Wizard dialog boxes will ask you a series of questions that you need to complete to create the database. The window currently displayed is used to create the structure of the table. To do this you need to specify the fields to be used in the table.

The address table template already includes all the fields that are checked in the Fields in the Table list box. Some fields are not checked and can be added to the table if desired.

Scroll the list box using the scroll bar to see additional fields.

This window also asks if you want sample data in your database to show you how to use the database. In response to this question,

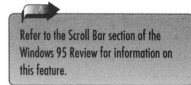

Refer to the Scroll Bar section of the Windows 95 Review for information on this feature.

Select: Yes, include sample data.

To accept the default selected fields and move on to the next window,

Choose: Next >

The dialog box on your screen should be similar to Figure 1-6.

Figure 1-6

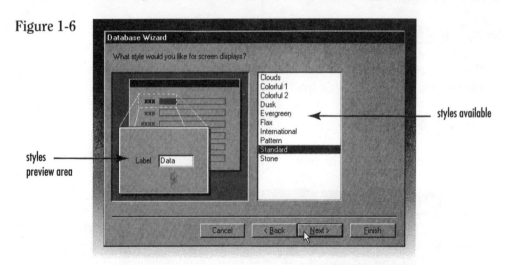

In this window you are asked to select a screen display style to display the information.

> This lab will use the Colorful 2 style.

Select each style and preview how it will appear. Then select a style of your choice.

Choose: Next >

> You will learn about creating reports in Lab 4.

The next window asks you to pick a design for printed reports.

Preview and select a design of your choice.

> This lab will use the Casual design.

Choose: Next >

The title "Address Book" is proposed for the title of the database, and you are asked if you want to include a picture. To accept the defaults,

Choose: Next >

The final Database Wizard window is displayed.

Choose: Finish

Two progress bars show you what parts of the database are being created and their progress toward completion. When completed, your screen should be similar to Figure 1-7.

> It may take your computer system several minutes to create the database.

Figure 1-7

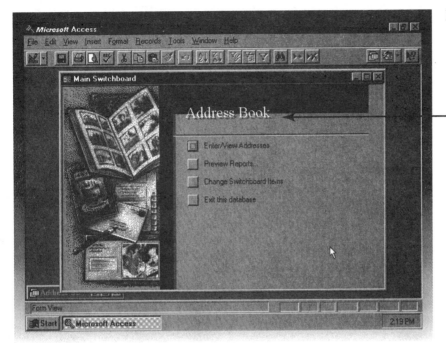

address book
Switchboard

Many databases include a startup window, called the **Switchboard**, that makes it easy to move from one task to another in the database. The Switchboard is automatically created whenever a Database Wizard is used.

Choose: Enter/View Addresses

The window on your screen should be similar to Figure 1-8.

Figure 1-8

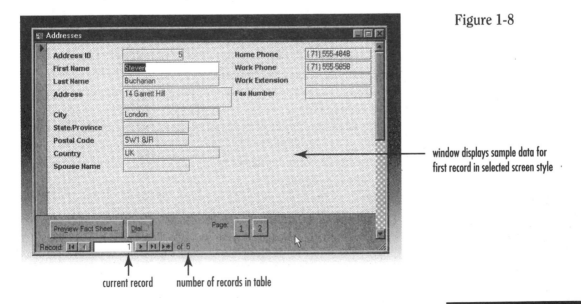

window displays sample data for
first record in selected screen style

current record   number of records in table

The window displays the sample data for the first record of five records in the Address Book table. The record is displayed in the screen display style you selected. To see the second page of information for this record,

You could also press [Page Down].

Click:

Click ⊠ to close the window.

Close the window.

The Switchboard window is displayed again. To see the reports that are generated from the table data,

Choose: Preview Reports

You can generate four different reports from the information in the database. To see a report of the data organized by last name,

Choose: Preview the Addresses by Last Name Report

The window on your screen should be similar to Figure 1-9.

Figure 1-9

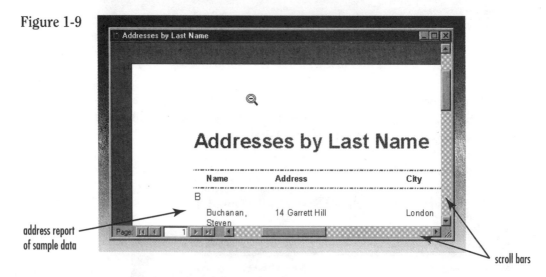

address report of sample data

scroll bars

To see the entire report, scroll the window using the scroll bars.

All five sample records that are in the table are arranged in alphabetical order by last name.

Close the window.

Choose: Return to Main Switchboard
Choose: Exit this database

Note: If you are ending your lab session now, follow the directions on page DB50 to exit Access. When you begin Part 2, load Access and close the startup dialog box.

Now that you have learned how a database is created with the Database Wizard and have seen many of the database features available in Access, you are ready to begin creating the database for The Sports Company employees.

Part 2

Planning a Database

The Sports Company plans to use Access to maintain several different types of databases. The database you will create will contain information about each Sports Company employee. Other plans for using Access include keeping track of preferred customers and inventory. To keep the different types of information separate, the company plans to create a database for each group.

Because Access does not have a database template that you can use to create the employee database, you will need to create a custom database from scratch. Creating a new database follows several basic steps.

Concept 3: Database Development

The development of a database follows several steps: planning, creating, entering data, editing, form design, data analysis, report design, and printing.

Planning: The first step in the development of a database is to understand the purpose of the database and to plan what information your database should hold and the output you need from the database.

Creating: After planning the database, you create tables to hold data by defining the table structure.

Entering Data: Once a table has been set up, you enter the data to complete each record.

Editing: Making changes to your tables is called editing. While entering data, you are bound to make typing and spelling errors that need to be corrected. This is one type of editing. Another is to revise the structure of the tables by adding, deleting, or redefining fields of information.

Creating Forms: After you create a table, you can create a form for easier data entry. Forms also make editing easier.

Analyzing Data: To analyze the data stored in your tables, you ask questions, called queries, of the table data. The results of queries allow you to look at only selected data or to view data in a specific format. For example, you can examine data to determine the largest sales, monthly birthdays, or to make projections.

Creating Reports: To be able to print your data in a professional and attractive format, you create reports. Reports allow you to customize the appearance of the data.

Previewing and Printing: The last step is to print a hard copy of the database or report. This step includes previewing the document onscreen as it will appear when printed. Previewing allows you to check the document's overall appearance and to make any final changes needed before printing.

You will find that you will generally follow these steps in order as you create your database. However, you will probably retrace steps as the final database is developed.

Your first step is to plan the design of your database tables: how many tables, what data they will contain, and how they will be related. You need to decide what information each table in the employee database should contain and how it should be structured or laid out.

You can obtain this information by analyzing the current recordkeeping procedures used throughout the company. You need to understand the existing procedures so your database tables will reflect the information that is maintained by different departments. You should be aware of the forms that are the basis for the data entered into the department records, and of the information that is taken from the records to produce periodic reports. You also need to find out what information the department heads would like to be able to obtain from the database that may be too difficult to generate using their current procedures.

After looking over the existing recordkeeping procedures and the reports that are created from the information, you decide to create several separate tables of data in the database file that have the employee number as the common field. Creating several smaller tables of related data rather than one large table makes it easier to use the tables and faster to process data. This is because you can join several tables together as needed.

You decide to include the data currently maintained in the personnel folder on each employee in one table. After having carefully considered the available data on each employee, you decide to include the following fields:

Employee ID
Date Hired
Last Name
First Name
Street
City
State
Zip Code
Birth Date

Creating a Database

Now that you have decided on the fields you want to include in the table, you are ready to create a new database using the Blank Database template.

Click: New Database

Select: Blank Database

Choose: OK

The File New Database dialog box is displayed. Just as when you created the Address Book database, the first step is to specify a name for the database file and the location where you want the file saved. By default Access uses the name db1. You want the program to store the database on your data disk using the name Employee Data.

> The number in the default filename on your screen may be different.

Replace the default database filename with Employee Data.

If necessary, change the location to save your file to the drive containing your data disk.

> The filename can be entered in either upper-case or lowercase letters, but the name will be stored and displayed the way you type it.

Choose: Create

After a few seconds, the Database window shown in Figure 1-10 is displayed.

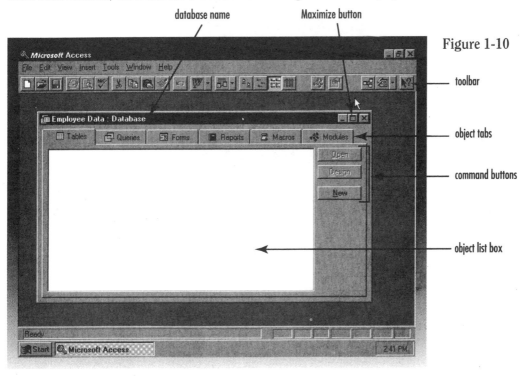

Figure 1-10

The name of the database, Employee Data, followed by the name of the window, appears in the window title bar. The Database window is the command center. From this window you can create and use any database object.

Concept 4: Objects

An **object** is an item made up of many elements, such as a table or report, that you create, select, and manipulate as a unit. The **object tabs** at the top of the Database window are used to select the type of object you want to use. The currently selected object tab is Tables. The table object is the basic unit of a database and must be created first, before any other types of objects are created. The object list box under the object tabs normally displays a list of objects associated with the selected object tab. The Tables object list box is empty because you have not created any tables for this database yet.

Access displays each different type of object in its own window. You can display multiple object windows in the work area; however, you cannot open more than one database file at a time.

Creating a Table

After naming the database, your next step is to create the table to hold the employee data. The only available command button in the Database window is New. This is because you cannot use any of the other buttons in this window until you have created a database table. To begin creation of the table,

Choose: New

The New Table dialog box on your screen should be similar to Figure 1-11.

Figure 1-11

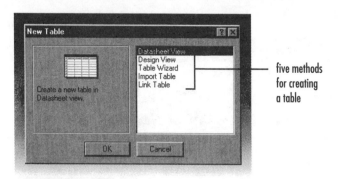

five methods for creating a table

> Access includes 19 different Wizards that can be used to create different Access objects.

This dialog box has five options that provide different ways to create a table. The first three, Datasheet View, Design View, and Table Wizard, are the most commonly used. The Table Wizard option starts the Table Wizard feature. This feature lets you select from 45 predesigned database tables and creates a table for you based upon your selections. The Datasheet and Design View options open different view windows in which you can create a new custom table from scratch.

Concept 5: Views

Access allows you to view the objects in your database in several different window formats, called views. The basic views are described in the table below.

View	Use
Design view	Allows you to create a table, form, query, or report.
Datasheet view	Provides a row-and-column view of the data in tables, forms, and queries.
Form view	Displays your data in a form.
Print Preview	Displays a form, report, or datasheet as it will appear when printed.
Layout Preview	Uses sample data to demonstrate the appearance of a completed report.

Each view includes it own menu and toolbar designed to work with the object in the window. The views available change depending on the type of object you are using.

To create the table in Design view,

Select: Design View

Choose: ▭ OK ▭

The table Design view window on your screen should be similar to Figure 1-12.

The Table Design View Window

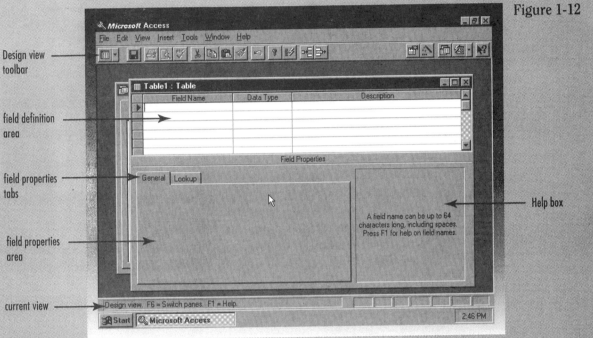

Figure 1-12

Design view toolbar

field definition area

field properties tabs

field properties area

current view

Help box

In table Design view you can create and modify the structure of your table. This view automatically displays a Table Design toolbar that contains the standard buttons as well as buttons that are specific to the table Design view window. These buttons are identified below.

> The status bar displays the name of the view you are using.

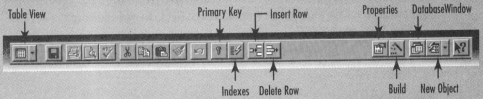

Table View   Primary Key   Insert Row   Properties   DatabaseWindow

Indexes   Delete Row   Build   New Object

The table Design view window is divided into two areas. The upper portion consists of a grid with three columns: Field Name, Data Type, and Description. Each row is where a field is defined by entering the required information in each of the columns.

The lower area consists of two tabs: General and Lookup. This area will display the field properties or settings associated with the selected field. To the right of the tabs is a Help box that provides information on the task you are performing in the window.

Defining the Table Structure

The insertion point is positioned in the Field Name box of the first row ready for you to define the first field. The Help box displays a brief description of the rules for entering a valid field name.

> ### Concept 6: Field Names
>
> A **field name** is used to identify the data stored in the field. A field name should be descriptive of the contents of the data to be entered in the field. It can be up to 64 characters long and can consist of letters, numbers, spaces, and special characters, except a period (.), an exclamation point (!), an accent grave (`), and brackets ([]). You also cannot start a field name with a space. Examples of field names might include Last Name, First Name, Address, Phone Number, Department, Hire Date, or other words that describe the data. It is best to use short field names to make the tables easier to manage.

The first field of data you will enter in the table is the employee number. The employee number is assigned to each employee when hired. Each new employee is given the next consecutive number, so no two employees can have the same number. It is a maximum of four digits.

You have decided to name the field "Employee Number." The name can be typed in either uppercase or lowercase letters. Access will display the characters exactly as you enter them. To enter the first field name in the Field Name column,

Type: **Employee Number**

As you type, the insertion point moves to show you where the next character you type will appear. The ▶ to the left of the field name indicates the current field. This is the field that will be affected by your next action.

Since the data you will enter in this field is a maximum of four characters, you decide to change the field name to Employee ID, so the field name is closer in size to the data that will be entered in the field. To edit the entry,

The `Backspace` key will delete the characters to the left of the insertion point, and the `Delete` key will delete characters to the right.

Press: `Backspace` **(6 times)**
Type: **ID**

Now that the field name is correct, to indicate you are finished entering the field name,

Press: `←Enter`

The window on your screen should be similar to Figure 1-13.

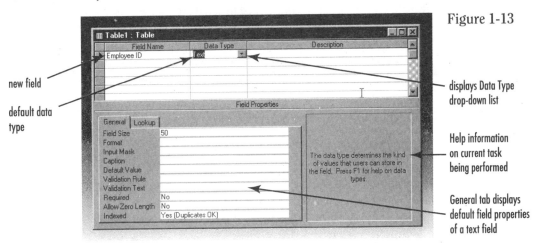

Figure 1-13

new field

default data type

displays Data Type drop-down list

Help information on current task being performed

General tab displays default field properties of a text field

The insertion point has moved to the Data Type column where the default data type of "Text" is automatically entered.

Display the Data Type drop-down list.

Concept 7: Data Types

The **data type** defines the type of data the field will contain. Access uses the data type to ensure that the right kind of data is entered in a field. It is important to choose the right data type for a field before you start entering data in the table. You can change a data type after the field contains data, but if the data types are not compatible, such as a text entry in a field whose data type accepts numbers only, you may lose data. Nine data types are described below.

Data Type	Description
Text	Text entries (words, combinations of words and numbers, numbers that are not used in calculations) up to 255 characters in length (this is the default). Names and phone numbers are examples of Text field entries. Text is the default data type.
Memo	Text that is variable in length and usually too long to be stored in a Text field. A maximum of 64,000 characters can be entered in a Memo field.
Number	Digits only. Number fields are used when you want to perform calculations on the values in the field. Number of Employees is an example of a Number field entry.
Date/Time	Any valid date. Access only allows dates from January 1, 100 to December 31, 9999. Access correctly handles leap years and checks all dates for validity. You cannot set the field size in Date/Time fields.
Currency	Exactly like Number fields, but formatted to display decimal places and a currency symbol. You can change the number of decimal places but not the field size in a Currency field.
AutoNumber	A unique, sequential number that is automatically incremented by one whenever a new record is added to a table.
Yes/No	Accepts only Yes/No, True/False, or On/Off entries. You cannot change the field size for a Yes/No field.
OLE Object	An object, such as a graphic (picture), sound, document, or spreadsheet, that is linked to or embedded in a table.
Lookup Wizard	A list of options you choose from another table in the database. Choosing this data type starts the Lookup Wizard.

Even though a field such as the Employee ID field may contain numeric entries, unless the numbers are used in calculations the field should be assigned the Text data type. This allows other characters, such as the parentheses or hyphens in a telephone number, to be included in the entry. Also, by specifying the type as Text, any leading zeros (for example, in the zip code 07739) will be preserved, whereas leading zeros in a Number type field are dropped (which would make this zip code incorrectly 7739).

To close the Data Type list and accept Text as the data type,

Press: Esc

In the bottom half of the screen, notice that the General tab displays the default field properties associated with a Text data type.

Concept 8: Field Properties

Field properties are a set of characteristics that are associated with each field and that vary with the type of field. Each data type has a different set of field properties. Setting field properties enhances the way your table works. Some of the more commonly used properties and their functions are described below.

Property	Function
Field Size	Sets the maximum size of data that can be entered in the field.
Format	Specifies how data displays in a table and prints.
Input Mask	Simplifies data entry and specifies how data displays in a text box.
Decimal Places	Displays a specific number of places after the decimal point when using a format for a Number or Currency field.
Caption	Specifies a field label other than the field name.
Default Value	Automatically fills in a certain value for this field in new records as you add to the table. You can override a default value by typing a new value into the field.
Validation Rule	Limits data entered in a field to values that meet certain requirements.
Validation Text	Specifies the message to be displayed when a field, control, or record does not satisfy the associated Validation Rule.
Required	Specifies whether or not a value must be entered in a field.
Allow Zero Length	Specifies whether or not an entry containing no characters is valid.
Indexed	Sets a field as an index field (a field that controls the order or records). Speeds up searches on fields that are searched frequently.

The field size setting for Text fields can be between 1 and 255 spaces.

The **field size** property controls the number of characters that can be entered in a field. By default Access sets a Text field size to 50. Although Access uses only the amount of storage space necessary for the text you actually store in a Text field, setting the field size to the smallest possible size can decrease the processing time required by the program. Additionally, if the field data to be entered is a specific size, setting the field size to that number restricts the entry to the maximum number.

Since the Employee ID field will contain a maximum of four characters, you want to change the field size from the default of 50 to 4. With the mouse pointer shaped as an I-beam,

Click: **Field Size property box**

The insertion point moves to the Field Size property box, and the Help box displays information about this feature.

Replace the default entry with the number 4.

This is the only field property that you want to change. To continue defining the Employee ID field, you will enter a description of the field in the Description text box. Although it is optional, a field description makes the table easier to understand and update because the description displays in the status bar when you enter data into the table.

Click in the Description text box for the Employee ID field, and enter the description "A unique 4-digit number assigned to each employee as hired."

Next you want to make this field a primary key field.

> You can also press F6 to switch between the upper and lower areas of the dialog box.

> Clicking on the left edge of a field or property text box when the mouse pointer is a ↗ will select the entire entry in the box.

> Text in the Description box scrolls horizontally as needed.

Concept 9: Primary Key

A **primary key** is a field that uniquely identifies each record. Most tables have at least one field that is selected as the primary key. The data in the primary key field must be unique for each record. For example, a table that contains the Social Security number for each employee could be selected as the primary key field because the data in that field is unique for each employee. Other examples of a primary key field are parts numbers or catalog numbers.

A primary key prevents duplicate records from being entered in the table and is used to control the order in which records display in the table. This makes it faster for databases to locate records in the table and to process other operations. The primary key is also used to create a link between tables in a database.

Although any field can be the primary key field, traditionally the first field or group of fields in the table is the primary key field.

To define the field as a primary key,

Click: **Primary Key**

> The menu equivalent is <u>E</u>dit/Primary <u>K</u>ey.

Your screen should be similar to Figure 1-14.

Figure 1-14

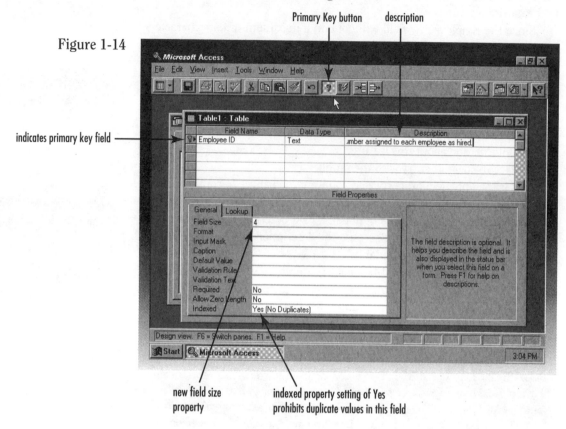

indicates primary key field

Primary Key button   description

new field size property

indexed property setting of Yes prohibits duplicate values in this field

The primary key icon appears in the column to the left of the field name, showing that this field is a primary key field. Now that this field is the primary key field, also notice that the indexed property setting has changed to Yes (No Duplicates). This setting prohibits duplicate values in a field.

You have completed defining the first field. To move to the next row to define the second field,

Press: ⏎Enter

The second field will contain the date the employee was hired. To enter the second field name,

> Using Tab⭲ or → has the same effect as pressing ⏎Enter; it moves the insertion point to the next column to the right. ⇧Shift + Tab⭲ or ← moves the insertion point to the left one column.

Type: **Date Hired**
Press: Tab⭲ **or** →

Access is waiting for you to define the data type. This field will display the date the employee started working at The Sports Company in the form of month/day/year. The data type that will display the date in this format is Date/Time. From the Data Type list box,

> You can also enter the data type by typing the first character of the data type option. For example, you can enter "d" for Date/Time.

Select: **Date/Time**

The default field properties for the selected data type are displayed. This time you want to change the format or layout of the field.

Switch to the Field Properties section and select the Format property box. Open the drop-down list of Format options.

The window on your screen should be similar to Figure 1-15.

Figure 1-15

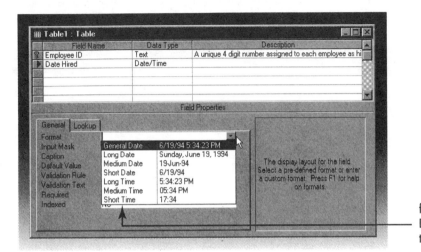

format options for Date/Time data type field

The seven Date/Time format options and examples of how they will appear are displayed. You want the date to display as mm/dd/yy, regardless of how the date is entered. To set this format,

Choose: Short Date

Next you want to enter a description for this field. Because there are many ways a date can be entered, you want the description to describe the acceptable types of date entries.

In the Description text box of the Date Hired field, enter the description "Acceptable entry formats are 4/4/97, Apr 4, 1997, or April 4, 1997."

Press: ⏎Enter

Now you are ready to enter the third field. This field will hold the employee's last name. To specify the name of the third field,

Type: Last Name
Press: ⏎Enter

The default data type, Text, is acceptable for this field. Additionally, because the length of all the names is not known, you will leave the field size setting at its default size of 50.

Press: ⏎Enter

In this case you feel the field name is descriptive of the field contents and a description is not needed. To leave the description blank,

Press: [←Enter]

In the same manner, enter the information shown below for the next seven fields. If you make a typing mistake use [Backspace] and [Delete] to correct errors.

Field Name	Data Type	Description	Field Size/Format
First Name	Text		50
Street	Text		50
City	Text		50
State	Text	A 2-character abbreviation entered in all capital letters.	2
Zip Code	Text	Use the 9-digit zip code if available.	10
Phone Number	Text	Enter using the format (555)555-5555.	15
Birth Date	Date/Time	Acceptable entry formats are 4/4/97, Apr 4, 1997, or April 4, 1997	Short Date

> You can copy the description from the Date Hired field to the Birth Date field. Refer to the Cut, Copy, and Paste section of the Windows 95 Review for information on this feature.

When you have completed the seven additional fields, the window on your screen should be similar to Figure 1-16.

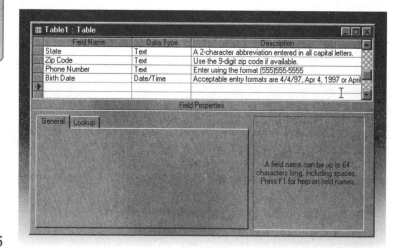

Figure 1-16

> You may need to scroll the Field Name grid to see the Last Name field.

After looking over the table, you decide to change the field sizes of the Last Name, First Name, and City fields to 20-character entries.

Move to: **any column in the Last Name field**

The field properties for the Last Name field are displayed.

Change the field size to 20.

In a similar manner, change the field size for the First Name and City fields to 20. Carefully check your screen to ensure that each field name and field type were entered correctly and make any necessary corrections.

Saving the Table Structure

Once you are satisfied that your field definitions are correct, you can save the table design by naming it.

Click: Save

In the Save As dialog box, you want to replace the default name, Table1, with a more descriptive name.

> ### Concept 10: Table Names
>
> Each table in a database is assigned a name. The name should be descriptive of the contents of the table. A table name follows the same set of standard naming conventions or rules that you use when naming fields. The name can be a maximum of 64 characters and can be any combination of letters, numbers, spaces (except at the beginning of the name), and special characters except a period, exclamation point, accent grave (`) and brackets ([]). It is acceptable to use the same name for both a table and the database, although each table in a database must have a unique name. The table name can be entered in either uppercase or lowercase letters. Avoid long names that may be difficult to remember.

You will save the table using the table name Employees.

Type: Employees
Choose: OK

The table structure is saved with the database file. You have created a table named Employees in the Employee Data database file.

Note: If you are ending your lab session now, close the Design window and exit Access following the directions on page DB50. When you begin Part 3, load Access and open the file Employee Data from your data disk. Then choose Design from the Tables tab of the Database window.

Part 3

Switching Views

Now that the table structure is defined and saved, you can enter the employee data into the new table. You enter and display data in the table in Datasheet view.

> Clicking in the text entry areas, when the mouse pointer shape is an I-beam, displays the insertion point at that location. The insertion point can also be moved within a text box using → or ←.

> To delete an entire field, move to the field and choose **E**dit/Delete **R**ow.

> The menu equivalent is **F**ile/**S**ave or Ctrl + S.

Clicking the ⬛ next to the Table View button will display a drop-down list of available views.

The menu equivalent is **V**iew/Data**s**heet.

The Table View button is a toggle button that switches between the different available views. The graphic in the button changes to indicate the view that *will be* displayed when selected. The Table View button appears as 🔲 for Design view and 🔲 for Datasheet view.

To view the Employees table in Datasheet view,

Click:  **Datasheet View**

The table is now displayed in Datasheet view as shown in Figure 1-17.

The Datasheet View Window

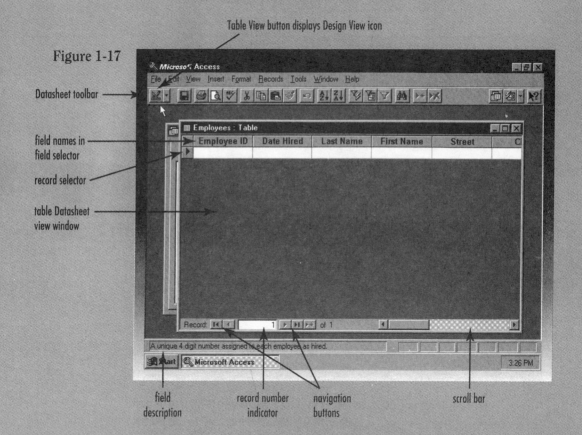

Figure 1-17

In table Datasheet view you can enter and delete records and edit field data in existing records. The menu bar contains menus that can be used in this view. In addition, this view automatically displays a table Datasheet toolbar containing the standard buttons as well as buttons that are specific to the table Datasheet view window. These buttons are identified below.

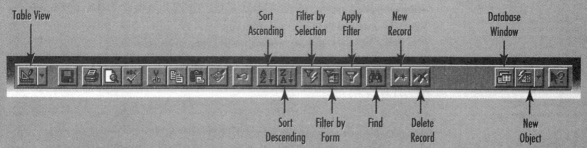

Datasheet view displays the table data in a row-and-column format. The field names you entered in Design view are displayed as column headings in the window. This area is called the **field selector** for each column. Below the field selector is a blank row where you will enter the data for a record. To the left of the row is the **record selector column**. The triangular symbol ▶ in this column indicates which record is the **current record**.

The bottom of the window displays a horizontal scroll bar, navigation buttons, and a record number indicator. The **record number indicator** shows the number of the current record as well as the total number of records in the table. Because the table does not yet contain records, the indicator displays "Record: 1 of 1" in anticipation of your first entry. On both sides of the record number are the **navigation buttons**. You use these buttons to move through the records with a mouse. You use the scroll bar to scroll the window horizontally to display fields that are out of view.

> You will learn about using the navigation buttons in Lab 2.

The status bar displays the description for the field where the insertion point is located. Since it is in the Employee ID field column, the description you entered for this field is displayed.

Only the first few field names are visible because there is not enough space in the Employees table window to display all the fields.

To see more information in the window, maximize the window.

Now that you can see several more field columns, you notice that the column widths are all the same, even though you set different field sizes in the Design window. This is because the Datasheet view window has its own default column width setting. You will learn how to change the column width later in this lab.

> Refer to the Sizing Windows section of the Windows 95 Review for information on this feature.

Entering Data

The insertion point is positioned in the Employee ID field, indicating the program is ready to accept data in this field. The description in the status bar provides the user with information about the data that should be entered in the field. The data you will enter for the first record is as follows:

Field Name	Data
Employee ID	1151
Date Hired	October 14, 1990
Last Name	Anderson
First Name	Susan
Street	4389 S. Hayden Rd.
City	Mesa
State	AZ
Zip Code	85205-0346
Phone Number	(602)555-1950
Birth Date	June 14, 1965

When you enter data in a record, it should be entered accurately and consistently as described in the Data Entry Guidelines concept box.

Concept 11: Data Entry Guidelines

The data you enter in a field should be typed exactly as you want it to appear. This is important because any printouts of the data will display the information exactly as entered. It is also important to enter data in a consistent form. For example, if you decide to abbreviate the word "Street" as "St." in the Street field, then it should be abbreviated the same way in every record where it appears. Also be careful not to enter a blank space before or after a field entry. This can cause problems when using the table to locate information.

If data is entered accurately and in a consistent manner, it is easier to locate information and to create accurate reports from the data in the table. Access also provides a variety of ways to control how data is entered in a database, which help ensure accurate data entry. You will learn about many of these features next and in Lab 2.

To enter the Employee ID for the first record,

Type: 1

Your screen should be similar to Figure 1-18.

record entry in progress

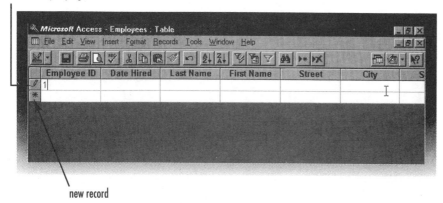

Figure 1-18

new record

Notice that as soon as you entered the 1, a second row appears in the table. The * symbol in the record selector column indicates the end of the table or where a new record can be entered. In addition, the current record symbol has changed to a *↗*. This symbol means the record is in the process of being entered or edited and has not yet been saved.

To complete the Employee ID field data,

Type: **151**

To see what happens if you try to enter a number that is larger than the field size of 4 that you defined in Design view,

Type: **0**

The program will not accept an entry that is larger than the field size. The field size restriction helps control the accuracy of data by not allowing an entry larger than specified. To complete the entry,

Press: ⟨←Enter⟩

The data is entered in the field, and the insertion point has moved to the next field, Date Hired. To enter the date hired (it is intentionally incorrect) for this record,

Type: **10/41/90**
Press: ⟨←Enter⟩

Your screen should be similar to Figure 1-19.

Figure 1-19

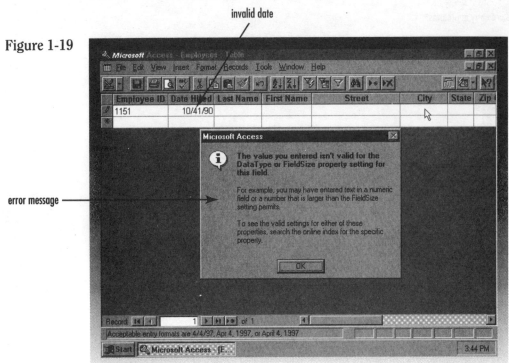

invalid date

error message

An informational message box is displayed. Access automatically performs some basic checks on the data as it is entered based upon the field type specified in the table design. This is another way Access helps you control data entry to ensure the accuracy of the data. In this case the date entered (10/41/90) could not be correct because there cannot be 41 days in a month. To close the message box,

Choose: OK

Editing Data

Next you need to edit the entry to correct it. How you edit data in Access depends on which mode of operation is active.

Concept 12: Modes

Two modes of operation, Edit mode and Navigation mode, control how you can move through and make changes to data in a table.

Edit mode is used to enter or edit data in a field. It is automatically active when you enter a new record into a table. In Edit mode the insertion point is displayed in the field so you can edit existing data or enter new data. To activate Edit mode in an existing record, click on the field when the mouse pointer is an I-beam. To position the insertion point in the field entry, click at the location where you want it to appear. The keyboard keys shown in the table below can also be used to move the insertion point in Edit mode and to make changes to individual characters in the entry.

Navigation mode is used to move from field to field and to delete an entire field entry. In Navigation mode the entire field entry is selected (highlighted), and the insertion point is not displayed. You move from field to field using the keyboard keys shown in the table below. The (Delete) key will clear the entire entry. To activate Navigation mode, point to the left edge of a field and click when the pointer displays as ⬦. Navigation mode is automatically active when you move using the keyboard keys. To switch between modes using the keyboard, press (F2).

Key	Edit Mode	Navigation Mode
← →	Moves insertion point left and right one character	Moves highlight forward or back a field
Home	Moves insertion point to beginning of field	Moves highlight to first field in current record
End	Moves the insertion point to the end of the field	Moves highlight to last field in current record
Delete	Deletes character to right of insertion point	Deletes entire field contents
Backspace	Deletes character to left of insertion point	Deletes entire field contents
Tab ⇄	Ends Edit mode and highlights next field	Moves highlight to next field

Because you are entering data in a new record, Edit mode is active.

Position the insertion point and use the (Backspace) or (Delete) key to delete the error. Then change the 41 to 14.

> If you want to cancel your changes in the current field, press (Esc).

Press: (↵Enter)

The corrected date is accepted, and the insertion point moves to the Last Name field. Because no description was entered for this field, the status bar displays "Datasheet view" instead of a field description. To enter the last name data,

> You can also press [Tab ⇆] to move to the next field. [→] will move to the next field if the insertion point is at the end of the entry or you are in Navigation mode.

> The fields will scroll on the screen as you move to the right.

Type: **Anderson**
Press: [←Enter]

Enter the data shown below for the remaining fields, typing the information exactly as it appears.

Field Name	Data
First Name	Susan
Street	4389 S. Hayden Rd.
City	Mesa
State	AZ
Zip Code	85205-0346
Phone Number	(602)555-1950
Birth Date	6/14/65

To complete the record,

Press: [←Enter]

Your screen should be similar to Figure 1-20.

Figure 1-20

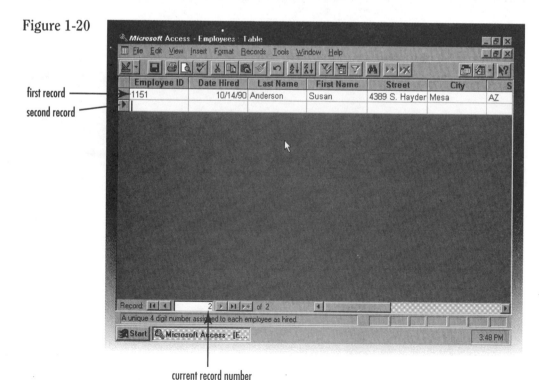

first record

second record

current record number

The data for the first record is complete. The insertion point moves to the first field on the next row and waits for input of the employee number for the next record. As soon as the insertion point moves to another record, the data is saved on the disk and the number of the new record appears in the status bar. The second record was automatically assigned the record number 2.

Next you will check the first record for accuracy.

Point to the left end of the Employee ID field for the first record. When the mouse pointer appears as ⊕, click the mouse button.

The entire field is selected (highlighted), and you have activated Navigation mode. If you type, the entire selection will be replaced with the new text. If you press → or ←, you will move field by field through the record.

Press: → **(4 times)**

The Street field is selected. To change to Edit mode to check the entire field contents,

Click: the Street field with the mouse pointer shape as an I-beam

The insertion point is positioned in the field, and you have activated the Edit mode. Now you can edit the field contents if necessary.

Then, because the field column is too small to see the entire field contents, you want to position the insertion point at the end of the address so that you can check the rest of the entry.

Press: End

The text scrolled in the field, and the insertion point is positioned at the end of the entry.

If the entry contains an error, correct it.

To move to the next field,

Press: Tab ↹

Check the first record for accuracy and edit as needed. You can also use the horizontal scroll bar to scroll the window to check fields that are not visible.

> You could also press ↑ to move up one record to change to Navigation mode.

> Refer to Concept 12 to review the Access modes.

> You can also press ←Enter or Tab ↹ to move to the next field in Navigation mode.

> You could also press F2 to switch to Edit mode.

> ⇧ Shift + Tab ↹ moves one field to the left.

Enter the following data for the second record.

Field Name	Data
Employee ID	0434
Date Hired	June 4, 1991
Last Name	Long
First Name	William
Street	947 S. Forest St.
City	Tempe
State	AZ
Zip Code	86301-1268
Phone Number	(602)555-4494
Birth Date	April 20, 1970

To complete the record,

Press: ⏎Enter

Your screen should be similar to Figure 1-21.

Figure 1-21

second record

When you have completed entering the data for the second record, Access is ready for you to enter the data for the third record.

Check the second record for accuracy and edit it if necessary.

Adjusting Column Widths

As you have noticed, some of the fields (such as the Street field) do not display the entire entry, while other fields (such as the State field) are much larger than the field's column heading or contents. This is because the default column width in Datasheet view is not the same size as the field sizes you specified in Design view.

Concept 13: Column Width

Column width refers to the size of each field column in Datasheet view. The column width does not affect the amount of data you can enter into a field, but does affect the data that you can see on the screen. The default column width in Datasheet view is set to display 15.6667 characters. You can adjust the column width to change the appearance of the datasheet. If you shorten the column width, you do not delete the actual data, even if the contents of the field are no longer visible on the datasheet. It is usually best to adjust the column width so the column is slightly larger than the column heading or longest field contents, whichever is longer. Do not confuse column width with field size. Field size is a property associated with each field; it controls the maximum number of characters that you can enter in the field. If you shorten the field size, you can lose data already entered in the field.

First you will increase the width of the Street field so the entire address will be visible.

Point to the right border line of the column heading of the Street field name.

When the mouse pointer changes to ↔, you can drag the right column border line in either direction to increase or decrease the column width. As you drag, a column line appears to show you the new column border. When you release the mouse button, the column width will be set.

Drag the right column border of the Street field column to the right until you think it will be large enough to display the field contents. If it is too wide or not wide enough, adjust it again.

Your screen should be similar to Figure 1-22.

> You can also adjust the column width to a specific number of characters using the Column Width command in the Format menu.

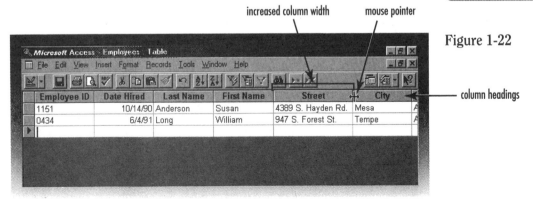

Figure 1-22

The width of the Street column has increased to the size you specified.

Rather than change the widths of all the other columns individually, you can select all columns and change their widths at the same time. To select multiple columns, point to the column headings in the field selector area of the first column you want to select.

Point to the Employee ID field name, but do not click yet.

When the mouse pointer changes to ↓, it indicates that the column will be selected if you click on it. To select multiple columns, click and, without releasing the mouse, drag across the column headings.

DATABASE

> The fields will scroll horizontally in the window as you drag to select the columns.

>
> The keyboard equivalent for selecting columns is to select a field entry in the first column, press Ctrl + Spacebar, then press ⇧Shift + the appropriate arrow key to select multiple columns.

selected columns ───

Drag to the right across all column headings to select them all.

Use the scroll bar to bring the first field column back into view in the window.

Your screen should be similar to Figure 1-23.

mouse pointer

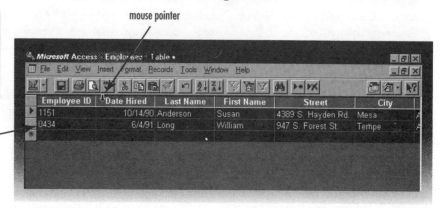

Figure 1-23

> Clicking the box to the left of the first field name will select the entire table.

> The menu equivalent is Format/Column Width/Best Fit. The Column Width command is also on the shortcut menu when an entire column is selected.

Multiple columns are highlighted. Now, if you were to drag the column border of any selected column, all the selected columns would change to the same size. In addition to dragging the column border to increase or decrease the column width, you can double-click the column border to activate the Best Fit feature. The **Best Fit** feature automatically adjusts the column widths of all selected columns to accommodate the longest entry or column heading in each of the selected columns.

Double-click any selected column border with the mouse pointer as ↔.

Your screen should be similar to Figure 1-24.

Figure 1-24

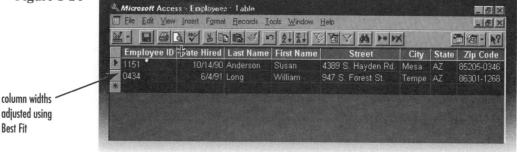

column widths adjusted using Best Fit

> Clicking anywhere will clear the selection.

The columns have been automatically adjusted to different sizes depending on their contents.

Now that you can see the complete contents of each field, check each of the records again and edit any entries that are incorrect.

Add the following record to the table as record 3.

Field	Date
Employee ID	0434
Date Hired	April 12, 1991
Last Name	Bergstrom
First Name	Drew
Street	8943 W. Southern Ave.
City	Mesa
State	AZ
Zip Code	84101-8475
Phone Number	(602)555-8201
Birth Date	August 7, 1961

To complete the record,

Press: ⏎Enter

As soon as you complete the record, the error message dialog box shown in Figure 1-25 is displayed.

Figure 1-25

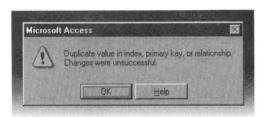

This message displays whenever a duplicate value is located in a key field. The key field is Employee ID. You realize you were looking at the employee number from the previous record when you entered the employee number for this record. The employee number should be 0234. To clear the message,

Choose: OK

Change the Employee ID for record 3 to 0234.

Press: ↓

The record is accepted with the new employee number. Notice that the address for this record does not fully display in the Street field. It has a longer address than either of the other two records.

> Double-click the right border of a field to best-fit a single column.

To fully display the Street field data, best fit the field again.

When you add new records in Datasheet view, the records display in the order you enter them. However, they are stored on disk in order by the primary key field. You can change the display on the screen to reflect the correct order by using the ⇧Shift + F9 key combination.

Press: ⇧Shift + F9

Your screen should be similar to Figure 1-26.

Figure 1-26

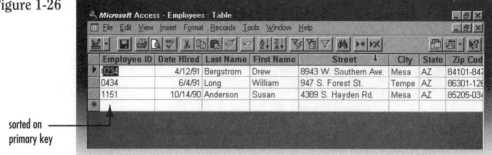

sorted on primary key

The records are now in order by employee number. This is the order determined by the primary key field.

> The table order is also updated when you close and then reopen the table.

Using the Data Entry Command

Next you want to add several more employee records to the table. Another way to add records is to use the Data Entry command on the Records menu. This command does not display existing records, which prevents accidental changes to the table data. To use the Data Entry command,

Choose: Records/Data Entry

Your screen should be similar to Figure 1-27.

Figure 1-27

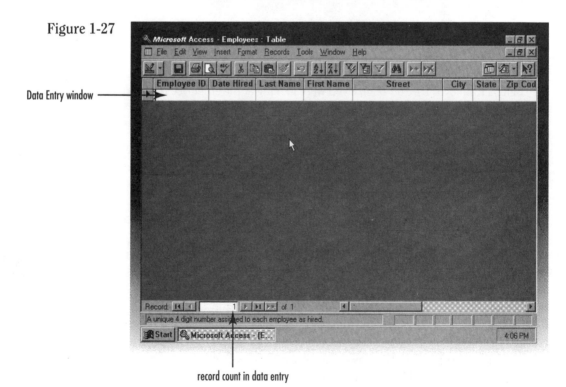

Data Entry window

record count in data entry

The existing records are hidden and the only row displayed is a blank row where you can enter a new record. The status bar displays "1 of 1." This number reflects the number of new records as they are added in Data Entry rather than all records in the table.

Enter the two records below.

Field	Record 1	Record 2
Employee ID	0839	0728
Date Hired	August 14, 1991	July 15, 1991
Last Name	Artis	Toroyan
First Name	Jose	Lucy
Street	358 Maple Dr.	2348 S. Bala Dr.
City	Scottsdale	Tempe
State	AZ	AZ
Zip Code	85205-6911	85301-7985
Phone Number	(602)555-0091	(602)555-9870
Birth Date	December 10, 1963	March 15, 1961

Enter a final record using your first and last name. Enter 9999 as your employee number and the current date as your date hired. The information you enter in all other fields can be fictitious.

Best Fit the City column and any other columns that do not fully display the field contents.

Check each of the records and correct any entry errors.

Now that you have entered the new records, you can redisplay all the records in the table. To do this,

Choose: Records/Remove Filter/Sort

Your screen should be similar to Figure 1-28.

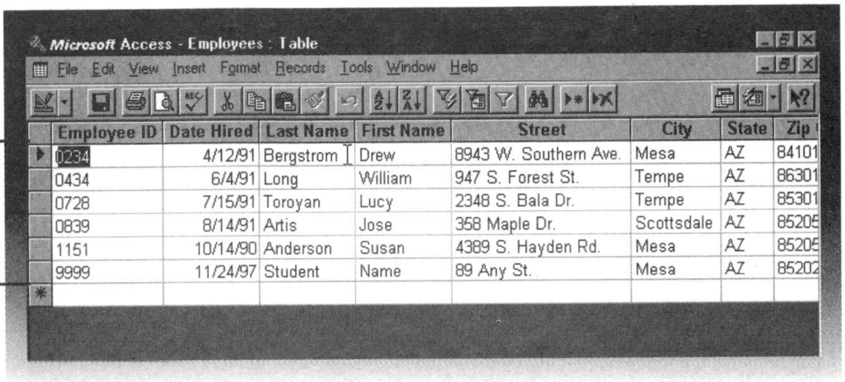

Figure 1-28

records in sorted order by Employee ID

The new records are added to the table in order by employee number. If you had added these records in Datasheet view, they would not appear in key field order until you updated the table display. This is another advantage of using Data Entry.

Previewing and Printing the Table

If you have printer capability, you can print a copy of the records in this table. Before printing the table, you will preview how the table will look when printed. Previewing the document displays each page of your document in a reduced size so you can see the layout. Then, if necessary, you can make changes to the layout before printing, to both save time and avoid wasting paper.

To preview the Employee table,

> The menu equivalent is File/Print Preview.

Click: 📇 **Print Preview**

Your screen should be similar to Figure 1-29.

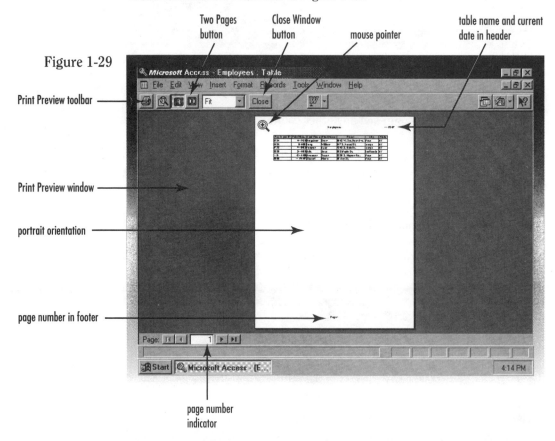

Figure 1-29

Two Pages button

Close Window button

mouse pointer

table name and current date in header

Print Preview toolbar

Print Preview window

portrait orientation

page number in footer

page number indicator

The Print Preview window displays a reduced view of how the table will appear when printed.

The window includes its own menus and toolbar. The toolbar buttons are identified below.

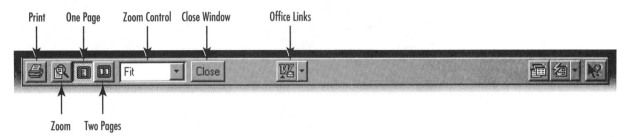

The document will be printed using the default report and page layout settings, which include such items as 1-inch margins, the table name and date displayed in a header, and the page number in a footer. Notice, however, that because the table is too wide to fit across the width of a page, only the first seven fields are displayed on the page. The rest of the table will be printed on a second page. To see both pages,

Click: [ ] **two pages**

The last three field columns display on this second page. You would like to print the table on a single page. One way to do this is to change the page orientation. **Orientation** refers to the direction text prints on a page. Normal orientation is to print across the width of an $8^{1}/_{2}$-inch page. This is called **portrait** orientation. You can change the orientation to print across the length of the paper. This is called **landscape** orientation. Using landscape orientation lets more information appear on the page because you are printing across the 11-inch length of the paper.

To change the orientation,

Choose: File/Page Setup

The Page Setup dialog box provides two groups of options identified by tabs.

If necessary, choose the Page tab.

The default orientation setting, Portrait, is selected. To change the orientation to Landscape,

Select: **Landscape**
Choose: OK

Your screen should be similar to Figure 1-30.

Figure 1-30

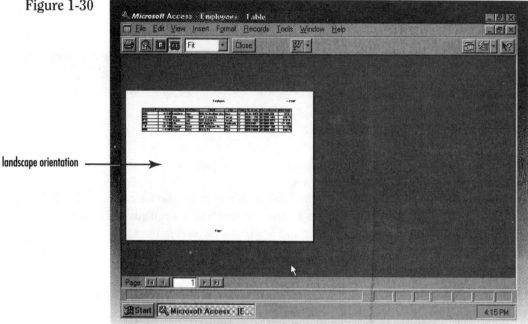

landscape orientation

You will learn about other Print Preview features in Lab 2.

The Print Preview window now shows how the table will appear when printed using landscape orientation. The entire table easily fits across the length of the page.

Now you are ready to print the table. The 🖶 Print button on the toolbar will immediately start printing the report using the default print settings. To check the print settings first, you need to use the Print command on the File menu.

If necessary, make sure your printer is on and ready to print.

The shortcut for the Print command is
Ctrl + P.

Note: Please consult your instructor for printing procedures that may differ from the directions below.

Choose: File/Print

The Print dialog box on your screen should be similar to Figure 1-31.

current printer   Printer Name drop-down box

Figure 1-31

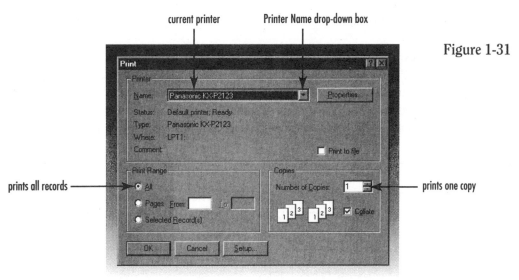

prints all records

prints one copy

From this dialog box you need to specify the printer you will be using and the print settings. The printer that is currently selected is displayed in the Name drop-down list box in the Printer section of the dialog box.

If you need to change the selected printer to another printer, open the Name drop-down list box and select the appropriate printer (your instructor will tell you which printer to select).

The Page Range area of the Print dialog box lets you specify how much of the document you want printed. The range options are described in the table below:

Option	Action
All	Prints entire document
Pa**g**es	Prints page numbers you specify in From and To text boxes
Selected **R**ecord(s)	Prints selected (highlighted) records only

The default range setting, All, is appropriate.

The Copies area of the dialog box is used to specify the number of copies you want printed. The default prints one copy. To print the table,

Choose: OK

Your printer should be printing out the table. The printed copy should be the same as displayed in the Print Preview window.

To close the Print Preview window and return to the Datasheet view,

Click: Close

The menu equivalent is **V**iew/Data**s**heet.

Closing the Table and Exiting Access

To close the table,

The menu equivalent is <u>F</u>ile/<u>C</u>lose or
Ctrl + W.

Click: ▧ **Close (in the Table window)**

Because you changed the column widths of the table in Datasheet view, you are prompted to save the layout changes you made before the table is closed. If you do not save the table, your column width settings will be lost.

Choose: **<u>Y</u>es**

The Database window is displayed again. The name of the table you created appears in the Table object list. Now the Open and Design command buttons can be used to modify the selected table in the list box.

   To quickly redisplay the table of employee records,

Choose: **<u>O</u>pen**

The table of employee records is displayed in Datasheet view again, just as it did before you saved and closed the table. To close the table again,

Choose: ▧ **Close (in the Table window)**

Notice that this time you were not prompted to save the table because you did not make any changes.

   You will continue to build and use the table of employee records in the next lab.

   To exit Access and return to the Windows 95 desktop,

The menu equivalent is <u>F</u>ile/E<u>x</u>it or
Alt + F4.

Click: ▧ **Close (in the Access window title bar)**

Do not remove your data disk from the drive
until you close the Access application window.

LAB REVIEW

Key Terms

Best Fit (DB42)
column width (DB41)
current record (DB33)
data type (DB25)
database (DB10)
Database Wizard (DB13)
Datasheet view (DB22)
Design view (DB22)
Edit mode (DB37)
field (DB10)
field name (DB24)
field property (DB26)

field selector (DB33)
field size (DB26)
Form view (DB22)
landscape (DB47)
Layout Preview (DB22)
navigation buttons (DB33)
Navigation mode (DB37)
object (DB21)
object tab (DB21)
orientation (DB47)
portrait (DB47)

primary key (DB27)
Print Preview (DB22)
record (DB10)
record number indicator (DB33)
record selector column (DB33)
relational (DB10)
startup window (DB12)
Switchboard (DB17)
table (DB10)
template (DB14)
work area (DB13)

Command Summary

Command	Shortcut	Toolbar	Action
File/**N**ew Database	Ctrl + N	🔳	Creates a new database
File/**C**lose	Ctrl + W	❎	Closes open window
File/**S**ave	Ctrl + S	🔳	Saves table
File/Page Set**u**p			Displays Page Setup dialog box
File/Print Pre**v**iew		🔳	Displays file as it will appear when printed
File/**P**rint	Ctrl + P	🔳	Prints contents of file
File/E**x**it	Alt + F4	❎	Closes Access and returns to Windows 95 desktop
Edit/Primary **K**ey		🔳	Defines a field as a primary key field
View/Data**s**heet		🔳	Displays table in Datasheet view
F**o**rmat/**C**olumn Width			Changes width of table columns in Datasheet view
Records/**R**emove Filter/Sort			Displays all records in table
Records/**D**ata Entry			Hides existing records and enters Data Entry mode

Matching

1. Best Fit	_____	**a.** attributes of a field that affect its appearance or behavior
2. database	_____	**b.** controls the type of data a field can contain
3. field property	_____	**c.** an organized collection of related information
4. primary key	_____	**d.** insertion point is on record 1 of four records
5. record	_____	**e.** feature used to adjust column width to largest entry
6. landscape	_____	**f.** collection of related fields
7. field	_____	**g.** field used to order records
8. 1 of 4	_____	**h.** displays table in row and column format
9. Datasheet view	_____	**i.** specific item of information contained in a record
10. data type	_____	**j.** orientation that prints document across length of page

Fill-In Questions

1. Identify the parts of the Access screen by entering the correct term for each item.

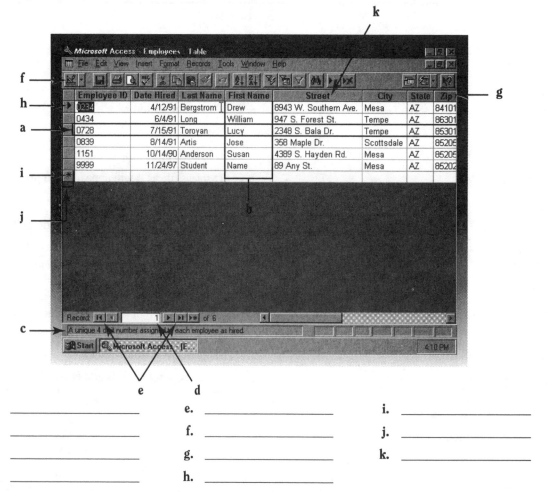

a. _____	**e.** _____	**i.** _____
b. _____	**f.** _____	**j.** _____
c. _____	**g.** _____	**k.** _____
d. _____	**h.** _____	

2. Complete the following statements by filling in the blanks with the correct terms.

a. A _____ is a collection of organized information. The information is stored in _____.

b. Relational databases define _____ between tables by having common data in the tables.

c. The first step in developing a database is _____.

d. The _____ defines the type of data that can be entered in a field.

e. An _____ is an item made up of different elements.

f. The set of characteristics associated with a field are the _____.

g. A descriptive label called a _____ is used to identify the data stored in a field.

h. The _____ data type is used to format numbers with dollar signs and decimal places.

i. A _____ is a field that uniquely identifies each record in a table.

j. _____ view allows the user to enter, edit, and delete records in a table.

Discussion Questions

1. Discuss several uses you may have for a relational database. Then explain the steps you would follow to create the first table.

2. Discuss why it is important to plan a database before creating it. How can proper planning save you time later?

3. Discuss the difference between Edit mode and Navigation mode.

4. Design view and Datasheet view are two of the Access views. Discuss when it would be appropriate to use each of these views.

5. Discuss why it is important to choose the correct data type for a field. What may happen to the data if you change the data type?

Hands-On Practice Exercises

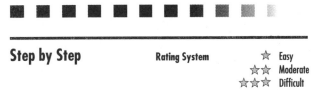

Step by Step	**Rating System**	☆ Easy
		☆☆ Moderate
		☆☆☆ Difficult

1. There are many ways to customize the tables you create using Access. In this exercise you will use the Access Help system to search for information on the ways you can customize Access tables.

a. Open the Access Help Answer Wizard.

b. Request Help information on customizing tables.

c. Based on the Help information you find, list four ways you can customize a table in Design view.

2. Debbie started a commercial cleaning business while she was in college. Her business has now grown to a full-service company with four other employees, and she wants to computerize her business records. Debbie wants to start by transferring her client records to Access.

a. Help Debbie create a database named Cleaning Service Records. Design a table using the field information defined below.

Field Data	Type	Field Size	Description
Client #	Text	5	5-digit unique number
Company	Text	50	
Contact	Text	50	First & Last Name of contact person
Address	Text	50	
City	Text	50	
State	Text	2	2-letter abbreviation entered in all capital letters
Zip Code	Text	5	5-digit number
Phone	Text	8	8-digit number in format 123-4567
Cleaning Day	Text	3	3-letter day code: MON, TUE, WED, THU, FRI, SAT, or SUN
Square Ft	Number		
Rate	Currency		

b. Make the Client # field the primary key field.

c. Save the table as Clients.

d. Enter the following records into the table:

Record 1	Record 2
95037	94103
St. John & Associates Law Offices	The Sports Company
Kelley St. John	[your name]
13271 N. Central Ave.	8915 E. Hayden Rd.
Phoenix	Scottsdale
AZ	AZ
84137	85254
555-7991	555-1294
FRI	WED
5000	20000
$150	$500

Record 3

96052
TechnoBabble Electronics
Eddie Fitzpatrick
9860 E. Chandler Blvd.
Chandler
AZ
85601
555-9876
MON
10000
$250

e. Adjust the column widths appropriately.

f. Print the table. Save and close the table.

3. Michael is the human resources manager for a small resort. The resort used to be run by a family, but due to a growing interest in working dude ranches, the resort owners have hired a considerable number of employees over the past two years. One of Michael's responsibilities is to maintain employee records. To help him keep track of the employee information, Michael wants to create an Access database.

a. Help Michael create a database named Resort Records. Design a table using the field definitions shown below.

Field	Data Type	Field Size	Description
Employee #	Text	3	3-digit unique number
Last Name	Text	50	
First Name	Text	50	
Middle Initial	Text	1	1 character only
Address	Text	50	Complete address with city, state, and zip code included
Date Hired	Date	Short Date	
Department	Text	50	

b. Make the Employee # the key field.

c. Save the table as Staff Records.

d. Enter the following records into the table:

Record 1

015
[your last name]
[your first name]
W
34 Maple Dr., Scottsdale, AZ 85259
[current date]
Administration

Record 2

131
Johnson
Samantha
T
984 Mountainside Way, Phoenix, AZ 85101
5/31/95
Housekeeping

Record 3

216
Wesley
William
P
9742 S. Gifford Lane, Mesa, AZ 85039
October 12, 1994
Sales

Record 4

139
Feldman
Annie
K
8217 E. University Ave., Tempe, AZ 85210
2/7/96
Reservations

e. Adjust the column widths appropriately.

f. Print the table. Save and close the table.

On Your Own

4. James works at a small office supply store. He needs to create a database to keep track of the store inventory.

Help James create a database named Office Supplies to track item numbers (5-digit unique numbers), item names, quantity on hand, and item cost. The database table, named Inventory, should have a primary key. Enter five sample inventory items into the database. Enter your name in the sixth record item name field. Print the table, save any changes, and close the table.

5. Michelle owns a small catering business servicing business clients. Her business is growing and she is considering bringing in a partner to help with the workload. Michelle has a list of regular clients, and wants to use her computer and Microsoft Access to maintain her client records.

Help Michelle create a database named Catering Business to keep track of her clients. The table, named Customers, should include each customer's identification number, company, contact, address, phone number, preferred theme, and favorite dish. Enter five records to the table using fictitious data. The last record should include your name. Print the table. Save and close the table.

6. Create a new database named Lab1PE6 using the Blank Database template. Use the Table Wizard to help you create a table by selecting one of the table samples of your choice from the Personel category. Include your name in the table name. Follow the directions in each step of the Table Wizard and make appropriate selections to create your table. Add five records to the table. Adjust column widths as needed. Preview and print the table using the appropriate orientation.

Concept Summary

1 Creating a Database

Templates

Every Access database is based on a template file that includes predefined settings that are used to define the default characteristics of a database.

Database

A database is an organized collection of information.

Database Development

The development of a database follows several steps: planning, creating, editing, form design, data analysis, report design, and printing.

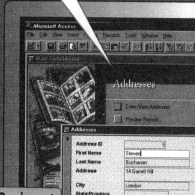

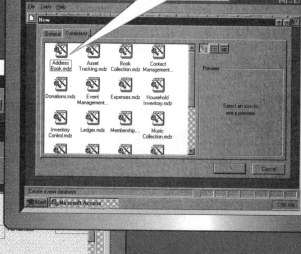

Field Names

A field name is used to identify the data stored in a field.

Data Types

The data type defines the type of data the field will contain. There are nine data types with Text as the default data type.

Primary Key

A primary key is a field that uniquely identifies each record. It is usually the first field in the table.

Field Properties

Field properties are a set of characteristics that are associated with each field, such as field size.

Views

Access allows you to view objects in your database in several different window formats called views. There are several basic views: Design view, Datasheet view, Form view, Print Preview, and Layout Preview.

DB56

Objects

A database file is made up of many different types of objects, such as tables, forms, and reports.

Table Names

Each table in a database must have a unique name and it should be descriptive of the data to be stored in the table.

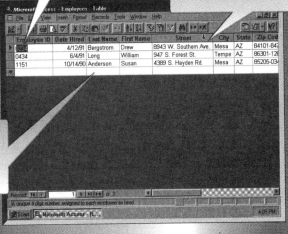

Concepts

Database
Templates
Database Development

Objects
Table Names

Field Names
Data Types
Field Properties
Primary Key
Views

Data Entry Guidelines
Modes
Column Width

Modes

Two modes of operation, Navigation mode and Edit mode, control how you can move through and make changes to the data in a table.

Data Entry Guidelines

The data you enter in a field should be typed exactly as you want it to appear and in a consistent form.

Column Width

Column width refers to the size of each column in Datasheet view. It controls the amount of data you can see in the column.

Modifying a Table and Creating a Form

COMPETENCIES

After completing this lab, you will know how to:

1. Navigate in Datasheet view.
2. Change field properties.
3. Find and replace data.
4. Use Undo.
5. Insert a new field in a table.
6. Add validity checks.
7. Hide and redisplay fields.
8. Sort records.
9. Delete records.
10. Create and enhance a form.
11. Enter records in Form view.
12. Print and save a form.

As you have seen, creating a database takes planning and a lot of time to set up the structure and enter the data. Even with the best of planning, however, things change. A computerized database program makes life easier by allowing you to quickly modify a table and update the records.

Even more impressive, as you will see in this lab, is the program's ability to locate data stored in the database. This is where all the hard work of entering data pays off. With a click of a button you can find data that might otherwise take hours to locate. The end result both saves time and improves accuracy.

You will also see how you can make the data you are looking at onscreen more pleasing by creating a form. A form can include colors, text enhancements, graphic lines and boxes, and layout and design changes that greatly improve the onscreen display of information.

Concept Overview	
The following concepts will be introduced in this lab:	
1. Format Property	You can use the Format property to create custom formats that change the way numbers, dates, times, and text display and print.
2. Default Value Property	The Default Value property is used to specify a value to be automatically entered in a field when a new record is created.
3. Input Mask Property	An input mask is a pattern that controls the data that can be entered in a field.
4. Find and Replace	The Find and Replace commands make locating and/or replacing information in a table fast and accurate.
5. Undo	You can use Undo to cancel your last action as long as you do not make any other changes to the table.
6. Validity Checks	Access automatically performs certain checks, called validity checks, on values entered in a field to make sure that the values are valid for the field type.
7. Expressions	Expressions are combinations of symbols that produce specific results. They are used to create validity checks, queries, forms, and reports.
8. Sort	You can quickly reorder records in a table by sorting a table to display in a different record order.
9. Forms	Forms are database objects used primarily for data entry and making changes to existing records.
10. Fonts	Fonts include three elements: typefaces, type size, and type style. They can be used to enhance the appearance of tables, forms, and reports.

CASE STUDY

You have continued to work on your table of employee records by adding more records to the table. As you have used the table, you have noticed several errors in the records you entered that need to be corrected. You also realize that you forgot to include a field for the employee's sex. You will make these changes to modify the table. In addition, you have decided to create a customized entry form for the table.

Part 1

Opening an Existing Database

Load Access for Windows 95. Put your data disk in drive A (or the appropriate drive for your system).

The Startup dialog box is displayed. To use the Startup dialog box to open the database file of employee data,

Select: **Open an Existing Database**

The list box now displays the names of recently used database files. To open the database file that contains the additional employee records,

The menu equivalent is <u>F</u>ile/<u>O</u>pen Database.

Select: **More Files**

Choose: OK

The Open dialog box is displayed.

In the Look in text box, change the location to the drive containing your data disk.

The name of the database file you created in Lab 1 is displayed in the list box along with the other database files on your data disk. The database file that contains the additional employee records is named Employee Records. To use this database file,

You could also double-click the filename to both select and open it.

Select: **Employee Records**

Choose: Open

The Database window for the Employee Records file is displayed. The table with the additional employee records, Sports Company Employees, is the only table listed in the Tables object list box. To open this table,

Choose: Open

Your screen should be similar to Figure 2-1.

Figure 2-1

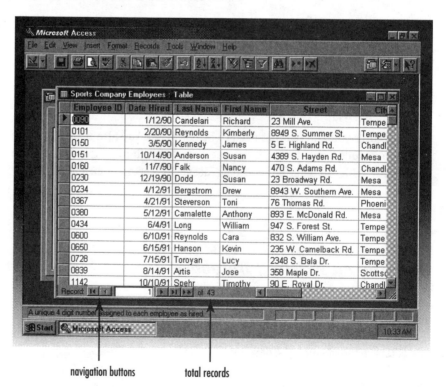

navigation buttons   total records

By default, the Datasheet view of the Table window is displayed. As you can see from the record number indicator, there are now 43 records in the table.

To enlarge the window to display more records, maximize the Datasheet window.

Moving Around a Large Table

In a large table, there are many methods you can use to quickly navigate through records in Datasheet view. You can always use the mouse to move from one field or record to another. However, if the information is not visible in the window, you must scroll the window first. The table below presents several keyboard methods that make navigation faster in Navigation mode.

Keys	Effect
Ctrl + Page Up	Left one window
Ctrl + Page Down	Right one window
End	Last field in record
Home	First field in record
Ctrl + End	Last field of last record
Ctrl + Home	First field of first record
Ctrl + ↑	Current field of first record
Ctrl + ↓	Current field of last record

The Navigation buttons in the status bar also provide navigation shortcuts. These buttons also move in Navigation mode and are described below.

Button	Effect
⏮	First record, same field
◀	Previous record, same field
▶	Next record, same field
⏭	Last record, same field
▶*	New (blank) record

> You can also type the record number you want to move to in the record indicator box of the status bar.

To see the next full window of records,

Press: Page Down

The next full window of records is visible. The first record in the window is now the current record.

Due to the number and width of the fields, not all fields can be displayed in the window at the same time. Rather than scrolling the window horizontally to see the additional fields, you can quickly move to the right a window at a time.

Press: Ctrl + Page Down

Your screen should be similar to Figure 2-2.

Figure 2-2

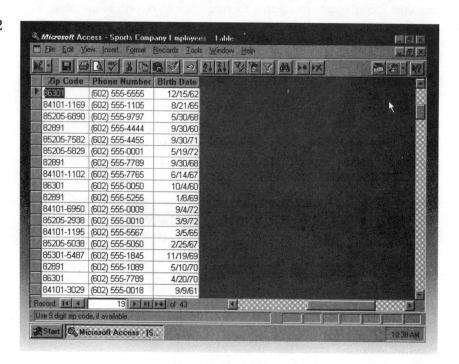

The contents of the first field in the window to the right are selected. To quickly move to the same field of the last record,

Click:

To move back to the first field of the first record,

Press: ⌃Ctrl + ⌂Home

Changing Field Properties

As you viewed the records in the database, you may have noticed that records 11, 22, and 25 have mixed-case entries in the State field. You would like all the state field entries to be in all uppercase letters. Also, rather than having to enter the same state for each record, you want the field to display the state AZ automatically. This will make data entry faster because all the stores are located in Arizona and it is unlikely that the employees will live in another state.

In Lab 1 you set the field properties of several fields. For example, you set the Employee ID field size to 4 so that a larger number could not be entered into the field. In addition, you set the format of the Date Hired field to display a date using the Short Date style. You can also set a field's property to automatically change the entry to uppercase characters.

To change the properties of a field, you use Design view.

Click:  **Design View**

Reminder: Move to anywhere in a field to display its properties.

Display the properties associated with the State field.

Your screen should be similar to Figure 2-3.

Figure 2-3

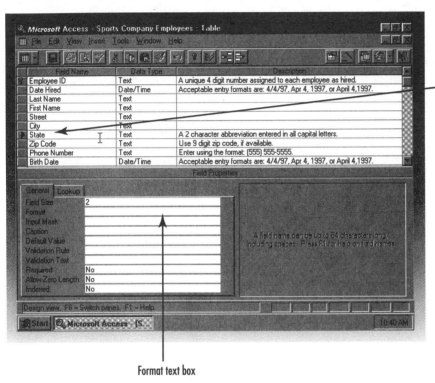

current field

Format text box

The Format property is used to customize the way an entry displays.

Concept 1: Format Property

You can use the Format property to create custom formats that change the way numbers, dates, times, and text display and print. Format properties do not change the way Access stores data, only how the data is displayed.

To change the format of a field, different symbols are entered in the Format text box. Text and Memo Data Types can use any of these four symbols:

Symbol	Description
@	A required text character or space. For example, the format property @@@-@@-@@@@ would display 123456789 as 123-45-6789. Nine characters or spaces are required.
>	Forces all characters to uppercase. For example, SMITH would be displayed whether you entered SMITH, smith, or Smith.
<	Forces all characters to lowercase. For example, smith would be displayed whether you entered SMITH, smith, or Smith.
&	An optional text character. For example, @@-@@& would display 12345 as 12-345 and 12.34 as 12-34. Four out of five characters are required and a fifth is optional.

To enter the symbol to change all entries in the field to uppercase, move to the Format field property text box.

Type: **>**

Next you want to change the State field property to automatically display the default value of AZ.

Concept 2: Default Value Property

The Default Value property is used to specify a value that is automatically entered in a field when a new record is created. This property is commonly used when most of the entries in a field will be the same for the entire table. That default value then displays automatically in the field. When users add a record to the table, they can either accept this value or enter another value. This saves time while entering data.

Move to the Default Value field property text box.

Type: **AZ**

Your screen should be similar to Figure 2-4.

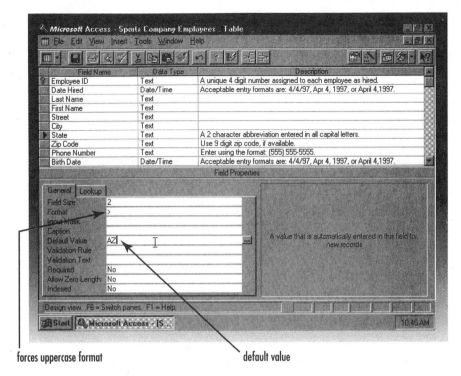

Figure 2-4

forces uppercase format   default value

While making this change, you decide to change the properties of the Zip Code field to make data entry easier.

Display the properties associated with the Zip Code field.

You want the Zip Code field to display the hyphen and restrict the entry to numbers only. Creating an input mask will set up the field in the desired manner.

Concept 3: Input Mask Property

An **input mask** is a pattern that controls the data that can be entered in a field. It consists of literal characters displayed in the field, and mask characters. **Literal characters** are characters such as parentheses used to surround the area code portion of a telephone number, or a hyphen used to separate the parts of the telephone number. **Mask characters** are symbols that control where the data is entered in the field, the type of data that can be entered, whether the data is required or optional, and the number of characters. They are not displayed in the field and are replaced by the entry as it is typed into the table.

Many of the most common mask characters are described below.

Character	Description
0	A required number entry 0 to 9 (plus (+) and minus (−) signs not allowed)
9	An optional number or space entry (plus and minus signs not allowed)
#	An optional number or space (spaces are displayed as blanks while in Edit mode, but blanks are removed when data is saved; plus and minus signs allowed)
L	A required letter entry (A to Z)
?	An optional letter entry (A to Z)
A	A required letter or digit entry
a	An optional letter or digit entry
&	A required entry of any character or a space
C	An optional entry of any character or a space
<	Causes all characters to be converted to lowercase
>	Causes all characters to be converted to uppercase
!	Causes the input mask to be displayed from right to left, rather than from left to right, when characters on the left side of the input mask are optional. Characters typed into the mask always fill it from left to right. You can include the exclamation point anywhere in the input mask.
\	Causes the character that follows to be displayed as the literal character (for example, \A displays as just A)

An input mast can have up to three parts. Each part is separated by a semicolon. For example, the input mask for a zip code field may be "00000-9999;0;_" The first part specifies the input mask itself (00000-9999). The second part specifies whether the literal display characters are stored in the table when you enter data. If you use 0 for this section, all literal display characters (for example, the hyphen in a zip code input mask) are stored with the value; if you enter 1 or leave this section blank, only characters typed into the control are stored. The third part specifies the character that is displayed while entering data to show the space where you should type a character in the input mask. For this section, you can use any character; if left blank, the default displays an underscore.

Move to the Input Mask field property text box.

The input mask for the Zip Code field will be 00000-9999;0. You will use zeros to restrict data entry to required numbers for the first five digits of the zip code entry. The last four numbers are optional, therefore you will use 9s as the character mask. The hyphen will be entered between the two parts of the zip code. The second part of the input mask, 0, will store the literal character (hyphen) as part of the value.

Type: **00000-9999;0**
Press: ⎡←Enter⎤

Your screen should be similar to Figure 2-5.

Figure 2-5

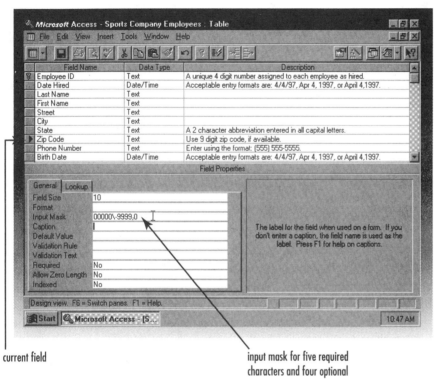

current field

input mask for five required
characters and four optional

Notice the \ character preceding the hyphen. The program enters the symbol for you to indicate that the hyphen is a literal character to display in the field.

You also decide to make a similar adjustment to the Phone Number field property. Rather than having to type the parentheses and hyphen, you want these to automatically display in the field. In addition, you want the field to accept numeric entries only. The input mask to make these changes is (000) 000-0000;0.

Change the input mask for the Phone Number field to (000) 000-0000;0.

To see how the new field property settings have changed the table,

Click: ▦ **Datasheet View**

A dialog box appears, advising you that the table must be saved before exiting Design view. This is because you have made changes to the structure of the table.

Choose: Yes

Move to the Phone Number field of record 1.

Your screen should be similar to Figure 2-6.

uppercase characters
in State field

input masks applied to Zip Code
and Phone Number fields

Figure 2-6

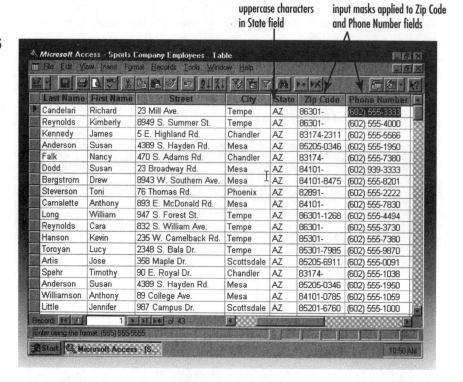

First, notice that the entry in the State field for record 11, which had lowercase characters, has been converted to uppercase characters. This change is a result of the format property setting you entered for the State field.

The Zip Code field displays the existing five-digit zip codes followed by the hyphen character as specified by the input mask for that field.

Because the entries in the Phone Number field already include the parentheses and hyphen, it is not possible to see the effect of the input mask on the field. However, when you enter a new record next, you will see how this mask helps data entry.

Move to a new blank record.

Notice that the new record displays "AZ" as the default value in the State field.

To see how the new format and input mask settings affect data input, enter the following new record:

You can click 📷 to quickly move to a new blank record.

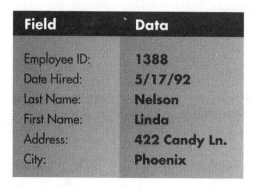

Field	Data
Employee ID:	1388
Date Hired:	5/17/92
Last Name:	Nelson
First Name:	Linda
Address:	422 Candy Ln.
City:	Phoenix

Because the state for this record is AZ, you can accept the default field value and skip this field. If the state were other than AZ, you could edit the entry.

Press: ⏎Enter

Next, in the zip code and phone number fields, you do not type the hyphens or parentheses, as they are supplied by the input mask. If you enter any characters except numbers in these fields, they will be rejected. Complete the record by entering the data shown below.

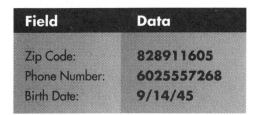

Field	Data
Zip Code:	828911605
Phone Number:	6025557268
Birth Date:	9/14/45

To complete this record and return to the first record,

Press: ⏎Enter
Press: Ctrl + Home

Finding and Replacing Data

Next you want to update the zip code field for the existing records. You have checked the zip code directory and found that all zip codes of 82891 have a four-digit extension of 1605.

Move to the Zip Code field of record 1.

To locate all the records with this zip code, you could look at the zip code field for each record to find the match and then edit the field to add the extension. If the table is small, this method would be acceptable. For large tables, however, this method could be quite time consuming and more prone to errors. A more efficient way is to search the table to find specific values in records and then replace the entry with another.

Concept 4: Find and Replace

One of the main advantages of a computerized database is the ability to quickly locate specific information. In addition, you can automatically replace the located information with new information. The Find command will locate all specified values in a field and the Replace command will both find a value and automatically replace it with another. For example, in a table containing supplier and item prices, you may need to increase the price of all items supplied by one manufacturer. To quickly locate these items, you would use the Find command to locate all records with the name of the manufacturer and then update the price appropriately. Alternatively, you could use the Replace command if you knew that all items priced at 9.95 were increasing to 11.89. This command would locate all values matching the original price and replace them with the new price. Finding and replacing data is fast and accurate, but you need to be careful when replacing not to replace unintended matches.

The Replace command will search the current field to find the specified data and replace it with other data.

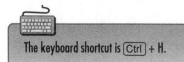

The keyboard shortcut is Ctrl + H.

Choose: Edit/Replace

The Replace in Field dialog box, shown in Figure 2-7 below, is displayed. It shows the name of the field it will search (the current field) in the title bar. In the Find What text box, you enter the text you want to locate.

Type: 82891- (do not press ←Enter)

After entering the text to find, do not press ←Enter because that would choose the Find Next command button and the search would begin.

Your screen should be similar to Figure 2-7.

enter replacement text   enter text to locate   field to search

Figure 2-7

search entire table   modify how search is conducted

You want to replace 82891- with 828911605. The replacement text must be entered exactly as you want it to appear in your document, excluding the hyphen that is entered by the input mask.

Press: Tab ⇆
Type: **828911605**

The Search drop-down list box displays All as the default setting. This setting searches through all records in the selected field of the table to find the specified value. You also can search down or up from the insertion point. The three other search options you can use to modify how the search is conducted are discussed below.

Option	Effect on Text	Example
Match Case	Finds only those text entries that have the same use of uppercase and lowercase text as the entry in the Find What dialog box. This option is off by default.	Enter "Southwest" in the Find What dialog box, turn on Match Case. You would not Locate "southwest."
Match Whole Field	Finds only whole words, not the same text string inside longer words. This option is on by default.	Enter "cat" in the Find What dialog box, turn on Find Whole Words Only. You would not locate "catastrophe" or "indicate."
Search Only Current Field	Searches only the field in which the pointer is currently located, ignoring other fields in the table. When not selected, this option searches all fields for each record in the table. This option is on by default.	If you Search Only the Last Name field for "Smith," you would locate only those individuals whose last names are Smith. You would not locate anyone living in Smith or on Smith Road.

The default settings for these options are appropriate. To begin the search,

Choose: Find Next

If necessary, move the dialog box so you can see the found entry.

Immediately the highlight moves to the first occurrence of text in the document that matches the find text and highlights it.

Your screen should be similar to Figure 2-8.

located match

Figure 2-8

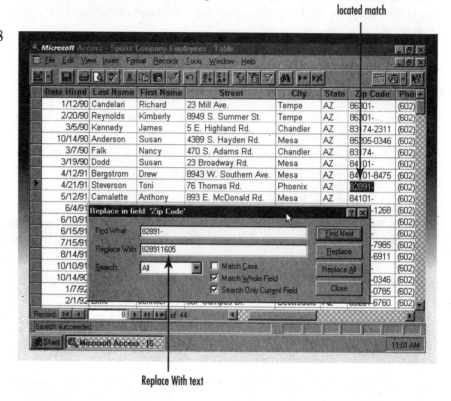

Replace With text

To replace the highlighted text,

Choose: Replace

Access immediately continues searching and locates a second occurrence of the entry. You decide the program is locating the values accurately, and it will be safe to replace all finds with the replacement value. To do this,

Choose: Replace All

It is much faster to use Replace All than to confirm each match separately. However, exercise care when using Replace All, because the search text you specify might be part of another word and you may accidentally replace text you want to keep.

When Access completes the search, you will see the message "You won't be able to undo this Replace operation." To approve the changes,

Choose: Yes

The Replace in Field dialog box is still displayed.

In the same manner, update the zip code for 86301 to include the extension 1268.

Close the Replace in Field dialog box.

Finding Data

A daily part of your job is to update employee records. Over the past few days you have received several change request forms to update the employee records. The first change request is for Carman Artis, who recently married and has both a name and address change.

To quickly locate the record, move to the Last Name field of record 1.

Click: **Find**

The menu equivalent is <u>E</u>dit/<u>F</u>ind or [Ctrl] + F.

The Find in Field dialog box, shown in Figure 2-9, is displayed.

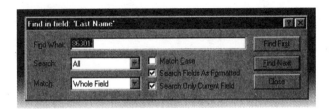

Figure 2-9

The Find in Field dialog box is very similar to the Replace dialog box. The Find What text box displays the last entry you made in that dialog box. To enter the new text to find,

Type: **artis**

Because the Match Case option is not selected, Find will look for an exact match regardless of uppercase or lowercase characters.

Choose: Find First

Access searches the table and moves to the first occurrence of the entry. The Last Name field is highlighted in record 14.

To edit the record, you need to close the dialog box.

Choose: Close

Note: If the Find command did not locate this record, reissue the command and make sure you enter the name Artis exactly as shown and are searching the Last Name field.

To change the last name to Richards,

Type: **Richards**
Press: [←Enter]

Using Undo

Now that the highlight is on the First Name field, you notice this is the record for Jose, not Carman. You changed the wrong record. You can use the Undo command to quickly undo this change.

> ### Concept 5: Undo
>
> As in all Windows 95 applications, Access includes an **Undo** feature. You can use Undo to cancel your last action as long as you do not make any other changes to the table. Even if you save the record or the table, you can undo changes to the last edited record by using the Undo Saved Record command on the Edit menu or by clicking 📷 Undo. Once you have changed another record or moved to another window, the earlier change cannot be undone. Neither Undo nor Undo Current Field/Record will undo deleted records. You can also use either command or button before leaving the field you are editing and the changes you have made will be undone.

To quickly undo the change made to this record,

> The menu equivalent is <u>E</u>dit/<u>U</u>ndo
> Current Field/Record or Esc.

Click: Undo

Your screen should be similar to Figure 2-10.

Figure 2-10

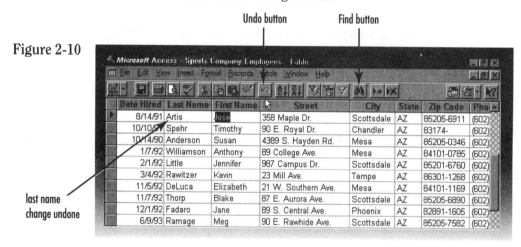

The original field value of "Artis" replaces "Richards."

To continue the search to locate the next record with the last name of Artis, move to the Last Name field of record 14.

Click: Find

The Find What text you entered is still displayed in the text box. To continue the search,

Choose: Find Next

The Last Name field contents of record 26 for Carman Artis is highlighted.

Close the Find in Field dialog box. Change the last name to Richards and the street to 5401 E. Thomas Rd.

Search the table for the following records and correct the entries.

Employee Name	Field	Correction
Adam Robson	Street	**4290 E. Alameda Dr.**
Kevin Hanson	City, Zip Code	**Scottsdale, 85205-3211**
Meg Ramage	Last Name	**Miller**

Reminder: The insertion point must be on the field you want to search before clicking 🔍 Find.

When you are done, return to the first field of record 1.

Inserting a Field

While continuing to use the table, you have realized that you need to include a field of information to hold each employee's gender. Although it is better to include all the necessary fields when creating the table structure, it is possible to add or remove fields from a table at a later time. To change the table structure,

If you remove a field, Access permanently deletes the field definition and any data in the field.

Click: 📐 Design View

After looking at the order of the fields, you decide to add the new field, Gender, between the Phone Number and Birth Date fields.

To add the new field to the existing structure, move to the Birth Date field.

You can also add or delete fields in Datasheet view.

Click: ▤ Insert Row

The Birth Date field has moved down one line to become the eleventh field, and a blank field line is ready to be defined as the tenth field.

Enter the new field information as follows:

The menu equivalent is Insert/Field. You can also use the Insert Field command on the Shortcut menu. ▤ or Edit/Delete Row removes a field.

Field Name:	**Gender**
Data Type:	**Text**
Description:	**Enter M for male or F for female.**
Field Size:	**1**
Format:	**>**

Your screen should be similar to Figure 2-11.

Insert Row button   Delete Row button

Figure 2-11

new field ──

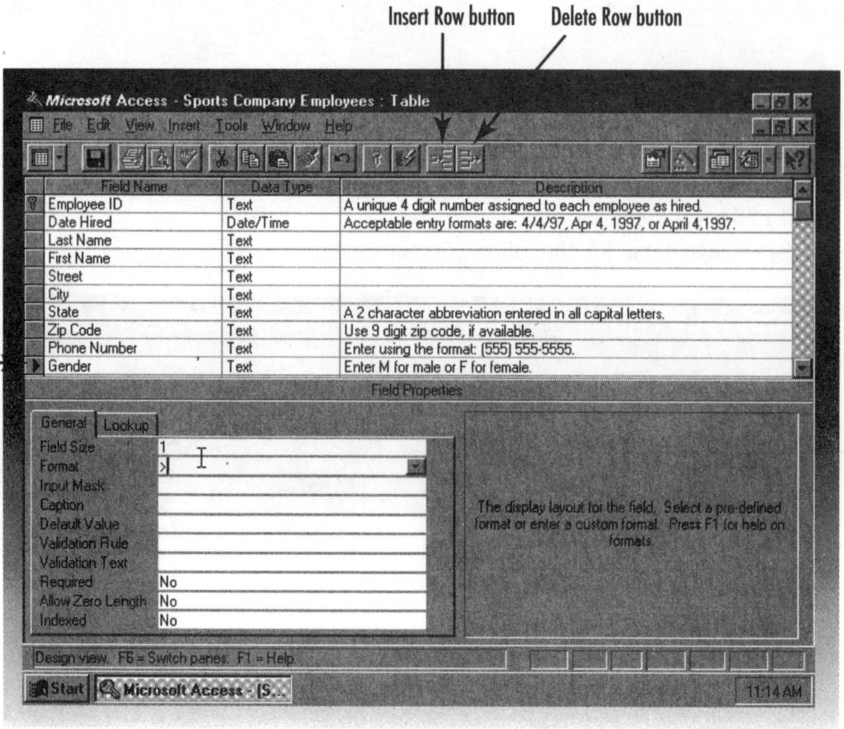

Adding Validity Checks

The only two characters you want the Gender field to accept are M for male and F for female. To specify that these two characters are the only entries acceptable in the field, you will include a validation rule and validation text field properties.

Concept 6: Validity Checks

Access automatically performs certain checks, called **validity checks**, on values entered in a field to make sure that the values are valid for the field type. A Text field type has few restrictions, but you can create your own validity checks for a field, which Access will apply during data entry. In this case you would like Access to allow only M or F to be entered in the field. A validity check is entered in the Validation Rule property box.

When you add a validity check, you can also add validation text in the Validation Text property box. **Validation text** appears in a message box if you attempt to enter invalid information in a text field for which you added a validity check. For example, if you added a validity check to a field to only allow the numbers 1 through 10, you might create validation text that would display the message, "The only valid entries for this field are numbers 1 through 10."

Move to the Validation Rule field property text box.

A validity check is set by entering an expression to describe acceptable values.

Concept 7: Expressions

Expressions are combinations of symbols that produce specific results. Expressions are used throughout Access to create validity checks, queries, forms, and reports. These are examples of possible expressions:

>=#1/1/95# AND <=#12/31/95#
="M" OR "F"
=[Sales Amount] + [Sales Tax]
="Tennis Rackets" OR "Racquetball Rackets"

You create an expression by combining identifiers, operators, and values to produce the desired result. An **identifier** is an element that refers to the value of a field, a graphical object, or property. In the expression =[Sales Amount] + [Sales Tax], [Sales Amount] and [Sales Tax] are identifiers that refer to the Sales Amount field values and Sales Tax field values.

An **operator** is a symbol or word that indicates that an operation is to be performed. The Access operators include = (equal to), <> (not equal to), >= (greater than or equal to), <= (less than or equal to), LIKE, OR, and AND. In the expression ="M" OR "F", the = sign and OR are operators. The = operator is assumed if no other operator is specified.

Values are numbers, dates, or groups of characters. Character groups such as "M", "F", "Tennis Rackets", or "Racquetball Rackets" are enclosed in quotation marks. Dates are enclosed in pound signs (#), as in >=#1/1/95# AND <=#12/31/95#.

To enter the expression for the validity check,

Type: =M or F
Press: ←Enter

The expression states that the acceptable values can only be equal to an M or an F. Notice that Access automatically added quotation marks around the two character strings and changed the "o" in "or" to uppercase (see Figure 2-12 on the next page). Because the Format property has been set to convert all entries to uppercase, an entry of m or f is also acceptable.

Next you can create an error message in the Validation Text field property text box to display if the wrong character is entered in the Gender field. If you do not specify a message, Access displays a default error message, which will not clearly describe the reason for the error.

Type: The only valid entries are M or F.

Your screen should be similar to Figure 2-12.

Figure 2-12

active field —

expression —

error message
text —

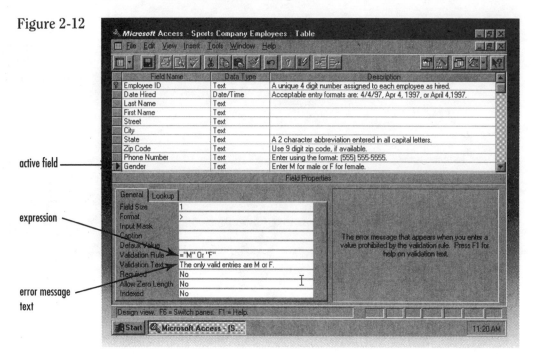

To save the table design changes,

Click: ▣ Save

A message box appears advising you that data integrity rules have been changed. When you restructure a table, you often make changes that could result in a loss of data. Changes such as shortening field sizes, creating validity checks, or changing field types can cause existing data to become invalid. Whenever you add or modify a validation rule, Access gives you the opportunity to check data within the affected field. At this point you can verify that all existing values match the new criteria (in other words, Gender equals M or F). You can also accept existing values without checking them, cancel the save, or call Help.

Because the field is new, there are no data values to verify, and a validation check is unnecessary. To continue,

Choose:

The new field is added to the table, and the changes to the file structure are saved.

Note: Through careful analysis and design of your database, you can avoid having to restructure your table and risk the potential loss of data.

To return to the Datasheet window,

Click: ▦ **Datasheet View**

Hiding and Redisplaying Fields

Next you want to enter data for the Gender field for each record. You can most likely tell the gender by looking at the employee's first name. For example, the first name for record 1 is Richard. Therefore the Gender field for record 1 should be M. If the name is not a good indicator of the person's gender, you could always verify the gender by checking the original employee data card.

Move to the Gender field for record 1.

Unfortunately, both the First Name and Gender fields are not visible on the screen. One quick way to view both fields is to hide the fields that are in between.

To hide the Street field through the Phone Number field, select the Street field through the Phone Number field.

Choose: F̲ormat/H̲ide Columns

> Drag in the column heads to select the fields.

Your screen should be similar to Figure 2-13.

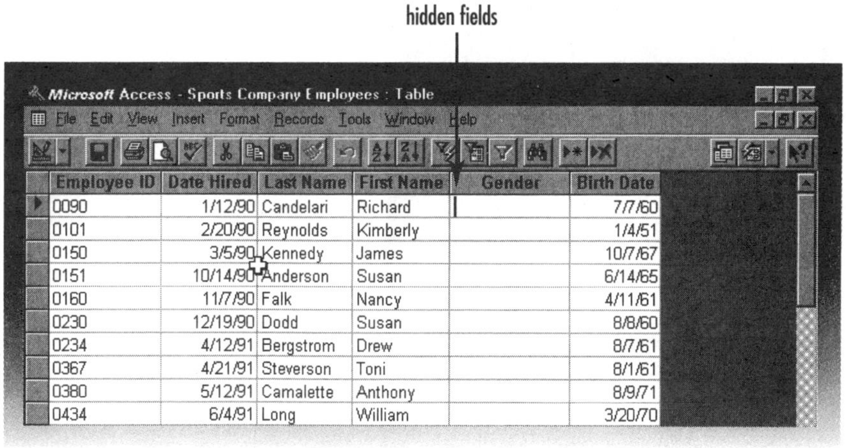

hidden fields

Figure 2-13

Now both the First Name and Gender columns are next to each other, making it easy to enter the gender while checking first names.

To verify that the validity check works, you will enter an invalid field value in the Gender field for the first record.

Type: g
Press: ←Enter

Access displays the error message you entered in the Validation Text box of the Design view. To clear the error message,

Choose: OK

To enter the correct gender,

Press: Backspace
Type: **m**
Press: ↓

The entry for the first record is displayed as an uppercase M.

Enter the Gender field values for the remaining records by looking at the First Name field to determine whether the employee is male or female.

Reduce the size of the Gender field using the Best Fit command.

To redisplay the hidden fields,

Choose: **Fo̲rmat/U̲nhide Columns**

The Unhide Columns dialog box on your screen should be similar to Figure 2-14.

Figure 2-14

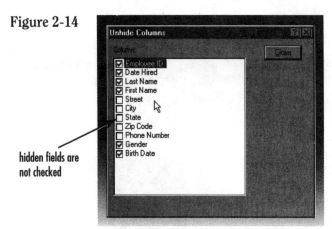

hidden fields are not checked

In this dialog box you need to select the fields you want to redisplay.

Select the five fields that do not display checkmarks.

Choose: Close

The fields are redisplayed.

Move to the first field of first record 1.

Sorting on a Single Field

As you may recall from Lab 1, the records are ordered by the primary key field, Employee ID, the first field in the table. The Accounting department manager, however, has asked you for an alphabetical list of all employees. To do this you can sort the records in the table.

Concept 8: Sort

You can quickly reorder records in a table by **sorting** a table to display in a different record order. Sorting data often helps you find specific information quickly. In Access you can sort data in ascending order (A to Z or 0 to 9) or descending order (Z to A or 9 to 0).

You can sort all records in a table by a single field, such as State, or you can select adjacent columns and sort by more than one field, such as State and then City. When you select multiple columns to sort, Access sorts records starting with the column farthest left, then moves to the right across the columns. For example, if you want to quickly sort by State, then by City, the State field must be to the left of the City column.

Access saves the new sort order with your table data and reapplies it automatically each time you open the table. To return to the primary key sort order, you must remove the temporary sort.

For the first sort, you want the records arranged in ascending alphabetical order (A through Z) by last name.

To do this, move to the Last Name field of any record.

Click:  **Sort Ascending**

The menu equivalent is <u>R</u>ecords/<u>S</u>ort/<u>A</u>scending.

Your screen should be similar to Figure 2-15.

Sort Ascending button

Sort Descending button

Figure 2-15

duplicate records

records sorted by last name

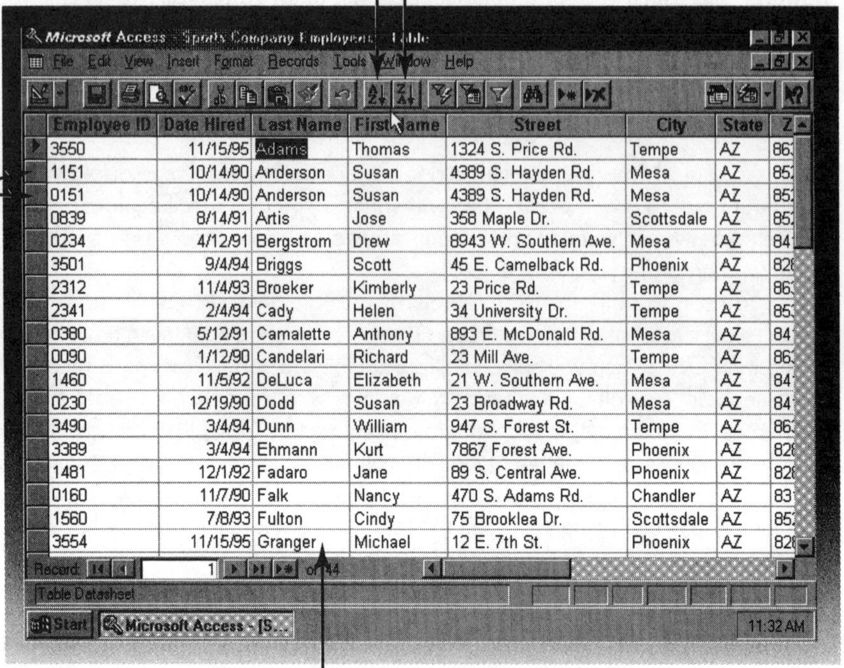

The employee records are displayed in alphabetical order by last name.

Deleting Records

Now that the records are alphabetically arranged, you immediately notice that Susan Anderson's record has been entered into the table twice. The records contain identical information in all the fields except for the Employee ID field. You think the same record was entered twice with different employee numbers. By checking the employee card, you determined that the record with the employee number of 1151 is incorrect. You need to delete the duplicate record.

Before you can delete a record, you must first select it. When a record is selected in Datasheet view, the active row is highlighted.

Point to the row selector of record 2 containing the employee number 1151.

The mouse pointer can have two shapes while positioned in the row selector. The ✛ indicates you can change the row height by dragging (similar to changing the column width), and the ➡ indicates you can select a record.

With the mouse pointer as ➡,

The menu equivalent is **E**dit/Se**l**ect Record or ⎍Shift + Spacebar in Navigation mode.

Click: the row selector for record 2

Your screen should be similar to Figure 2-16.

Cut button

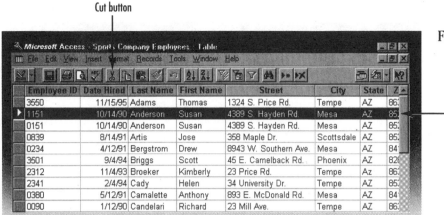

Figure 2-16

selected record

The entire record is selected. You are now ready to delete the record.

Click: **Cut**

As a precaution against accidentally deleting records, Access displays a warning message box. To indicate you want to permanently delete the record,

Choose:

Access deletes the entire record.

Sorting on Multiple Fields

Use the scroll box to scroll down to record 27.

Notice that the records for Kimberly and Cara Reynolds are sorted by last name but not by first name. You want the records that have the same last name to be further sorted by first name. To do this, you specify multiple sort fields.

When sorting on multiple fields, the fields must be adjacent to each other, and the most important field in the sort must be to the left of the secondary field. The Last Name and First Name fields are already in the correct locations for the sort you want to perform. To specify the fields to sort on, both columns must be selected.

Select the Last Name and First Name field columns.

The Last Name and First Name field columns should be highlighted.

Click:  **Sort Ascending**

The employee names still appear in alphabetical order by last name.

Scroll down to record 27.

The menu equivalent is **E**dit/Cu**t**, Ctrl + X, or Delete. The Cut command is also on the shortcut menu when a record is selected.

You cannot undo a deleted record.

As you drag the scroll box, the record location is displayed in the scroll tips box.

If the columns are not adjacent, you can hide the columns that are in between. If they are not in the correct order, you can move the columns. You will learn how to do this in Lab 3.

Your screen should be similar to Figure 2-17.

Figure 2-17

records sorted →
by last name and
by first name

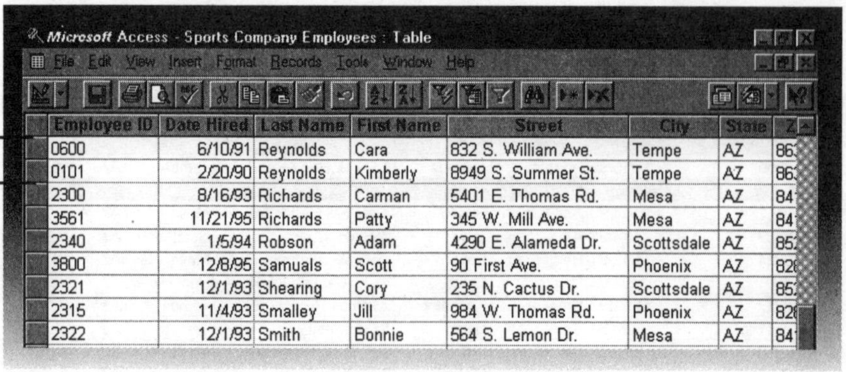

Employee ID	Date Hired	Last Name	First Name	Street	City	State	Z
0600	6/10/91	Reynolds	Cara	832 S. William Ave.	Tempe	AZ	86
0101	2/20/90	Reynolds	Kimberly	8949 S. Summer St.	Tempe	AZ	86
2300	8/16/93	Richards	Carman	5401 E. Thomas Rd.	Mesa	AZ	84
3561	11/21/95	Richards	Patty	345 W. Mill Ave.	Mesa	AZ	84
2340	1/5/94	Robson	Adam	4290 E. Alameda Dr.	Scottsdale	AZ	85
3800	12/8/95	Samuals	Scott	90 First Ave.	Phoenix	AZ	82
2321	12/1/93	Shearing	Cory	235 N. Cactus Dr.	Scottsdale	AZ	85
2315	11/4/93	Smalley	Jill	984 W. Thomas Rd.	Phoenix	AZ	82
2322	12/1/93	Smith	Bonnie	564 S. Lemon Dr.	Mesa	AZ	84

The records for Kimberly and Cara Reynolds are further sorted by first name.

As you can see, sorting is a fast, useful tool. The sort order remains in effect until you remove the sort or replace it with a new sort order. Although Access remembers your sort order even when you exit the program, it does not actually change the table records. You can remove the sort at any time to restore the records to the primary key sort order.

To remove the alphabetical sort on the first and last names and restore the primary key sort order,

Choose: Records/Remove Filter/Sort

The table displays the records in primary key sort order again.

Close the table and save your design changes.

The Database window should be displayed.

Note: If you are ending your session now, close the database file and exit Access. When you begin Part 2, load Access and open the Employee Records file.

Part 2

Creating a Form

One of your responsibilities is to make the database easy to use. You know from experience that long hours of viewing large tables can be tiring. Therefore you want to create an onscreen form to make this table easier to view and use.

Concept 9: Forms

Forms are database objects used primarily for data entry and making changes to existing records. Forms are based on an underlying table and include design elements such as descriptive text, titles, labels, lines, boxes, and pictures. Forms often use calculations as well, to summarize data that is not listed on the actual table, such as a sales total. Forms make working with long lists of data easier. They enable people to use the data in the tables without having to sift through many lines of data to find the exact record.

Forms are linked to the underlying table by using controls. **Controls** are items that can be selected and modified. Once a control is selected, it can be sized or moved. The most common type of control is a text box. A **text box** displays data from the table. The form usually includes a label with each text box. A **label** specifies the field name from the table or some custom name you want to display. This type of control is called a **compound control**.

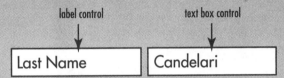

You can customize a form by adding lines, boxes, and pictures, as well as labels, descriptive text, and other messages for the user. Although you can print forms, they are designed primarily for onscreen use.

You can display a form in one of four different views: Form Design view, Form view, Form Datasheet view, and Form Preview. **Form Design view** allows you to create or design new forms. **Form view** displays records on the screen, most often one record at a time, for data entry or editing. **Form Datasheet view** provides a datasheet view of the form data. Although it appears similar to Table Datasheet view, Form Datasheet view includes all fields from the form, including calculated fields. **Form Preview** provides a visual representation of the form as it will appear when printed.

The form you want to create will be used by the Personnel department to add new employee records and to update existing employee records in the Sports Company Employees table. The input for the table comes from the paper Employee Data form that each employee fills out when hired. The paper form looks like this:

EMPLOYEE DATA
First Name:_____   Last Name: _____
Street:_____
City: _____   State: _____   Zip Code: _____
Phone Number: _____
Gender: _____   Birth Date: _____
For Personnel Use Only:
Employee ID: _____ Date Hired: _____

The order of information in the Employee Data form is different than the order that the data is entered into the table. To make the job of data entry easier, you want the table form to reflect the order of the paper form used by employees.

To create a form, open the Forms tab.

Choose: [New]

The New Form dialog box on your screen should be similar to Figure 2-18.

Figure 2-18

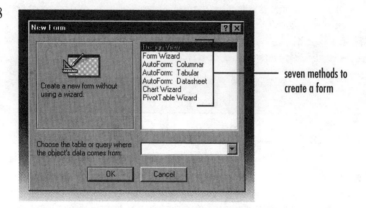

seven methods to create a form

This dialog box offers seven methods you can use to create a form. As you learned in Lab 1, Wizards guide you through the steps to create various database objects. You will use the Form Wizard to help you create this form.

Select: **Form Wizard**
Choose: [OK]

The first Form Wizard dialog box on your screen should be similar to Figure 2-19.

Figure 2-19

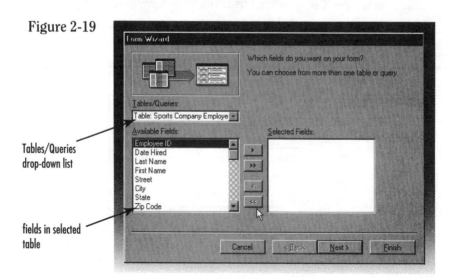

Tables/Queries drop-down list

fields in selected table

The dialog box displays the name of the current table, Sports Company Employees, in the Tables/Queries list box. This is the table that Access will use when creating the form. If your database contained multiple tables, you would display the Tables/Queries drop-down list to select a different table.

After selecting the table, you select the fields to include in the form. The fields from the selected table will appear in the Available Fields list box. The order in which you select the fields is the **tab order**, or the order in which the highlight will move through the fields on the form during data entry. You would like the order to be the same as the order on the paper form. To add the First Name field to the form first, from the Available Fields list box,

Select: **First Name**

The First Name field should be highlighted. To move the First Name field to the Selected Fields list box,

Click:

The dialog box on your screen should be similar to Figure 2-20.

> You can also double-click on each field name in the Available Fields list box to move the field name to the Selected Fields list box.

> The ⬛ button adds all available fields to the Selected Fields list.

Figure 2-20

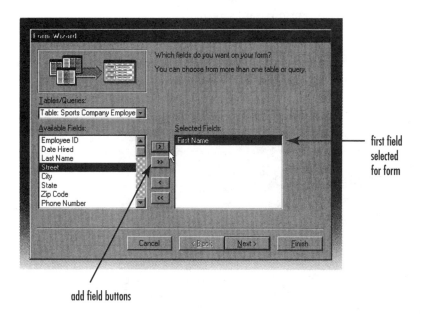

add field buttons

The First Name field is removed from the Available Fields list and added to the top of the Selected Fields list box.

In the same manner, select the fields in the order shown below and add them to the Selected Fields list.

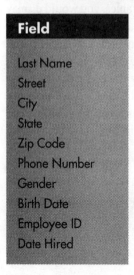

Field
Last Name
Street
City
State
Zip Code
Phone Number
Gender
Birth Date
Employee ID
Date Hired

The Available Fields list box should be empty, and the Selected Fields list box should list the fields in the selected order.

To move to the next Form Wizard screen,

Choose: Next >

The second Form Wizard dialog box on your screen should be similar to Figure 2-21.

Figure 2-21

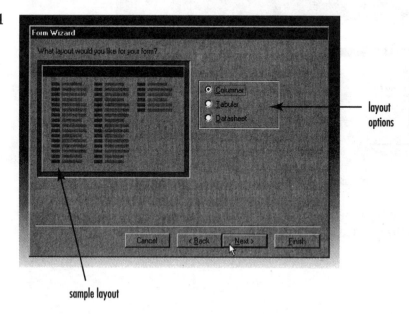

layout options

sample layout

In this dialog box you are asked to select the layout for the form. Three form layouts are available: Columnar, Tabular, and Datasheet. They are described in the table below.

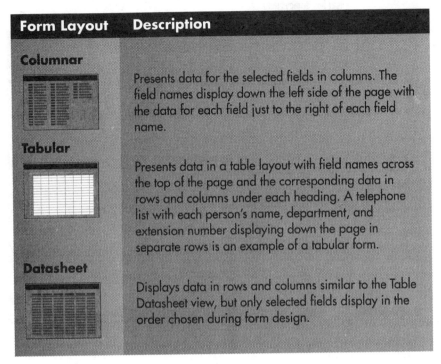

Form Layout	Description
Columnar	Presents data for the selected fields in columns. The field names display down the left side of the page with the data for each field just to the right of each field name.
Tabular	Presents data in a table layout with field names across the top of the page and the corresponding data in rows and columns under each heading. A telephone list with each person's name, department, and extension number displaying down the page in separate rows is an example of a tabular form.
Datasheet	Displays data in rows and columns similar to the Table Datasheet view, but only selected fields display in the order chosen during form design.

The columnar layout would appear most similar to the paper form currently in use by the personnel department.

Select: <u>C</u>olumnar

Choose: Next >

Next you need to select from ten different styles for your form. A sample of each style is displayed on the left side of the dialog box. They are the same styles you selected from when you created the Address Book in Lab 1. You will create the form using the Clouds style.

Select: Clouds

Choose: <u>N</u>ext >

Finally, you need to enter a form title. The form title is the name of the form. The Wizard uses the name of the table as the default title. To change the form's title,

Type: Employee Data Form

The other default setting in this screen will open the form with data in it. This setting is acceptable. To view the form,

Choose: <u>F</u>inish

The completed form is displayed in the Form view window.
    If necessary, maximize the Form window.
    Your screen should be similar to Figure 2-22.

text box displays data

Figure 2-22

field label
displays
field name

form

view

form record number indicator

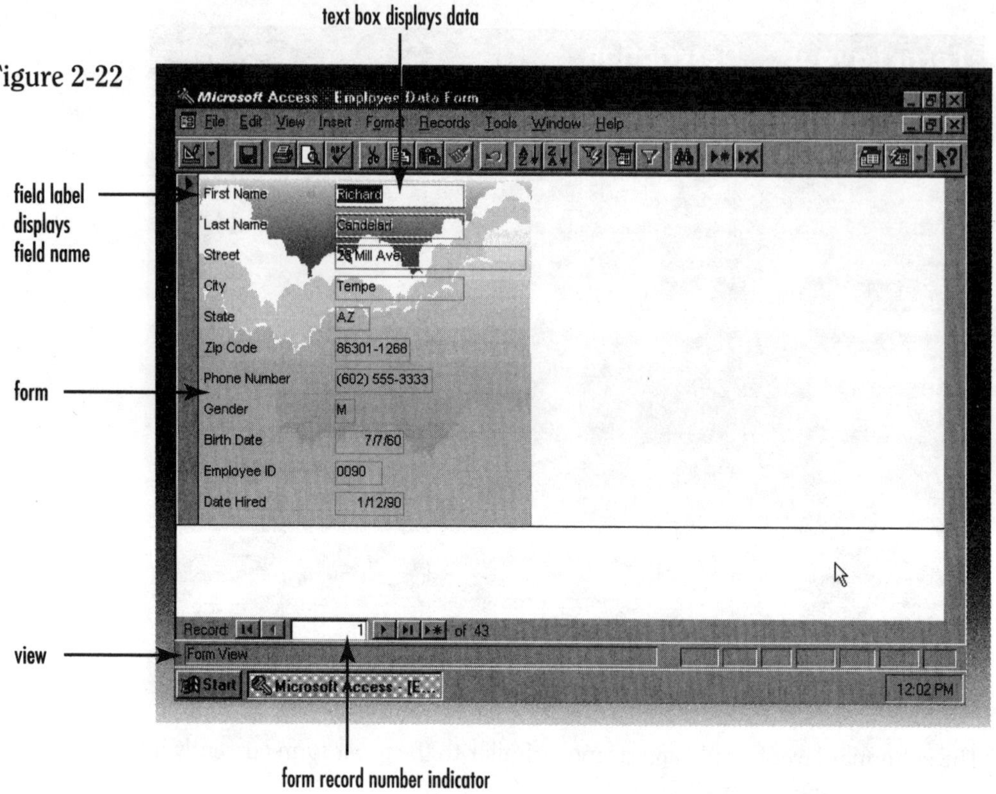

The form displays the selected fields in columnar layout using the Clouds form style. The field name labels are in a column along the left margin, and the field text boxes are in an adjacent column to the right. The employee information for Richard Candelari, record number 1, is displayed in the text boxes.

    You use the same navigation keys in Form view that you used in Datasheet view. You can move between fields in the form by using the navigation buttons at the bottom of the form, or the [Tab↹], [←Enter], [⇧Shift] + [Tab↹], and directional arrow keys on the keyboard. In addition, the [Page Up] and [Page Down] keys allow you to move between records in Form view.

    Move to record 2.

    Kimberly Reynolds' record is displayed in the form.

Changing the Form Layout

Now that you have looked at the first two records, you want to change the layout of the form to more closely resemble the paper entry form used in the Personnel department. To change the layout,

The menu equivalent is **V**iew/Form **D**esign.

Click: **Design View**

The Form Design view window on your screen should be similar to Figure 2-23.

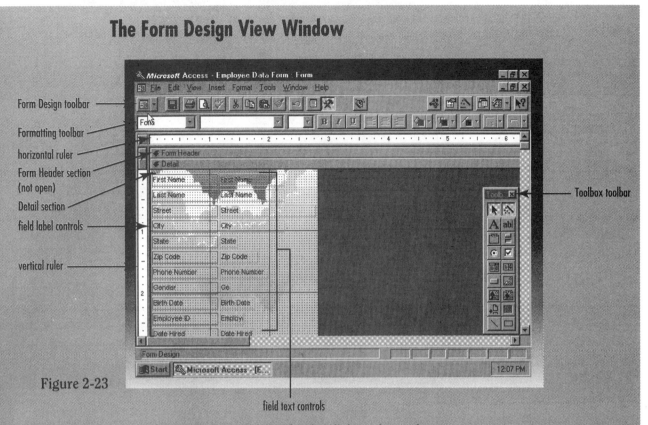

The Form Design View Window

Form Design toolbar

Formatting toolbar

horizontal ruler

Form Header section (not open)

Detail section

field label controls

vertical ruler

Toolbox toolbar

Figure 2-23

field text controls

Design view displays the form in a window that is bordered along the top by a horizontal ruler and along the left by a vertical ruler. The rulers help you correctly place items in the Form Design window.

The Form Design view automatically displays three toolbars: Form Design, Formatting, and Toolbox. The Form Design toolbar contains the standard buttons as well as buttons that are specific to the Form Design view window. These buttons are identified below.

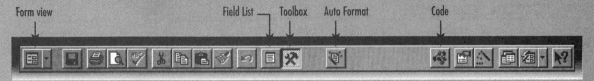

Form view   Field List   Toolbox   Auto Format   Code

The Formatting toolbar contains buttons that allow you to make text enhancements. The buttons on the Formatting toolbar are identified below.

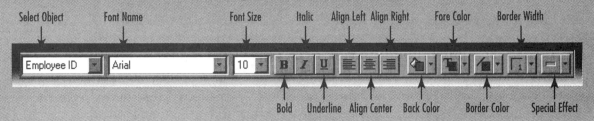

Select Object   Font Name   Font Size   Italic   Align Left   Align Right   Fore Color   Border Width

Bold   Underline   Align Center   Back Color   Border Color   Special Effect

The **Toolbox** toolbar contains buttons that are used to add and modify controls. The Toolbox buttons are identified below.

If the toolbox is not displayed, click Toolbox on the Form Design toolbar.

The Toolbox on your screen may be in a different location than in Figure 2-23. This is because a Toolbox can be moved and sized like any other window.

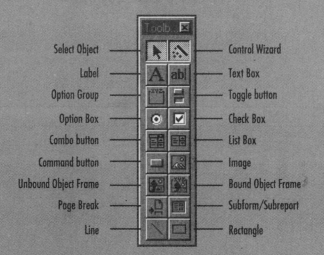

The Form Design window is divided into three areas, Form Header, Detail, and Form Footer. The contents of each section appear below the horizontal bar containing the name. The sections are described in the table below.

Section	Description
Form Header	An optional section that you can include to display information such as the form title, instructions, or graphics. The contents of a Form Header appear at the top of the screen or, if you print the form, at the top of the first page. Form Headers are not visible in Datasheet view, and do not scroll as you scroll through records. The Form Header currently contains no data.
Detail section	The area where the table data displays. The Detail section currently displays the controls for the Sports Company Employees table.
Form Footer	Another optional section that can include notes, instructions, or grand totals. Form Footers appear at the bottom of the screen or, if printed, at the end of the last page. Like Form Headers, Form Footers do not display in Datasheet view. The Form Footer section currently contains no data.

If necessary, scroll down to view the Form Footer section.

Refer to the Moving Windows section of the Windows 95 Review for information on this feature.

If necessary, move the Toolbox to the bottom right corner of the window.

Selecting Controls

Each field in the Form Design view is a control. You need to select controls in the form to modify them. To select the First Name control,

Click: **First Name label control**

Your screen should be similar to Figure 2-24.

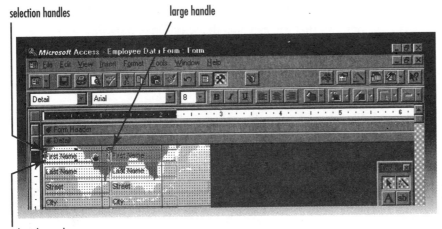

Figure 2-24

> Remember that the label controls are on the left in each set of controls.

> The mouse pointer must be ⩗ when selecting controls.

Notice that both the First Name label and text box controls are surrounded by small boxes. These boxes, called **selection handles**, are used to move and size controls. Selection handles surround a control only when the control is selected. The field name label control has eight handles and the text box control has one large handle. This indicates that the two controls will act as one when manipulated.

Click: **First Name text box control**

Now the text box control is surrounded by eight handles, and the label control has one handle. Whichever part of the field you click on is surrounded by eight handles, and the associated part of the field has one handle.

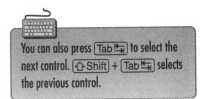

> You can also press [Tab ⇆] to select the next control. [⇧ Shift] + [Tab ⇆] selects the previous control.

Moving and Sizing Controls

Once you select a control, you can modify it by changing its location and size. The grid of dots helps you position the controls on the form. It not only provides a visual guide to positioning and sizing controls, but controls are "snapped" to the grid, or automatically positioned on the nearest grid line. You will rearrange the controls in the form as shown in Figure 2-25 on the next page.

You will begin by moving the Last Name controls to the right on the same line. When you move a selected control, use the ruler for location reference to help you align the rows and columns of controls. As you move the controls, the right edge of the form will expand to accommodate the new width of the design.

Select the Last Name controls.

Note: You can select either the label control or the text box control. Since the controls are connected, they will move together.

You will move the Last Name control to begin at the $2\frac{1}{2}$-inch position on the same line.

Position the mouse pointer on either the top or bottom border of the controls until the mouse pointer is a .

The indicates that you can drag the selection to move it.

Drag the control to the right until the left edge of the outline aligns with the $2\frac{1}{2}$-inch ruler position.

In the same manner, drag the First Name controls down the left margin of the form to the same line as the Last Name.

In a similar manner, move the other controls to the positions shown in Figure 2-25.

Your screen should be similar to Figure 2-25.

> You can also move controls without a mouse by using Ctrl + the directional arrow keys.

> The mouse pointer must be a when you drag the mouse to move a selected control.

> You can also delete controls by selecting them, then pressing Delete.

Figure 2-25

moved controls

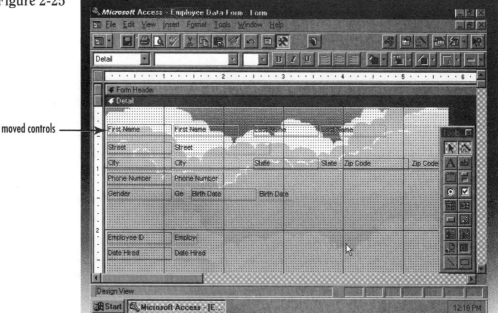

Next you will increase the size of the Street text box control.

Select the Street text box control.

When you position the mouse pointer on a handle, it changes to a ↔. The direction of the arrow indicates in which direction dragging the mouse will alter the shape of the object. This is similar to sizing a window.

Point to the middle handle on the right end of the Street text box control.

The mouse pointer is displayed as ↔.

Drag the control to the right until it aligns with the end of the Last Name text box control on the line above it.

Aligning Controls

Next, you need to align the First Name, Street, City, Phone Number, and Gender controls so they are even along the left edge. Rather than selecting each control individually and moving it, you can select several controls at the same time. When you select multiple controls, you can move all the selected fields as a group, align the selected controls so they are evenly spaced or in line one below the other, or make other changes to the entire group of controls.

To select multiple controls, press and hold down ⬆Shift, then click each control. When you have selected the controls you want, release ⬆Shift.

To select the controls you want to align,

Click: **the First Name control**
Press: ⬆Shift
Click: **the Street control**

Continue to hold ⬆Shift and click the City, Phone Number, and Gender controls, then release ⬆Shift.

To align the selected controls,

Choose: **F̱ormat/A̱lign/Ḻeft**

The controls all shift to the left and align with the control that was farthest left. Your screen should be similar to Figure 2-26.

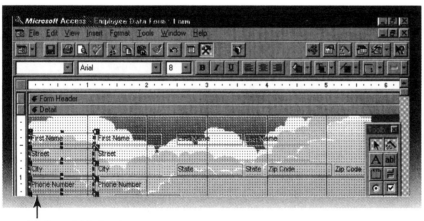

Figure 2-26

selected controls left-aligned

To deselect the controls, click any blank area of the form.

You now want to align all the controls in the upper section of this form so there is an even amount of space between each control. This vertical spacing can be adjusted between any group of selected controls.

Another way to select controls is to drag a selection box around the controls. To select the controls using this method, point to a blank area above the first control and drag until the box surrounds the controls you want to select.

When you release the mouse button, all the controls inside the box will be selected.

Using this method, select all the controls (excluding the Employee ID and Date Hired field controls) on the form.

To make the vertical spacing equal between the selected controls,

Choose: F̲ormat/V̲ertical Spacing/Make E̲qual

The vertical space between controls is adjusted to equal the greatest amount of existing vertical space between the selected controls.

Deselect the controls.

> You can fine-tune placement by selecting a control and using the ⌈Ctrl⌉ + directional keys to move it in increments.

Adding Text to a Form

Next you will add a control in the form header to display the form title. In addition, you want to add two subheads within the form to identify the personal data and company data areas. The Toolbox buttons let you add text, arrows, boxes, and other design elements to a form.

To add the form header, you first need to add a space in the Form Header area for a text label. You add space to the Form Header area by dragging the horizontal bar at the top of the Detail area down.

Point to the top of the Detail section bar until the mouse pointer is a ✛. Drag it down approximately 1/2 inch on the vertical ruler.

Your screen should be similar to Figure 2-27.

Figure 2-27

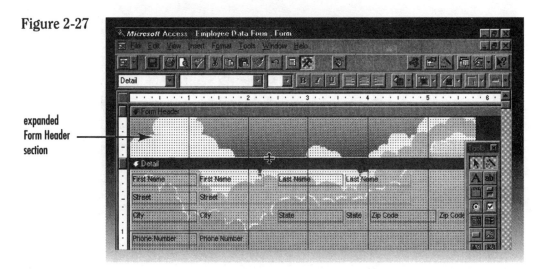

expanded
Form Header
section

To add the text for the form header, from the Toolbox,

Choose: [A] Label

Next you need to move the mouse to the location in the form where you want to enter the text. As you move the mouse in the window, the mouse pointer changes to ⁺**A** to remind you that you are adding text. You indicate where you want to begin entering the text by clicking on the location in the window.

Click in the Form Header area.

An insertion point is displayed in the form header, indicating that you can begin typing the descriptive label.

Type:　　**The Sports Company Employee Record**

The form title appears in a control box and can be sized and moved like any other control. To indicate the label is complete,

> You can edit text in controls just as you edit other text.

Press:　　⟮←Enter⟯

Now you will add another text label for the subheads in the Detail section.

Click:　　[A] **Label**

Click in the space above the First Name control in the Detail section.

Type:　　**Personal Data:**
Press:　　⟮←Enter⟯

In a similar manner, enter the subhead "Company Data:" in the space above the Employee ID control.

Your screen should be similar to Figure 2-28.

form header label control

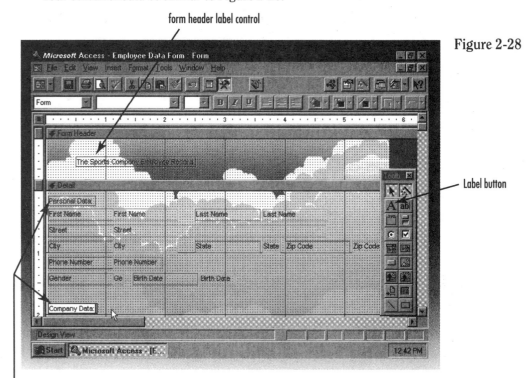

Figure 2-28

Label button

subhead label controls

Changing Fonts

You can further change the way a form appears by changing the fonts, colors, and styles of the text in the controls.

Concept 10: Fonts

One of the easiest and most creative ways you can enhance the tables, forms, and reports you create in Access is to change the font. A **font** is the way text appears when printed. The font includes three elements: typeface, type size, and type style.

A **typeface** is the design and shape of characters. The typefaces are named, such as Times Roman, Courier, Helvetica, and Arial. **Type size** refers to either the height or width of a character. Most characters are measured in **points**. A 72-point character is 1 inch tall. The width of a character, or **pitch**, is measured in characters per inch. The most common type size for text is 10 or 12 points, although headings can often be as large as 20 or 24 points.

Some fonts are **monospaced**, which means that the width of each character takes up the same amount of space. Courier New is a monospaced font that can be used to mimic text you see on a computer screen. Most fonts are **proportional**, which means that some letters, such as m or w, take up more space than other letters, such as i or t. Arial and Times New Roman are proportional fonts. Most fonts are also **scalable**, which means they can be printed in almost any point size, depending upon the capabilities of your printer. Nonscalable fonts are assigned a single point size.

Type style refers to the special attributes you assign to characters, such as bold, italic, or underline. You can also add color to the characters.

Several common fonts in different sizes and styles are shown in the table below.

Font Name	Font Size	Font Style
Arial	This is 12 pt. This is 18 pt.	**Bold 18 pt.**
Courier New	This is 12 pt. This is 18 pt.	**Bold 18 pt.**
Times New Roman	This is 12 pt. This is 18 pt.	**Bold 18 pt.**

Although you must apply font changes to entire controls rather than changing individual characters or words, you can apply multiple font changes to a table, form, or report by selecting and changing fonts for individual controls. In addition, you can change background colors on forms and reports. You should be careful, however, not to combine too many different fonts and colors or to use fancy fonts that might make it difficult to read the screen or are distracting to use for long periods of time.

The first text enhancement you want to make is to increase the font size of the text in all controls of the form. Larger fonts make it easier to read the data that is displayed in the form. To select all controls on the form,

Choose: Edit/Select All

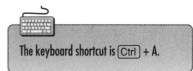

The keyboard shortcut is Ctrl + A.

All the controls in the form are selected and any formatting changes you make will apply to all controls until you clear the selection.

The **Formatting toolbar** buttons are used to make text enhancements, such as changing the font, font size, font style, or adding color. Notice that the Font Size button displays "8" as the point size of all text in the selected controls. You want to increase the font size to 10 points. To do this from the Font Size drop-down box,

Select: 10

The point size of all text in the selected controls is 10 points and much easier to read.

Clear the selection.

Next you want to make the form title an even larger font size.

Select the form header label control and change the font size to 20.

Now the font size is larger than the control box in which the label is displayed. You can size the control to fully display the label by dragging on the selection handles as you did earlier, or you can allow Access to automatically size the control around the new text. To automatically resize the control,

Remember, you must make font changes to all text in the control. You cannot change individual words or letters.

Choose: Format/Size/to Fit

You also want to make the title a different typeface. As you can see, the name of the default typeface, Arial, is displayed in the Font Name button.

Open the Font Name button and select Times New Roman as the typeface.

Move and adjust the size of the title control to center it in the Form Header section. Clear the selection.

The new typeface and size of the title greatly enhance the appearance of the form.

Your screen should be similar to Figure 2-29.

Figure 2-29

control sized to fit text
in larger type size

controls too small for text

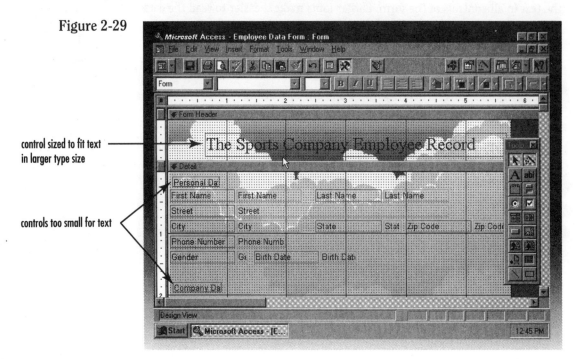

You also want to size the control boxes of the subheads and change their labels to bold to make them stand out from the rest of the text.

Select the Personal Data control.

Click: **B** Bold

Choose: F**o**rmat/**S**ize/to **F**it

In a similar manner bold and size the Company Data control.

If necessary, adjust the vertical placement and alignment of the two control labels.

Adding Text Color

You can also make controls more noticeable by adding color to their background, text, or borders. In addition, you can use special effects such as shadows to enhance the control border.

To improve the appearance of the form, you will make the text in the form header label red and add a shadow box to the control.

To add color, select the form header label control. Open the ▉ Fore Color drop-down menu.

A palette of 56 colors is displayed.

Choose: **red**

Then, to add the shadow effect, open the  Special Effect drop-down menu.
The menu displays six special effect options.

Choose: 　▣ **Shadowed**

Clear the selection.
Your screen should be similar to Figure 2-30.

color and shadow
added to control

Fore Color
button

Special Effect
button

Figure 2-30

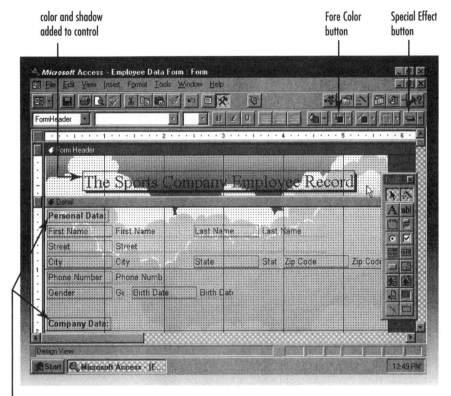

controls sized to fit and bold

The settings are applied to the selected control.
To see how the form will look onscreen, you will switch to Form view.

Click: 　▦ **Form View**

Your screen should be similar to Figure 2-31.

Figure 2-31

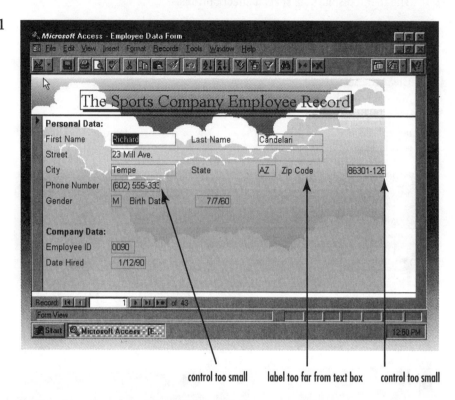

control too small   label too far from text box   control too small

The layout and design changes greatly enhance the appearance of the form. However, now you can also see that the Zip Code and Phone Number text box controls are not wide enough to display the data in the fields. You also notice that some of the text box controls are not very close to the label controls.

To make further changes to the form, switch back to Design view. Increase the size of the Zip Code and Phone Number text box controls.

Reduce the size of the State, Zip Code, and Birth Date label controls.

Now you need to move the text box controls closer to their labels.

Select the State control. Point to the larger handle of the State text box control. When the mouse pointer is a ♥, drag the control closer to the State label control.

In a similar manner, adjust the Zip Code and Birth Date text box controls.

Return to Form view.

> Depending on your screen display, other controls may not be wide enough. Make the necessary adjustments as you did for the Zip Code and Phone Number fields.

Your screen should be similar to Figure 2-32.

space between controls decreased

Figure 2-32

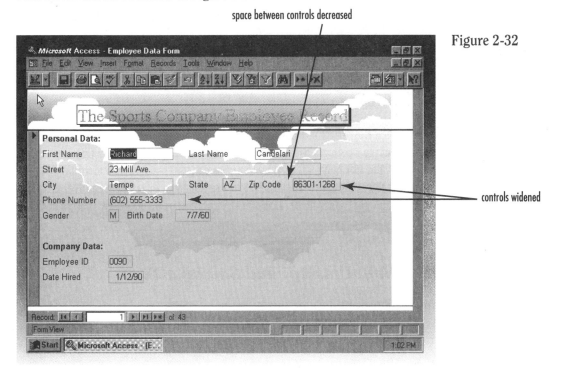

controls widened

Entering Records in Form View

Now that the custom form is complete, you can use it to enter new records.

Move to a new blank entry form and enter the following data for a new record.

Use ▶* New Record in the Form toolbar or the ▶* navigation button to display a blank form.

EMPLOYEE DATA	
First Name: **Brent**	Last Name: **Smith**
Street: **89 E. Southern Dr.**	
City: **Tempe** State: **AZ** Zip Code: **85301-2316**	
Phone Number: **(602)555-1234**	
Gender: **m** Birth Date: **April 13, 1971**	
For Personnel Use Only:	
Employee ID: **1027**	
Date Hired: **September 12, 1995**	

The input masks will appear in the form as you type in the field's control.

DATABASE

Using the form makes entering the new employee data much faster because the fields are in the same order as the information in the paper Employee Data form used by the Personnel department.

Enter another record using your special Employee ID 9999 and your first and last names. The data in all other fields can be fictitious, except enter the current date as your date hired.

To see the records you entered in Datasheet view, switch to Datasheet view. Scroll up a few rows to display both new records.

Notice that the field columns are in the same order as in the form. Form Datasheet view reflects the same layout as in the form. The Table Datasheet view, however, has not been affected by the changes you made in the form layout. Also notice that the new records are not in primary key order by employee number. When you open the table in Datasheet view, the new records will appear in primary key order.

Switch back to Form view.

Printing, Closing, and Saving a Form

You want to print the form displaying your record.

Display your record in the form.

To select your record,

> **Choose:**   <u>E</u>dit/Se<u>l</u>ect Record
> **Choose:**   <u>F</u>ile/<u>P</u>rint
> **Select:**   Selected <u>R</u>ecord(s)
> **Choose:**   OK

Your printer should print the form that contains your name.

Close the Form window.

A warning box prompts you to save your changes.

> **Choose:**    Yes

The Database window is displayed, showing the new form object name in the Forms tab object list.

Exit Access.

Display the View button drop-down list to see a list of available views.

You can also click in the vertical bar at the left edge of the Form window to select the record.

WARNING!

Do not remove your data disk from the drive until you exit Access.

LAB REVIEW

■ ■ ■ ■ ■ ■ ■ ■ ■ ■ ■

Key Terms

columnar form   (DB89)
compound control   (DB85)
control   (DB85)
datasheet form   (DB89)
Detail section   (DB92)
expression   (DB77)
font   (DB98)
form   (DB85)
Form Datasheet view   (DB85)
Form Design view   (DB85)
Form Footer   (DB92)
Form Header   (DB92)
Form Preview   (DB85)

Form view   (DB85)
Formatting toolbar   (DB99)
identifier   (DB77)
input mask   (DB66)
label   (DB85)
literal character   (DB66)
mask character   (DB66)
monospaced   (DB98)
operator   (DB77)
pitch   (DB98)
points   (DB98)
proportional   (DB98)
scalable   (DB98)

selection handle   (DB93)
sort   (DB81)
tab order   (DB87)
tabular form   (DB89)
text box   (DB85)
Toolbox   (DB92)
typeface   (DB98)
type size   (DB98)
type style   (DB98)
Undo   (DB74)
validation text   (DB76)
validity check   (DB76)
value   (DB77)

Command Summary

Command	Shortcut	Toolbar	Action
File/**O**pen Database	Ctrl + O		Opens existing database
Edit/U**n**do Current Field/Record	Esc		Cancels last action
Edit/Cu**t**	Ctrl + X, Delete		Deletes selected record
Edit/Delete **R**ow			Deletes selected field from table in Design view
Edit/Se**l**ect Record	⇧ Shift + Spacebar		Selects current record
Edit/Select **A**ll	Ctrl + A		Selects all controls on a form in Design view
Edit/**F**ind	Ctrl + F		Locates specified data
Edit/Re**p**lace	Ctrl + H		Locates and replaces specified data
View/Form **D**esign			Switches to Form Design view
Insert/**F**ield			Inserts a new field in table in Design view
F**o**rmat/**H**ide Columns			Hides columns in Datasheet view
F**o**rmat/**U**nhide Columns			Redisplays hidden columns in Datasheet view
F**o**rmat/A**l**ign/**L**eft			Aligns selected controls to left

Command	Shortcut	Toolbar	Action
F**o**rmat/**S**ize/to **F**it			Automatically resizes a control to fit around text
F**o**rmat/**V**ertical Spacing/Make **E**qual			Equalizes vertical space between selected multiple controls
Records/**S**ort/**A**scending		▨	Reorders records in ascending alphabetical order
Records/**R**emove Filter/Sort			Restores primary key sort order

Matching

1. operator

2. selection handles

3. ▨

4. =“Accounting” or “Finance”

5. control

6. >

7. sort

8. validity check

9. ▨

10. form

_____ a. links a form to the underlying table

_____ b. used to check that value entered in a field is valid for field type

_____ c. database object used primarily for onscreen display

_____ d. adds a text label control to form

_____ e. symbol, such as = or AND, that indicates operation to be performed

_____ f. example of an expression that would limit data that could be entered in a field

_____ g. toolbar button to locate specified data

_____ h. small boxes that surround a selected control

_____ i. changes display order of a table

_____ j. format character that forces all data in field to uppercase

Fill-In Questions

1. Complete the following statements by filling in the blanks with the correct terms.

a. A(n) _____ is a combination of symbols that produces specific results.

b. The _____ property is used to specify a value that is automatically entered in a field when a new record is created.

c. When _____ are performed, Access makes sure that the entry is acceptable in the field.

d. Records can be temporarily displayed in a different order by using the _____ feature.

e. Forms are primarily used for _____ and making changes to existing records.

f. The _____ property changes the way data appears in a field.

g. The three form layouts are _____, _____, and _____.

h. A(n) _____ is a pattern that controls the data that can be entered in a field.

i. When a form control in selected, it is surrounded by _____.

j. A(n) _____ is the design and shape of characters.

Discussion Questions

1. Discuss several different format properties and how they are used in a database.

2. Discuss why you would use input masks in a database. Give several examples of input masks and describe how they would affect the entry of data in a field.

3. Describe the Undo feature. What are some limitations of this feature in Access?

4. Discuss how validity checks work. What are some advantages of adding validity checks to a field? Include several examples.

5. Discuss the different ways records can be sorted. What are some advantages of sorting records?

Hands-On Practice Exercises

Step by Step

Rating System	
☆	Easy
☆☆	Moderate
☆☆☆	Difficult

1. You have just received a frantic call from James O'Dell at Valley of the Sun Office Supplies. He loves the database you helped him create, but his 10-year-old niece has been "helping" him enter data into his inventory table. He has discovered that it is a horrible mess. His niece put forth her best efforts, but there are numerous typographical errors in the table. James does not know how to edit his database.

    a. Open the Valley of the Sun Office Supplies database and the Inventory table, then help James straighten up his database by making these changes:

Item #78564	should read "clips," not "blips"
Item #28765	should indicate 10 Rolls/Box
Item #18719	has 8 pens in stock, not 863
Item #25743	price is $18.50 not $185.00

    b. Using the Find command, find item #53410 and enter the correct item number, 54301.

    c. James also wants to add a field property to the Item Name field to force the data in the field to display in all capital letters. Make the change.

    d. Enter your name in the item name field of a new record. Resize the Item Name column. Sort the table by Item Name, then print the table.

    e. Return the table to the primary key sort order.

    f. Close the table, saving any changes.

2. Michelle owns Food for Thought Catering. As her catering business continues to grow, she has established a reputation for excellent gourmet health foods. Nevertheless, she continues to serve whatever kinds of food her customers request. She wants your assistance to help her customize her database of client records.

    a. Open the Food for Thought Catering database and the Customers table.

    b. To help Michelle track which customers prefer healthy foods, in Table Design view, add a field after the Preferred Theme field. Use the following guidelines to define the new field:

Field name:	Healthy Foods
Data type:	Text
Description:	Does client prefer health-conscious foods?
Field size:	8
Format:	Display in all capital letters
Validation rule:	"Always" or "Never" or "Optional"
Validation text:	"Selection must be either Always, Never, or Optional"

    c. Update the table by entering an option in the Healthy Foods field for each record.

    d. Using the Form Wizard, create a columnar form. Use the Dusk style. Title the new form "Customer Information Form." In Design view, move the controls to make the computerized form look similar to Michelle's current paper form shown below. Also add the label for the title and a subhead for the Customer Preferences section of the form as shown in the paper form.

Customer Information Form

Customer #: _____
Company: _____
Contact:_____ Phone: _____
Address: _____

Customer Preferences

Healthy Food? _____
Preferred Theme? _____
Favorite Dish? _____

---

e. In Form Design view, make these enhancements to the form:

- Increase the font size for all controls to 12 points.

- Change the font for the Customer Information Form label control to a typeface of your choice and to 20 points, then size the control to fit.

- Change the font for the Customer Preferences label control to 14 points italic, then size the control to fit and underline the text.

f. Add these new customers to the table using the new form:

Customer Information Form

Customer #: 27691
Company: Desert Rescue Cleaning Service
Contact: Debbie Harrington Phone: 212-3999
Address: 6730 E. Ray Rd., Chandler, AZ 85601

Customer Preferences

Healthy Food? Always
Preferred Theme? Merry Maids
Favorite Dish? Souffle

Customer Information Form

Customer #: 41476
Company: Sunset Publishing
Contact: Jessica Herrera   Phone: 999-6110
Address: 3276 S. Rural Rd., Tempe, AZ 89562

Customer Preferences

Healthy Food? Always
Preferred Theme? Library
Favorite Dish? Spinach Salad

---

g. Adjust the size of any controls as needed to display the data appropriately.

h. Display the record for The Sports Company in the form. Change the contact name to your name. Print the record.

3. Eddie Fitzpatrick of TechnoBabble Electronics heard from Michelle at Food for Thought Catering that you are great with Access databases. Eddie needs you to help him customize the database that his cousin Teddy helped him set up. He has been putting in records, but doesn't know how to edit the data or to create a data entry form.

a. Open the TechnoBabble Electronics database and the Inventory table. Make these changes to the records:

Item #7195: change 100 to 133 in the Description field

Item #8031: change sEcurty to Security in the Description field

In all records where MPS is the supplier, change MPS to CTC

b. Teddy created sample entries for the table while Eddie was learning how to use the database. You now need to delete those records. Delete records for items #5640, #5926, and #6832.

c. Find item #8205 and change the cost from $200 to $150.

d. In Table Design view, add a field for the purchase price, between Cost and Quantity on Hand, with these specifications:

Field name: Purchase Price

Data type: Currency

Description: Cost to Customer

e. Add a field between Shelf Location and Supplier for the status of each item, indicating whether it is a regularly stocked item or a special order item. Use these specifications:

Field name: Status

Data type: Text

Description: What is the stocking status of this item?

Field size: 9

Format: Display in all capital letters

Default value: STOCK

Validation rule: Stock or SpecOrder

Validation text: Stocking status must be either Stock or SpecOrder

f. Change the Quantity on Hand field name to # On Hand, and the Shelf Location field name to Shelf. Change the supplies description to "3-character supplier code."

g. Add customer prices and stocking status to the existing data in the table.

h. Sort the table on the Description field, resize the columns, then print the table.

i. Return the table to the primary key sort order.

j. Create a columnar form for Eddie using the Form Wizard. Use the Colorful 1 background and name the form TechnoBabble Electronics Inventory List.

k. In Form Design view, move the controls so the form layout looks similar to Eddie's existing data entry form shown below. Add the label controls to display the form title and the Confidential subhead.

TechnoBabble Electronics Inventory List

Item #: _____

Description: _____

Shelf: _____   # On Hand: _____

Purchase Price: _____

Confidential

Supplier: _____

Status: _____   Cost: _____

---

l. In Form Design view, enhance the form by making these changes:

- Change the form title label text from white to yellow.
- Bold all controls in the form.
- Change all controls to 10-point Times New Roman.
- Change the text in the title control to a typeface of your choice and 18 points, then size the control to fit.
- Change the text in the Confidential control to 14-point Arial italic, then size the control to fit.
- Enlarge the status text box control.

m. Using the form, enter the following two new records:

TechnoBabble Electronics Inventory List

Item #: 2317
Description: Pager
Shelf: B-21   # On Hand: 4
Purchase Price: $74.50

Confidential
Supplier: CTC
Status: STOCK   Cost: 32.95

TechnoBabble Electronics Inventory List

Item #: 9611
Description: Keyboard, Electronic Music
Shelf: H-01   # On Hand: 1
Purchase Price: $324.35

Confidential
Supplier: MEE
Status: SPECORDER   Cost: $178.50

---

n. While looking at the form, you notice several controls are not sized appropriately for the data they display. Return to Display view and adjust the field controls as needed.

o. Use the Find command to locate the record for Item #3910. Add your name in the Description field. Select, then print the record. Close the form, saving any changes.

On Your Own

4. Debbie owns Desert Rescue Cleaning Service. Her commercial cleaning business is prospering, and she has asked you to help her by entering some new data and customizing her database of client records.

Open the Desert Rescue Cleaning Service database and the Clients table, then add five new records with either real or fictitious data. Change the contact in The Sports Company record to your name. Adjust the column widths as necessary.

Make any changes to the field properties that would make data entry easier, such as adding format properties or validation rules.

Use the Form Wizard to create a columnar form for data entry, named Desert Rescue Cleaning Service Client Data Form, arranging the controls to make data entry easy. Remember to add a title and any other helpful information on the form as a label.

Find the record for The Sports Company and print that form.

5. Michael has just contacted you from Go West Dude Ranch. The database you helped Michael create is working well, but he needs to make some changes. He is adding clients daily. Most of the clients are medium-sized companies who rent the Dude Ranch for special company functions, meetings, or other corporate events. Michael would like to track these customers. Help him with the database by making the following changes:

Open the Go West Dude Ranch database. Create a new table named Business Clients to track clients. Include an identification field and a contact person for each company. Remember to create a primary key field. Use appropriate field properties to make data entry easier.

Add three new business clients to the table. Adjust the display so that all information is displayed in each column. Sort the data by company name, then print the table. Return the order to primary key order. Remember to save any layout changes to the table.

Create a columnar form based on the Business Clients table for entering new clients into the table, and name it Go West Dude Ranch New Client Information. Enter three more new clients, including The Sports Company, making yourself the contact person for the company. Print that record form.

Create a columnar form named Go West Dude Ranch Employees, based on the Staff Records table, for the employees table that you helped Michael create earlier. You have agreed to take on another part-time job helping Michael out at the Dude Ranch in the Data Processing department, so enter a record for yourself using the new form, then print your record.

6. You are looking for a new job. To keep track of all the companies you have contacted, you decide to create a database file of this information.

Name the database file My Contacts. Create a table named Contacts that includes fields such as the company name, address, phone number, name of the contact person, and type of company. Include a field that is a unique number that you can assign each record. Make this field the primary key. Include other fields that you can use to track your status with the company—for example, fields that indicate the date a resume was sent, a phone contact was made, or the date of an interview.

Add appropriate field properties, such as formats, validation rules, and input masks. Enter at least five records. Print the table.

Create a columnar form named [Your Name] Employment Contacts. Use the form to add five additional records. Print one record.

Concept Summary

2 Modifying a Table and Creating a Form

Format Property

You can use the Format property to create custom formats that change the way numbers, dates, times, and text display and print.

Input Mask Property

An input mask is a pattern that controls the data that can be entered in a field.

Default Value Property

The Default Value property is used to specify a value to be automatically entered in a field when a new record is created.

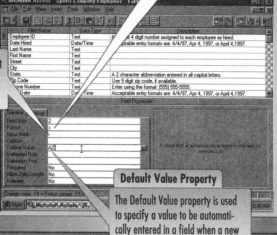

Concepts

Format Property
Default Value Property
Input Mask Property

Find and Replace
Undo

Validity Checks
Expressions

Sort

Forms
Fonts

Sort

You can quickly reorder records in a table by sorting a table to display in a different record order.

Employee ID	Date Hired	Last Name	First Name	Street	City	State	Z
3550	11/15/95	Adams	Thomas	1324 S. Price Rd.	Tempe	AZ	862
1151	10/14/90	Anderson	Susan	4389 S. Hayden Rd.	Mesa	AZ	852
0151	10/14/90	Anderson	Susan	4389 S. Hayden Rd.	Mesa	AZ	852
0839	8/14/91	Artis	Jose	358 Maple Dr.	Scottsdale	AZ	852
0234	4/12/91	Bergstrom	Drew	8943 W. Southern Ave.	Mesa	AZ	84
3501	9/4/94	Briggs	Scott	45 E. Camelback Rd.	Phoenix	AZ	820
2312	11/4/93	Broeker	Kimberly	23 Price Rd.	Tempe	AZ	862
2341	2/4/94	Cady	Helen	34 University Dr.	Tempe	AZ	862
0380	5/12/91	Camalette	Anthony	893 E. McDonald Rd.	Mesa	AZ	84
0090	1/12/90	Candelari	Richard	23 Mill Ave.	Tempe	AZ	862
1460	11/5/92	DeLuca	Elizabeth	21 W. Southern Ave.	Mesa	AZ	84
0230	3/19/90	Dodd	Susan	23 Broadway Rd.	Mesa	AZ	84
3490	3/4/94	Dunn	William	947 S. Forest St.	Tempe	AZ	862
3389	3/4/94	Ehmann	Kurt	7867 Forest Ave.	Phoenix	AZ	820
1481	12/1/92	Fadaro	Jane	89 S. Central Ave.	Phoenix	AZ	820
0160	3/7/90	Falk	Nancy	470 S. Adams Rd.	Chandler	AZ	83
1560	7/8/93	Fulton	Cindy	75 Brooklea Dr.	Scottsdale	AZ	852
3554	11/15/95	Granger	Michael	12 E. 7th St.	Phoenix	AZ	820

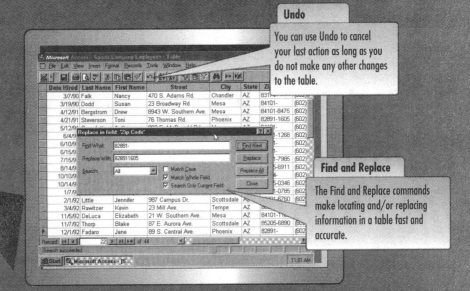

Undo

You can use Undo to cancel your last action as long as you do not make any other changes to the table.

Find and Replace

The Find and Replace commands make locating and/or replacing information in a table fast and accurate.

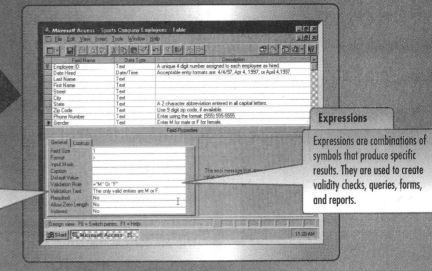

Validity Checks

Access automatically performs certain checks, called validity checks, on values entered in a field to make sure that the values are valid for the field type.

Expressions

Expressions are combinations of symbols that produce specific results. They are used to create validity checks, queries, forms, and reports.

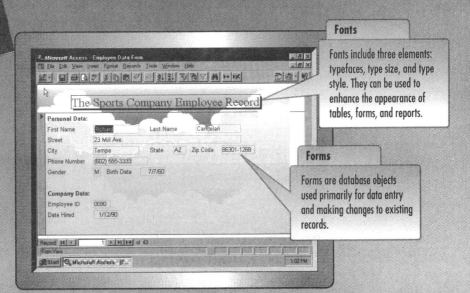

Fonts

Fonts include three elements: typefaces, type size, and type style. They can be used to enhance the appearance of tables, forms, and reports.

Forms

Forms are database objects used primarily for data entry and making changes to existing records.

Filtering and Querying Tables

You are probably now gaining an appreciation for how a database program makes many jobs easier and more efficient. Compiling, storing, and updating information in your database is useful only if you can find the information you need quickly, and can manipulate it and analyze it to answer specific questions.

In this lab you will learn to ask questions to get the information you need from your database tables. As you learn about the analytical features, think what it would be like to do the same task by hand. How long would it take? Would it be as accurate or as well presented? Your appreciation grows as you learn more about what the application can do for you.

Concept Overview

The following concepts will be introduced in this lab:

1. Filter — A filter is a restriction you place on records in the open datasheet or form to temporarily isolate a specified group of records.

2. AND and OR Operators — The AND and OR operators are used to specify multiple conditions that must be met for the records to display in the query datasheet.

3. Wildcard Characters — Wildcard characters are placeholders that represent any series of characters or any single character.

4. Queries — A query is a question you ask of a database that allows you to view data in different ways, to analyze data, and even to change existing data.

5. Joins and Relationships — You can bring information from different tables in your database together by defining a relationship to join the tables.

6. Calculated Field — To analyze data in a table, a variety of calculations can be made on data in fields and the results displayed in a query.

CASE STUDY

Now that you have the table of employee records structured the way you want, you will use the information to answer questions and create reports. You have also created several other tables that contain employee data such as pay rates and job titles. You will use the information in the tables to provide the answers to several inquiries about The Sports Company employees.

Part 1

Using Filter by Selection

Start Access for Windows 95. Put your data disk in the appropriate drive for your system.

You have continued to enter employee records into the Employees table. The updated table has been saved for you as Sports Company Employees in the Sports Company Personnel Records database on your data disk.

Open the Sports Company Personnel Records database file.

The Tables list box of the Database window displays the names of four tables in this database: Sports Company Employees, Weekly Hours Worked, Employee Pay Rates, and Employees by Department and Position. These tables will be used throughout the lab.

Open the Sports Company Employees table. If necessary, maximize the table Datasheet window.

This table now contains 72 records.

Add your information as a new record using your special ID number 9999 and the current date as your hire date.

While you are using the table, the store manager asks you for two items of information. The first is a request from an employee who wants to form a carpool. The employee wants to know the names of other employees who live in her town. The second is to help figure out the name of the employee who recently sent the manager a memo. The memo suggested how the warehouse could save time and money by changing one of the reporting procedures it uses. Although the first name in the memo is legible, the last name is not. The manager can only make out the first letter of the last name, C.

To answer both questions, you could sort the table and then write down the needed information. However, this could be time consuming if you had hundreds of employees in the table. A faster way is to apply a filter to the table records to locate this information.

Concept 1: Filter

A **filter** is a restriction you place on records in the open datasheet or form to quickly isolate and display a subset of records. A filter is created by specifying a set of limiting conditions, or **criteria**, you want records to meet in order to be displayed. A filter is ideal when you only want to display the subset for a brief time, then return immediately to the full set of records. You can print the filtered records as you would any form or table. A filter is only temporary and all records are redisplayed when you remove the filter or close and reopen the table or form. The filter results cannot be saved. However, the filter can be saved with the table and the results quickly redisplayed.

To find only those employees in the city of Chandler, you can quickly filter out all the other records using the Filter by Selection method. **Filter by Selection** is used when you can easily find and select an instance of the value in the table that you want the filter to use as the criteria to meet.

How the value is selected determines what results will be displayed in the subset. Placing the insertion point in a field selects the entire field contents. The filtered subset will include all records containing an exact match. Selecting part of a value in a field (by highlighting it) displays all records containing the selection in the subset. For example, in a table for a book collection, you could position the mouse pointer anywhere in a field for author Stephen King, choose the Filter by Selection command, and only records for books whose author matches the selected name, "Stephen King," would be displayed. Selecting the last name "King" would include all records for authors Stephen King, Martin Luther King, and Barbara Kingsolver.

You want to filter the table to display only those records with a City field entry of Chandler. To specify the city to locate, you need to select an example of the data in the table.

Move to the City field of record 3.

The City field contents, Chandler, is selected. To apply the filter,

> If the selected part of a value starts with the first character in the field, the subset displays all records whose values begin with the same selected characters.

> The menu equivalent is Records/Filter/ Filter By Selection.

Click: **Filter by Selection**

Your screen should be similar to Figure 3-1.

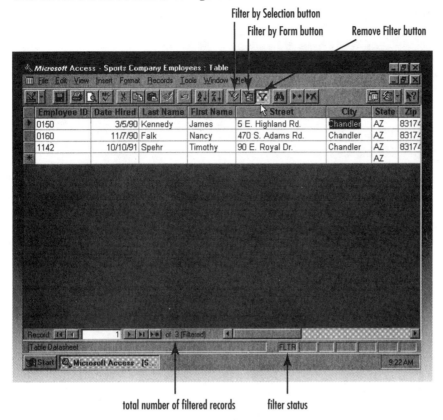

Filter by Selection button

Filter by Form button Remove Filter button

Figure 3-1

total number of filtered records   filter status

The datasheet displays only those records that contain the selected city. All other records are temporarily hidden. The status bar indicates the total number of filtered records and shows that the datasheet is filtered. You can print the filtered datasheet like any other datasheet.

To remove the filter,

Click:  **Remove Filter**

> The menu equivalent is **R**ecords/**R**emove Filter/Sort.

All the table records are redisplayed.

Using Filter by Form

After seeing how easy it was to locate this information, the manager asks you to also locate employees who live in the city of Mesa. This information may help in setting up the carpool, since the people traveling from the city of Chandler pass through Mesa on the way to the store. To find out this additional information, you need to use the **Filter by Form** method. This method allows you to perform filters on multiple criteria.

Click: 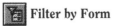 **Filter by Form**

> The menu equivalent is **R**ecords/**F**ilter/**F**ilter By Form.

The Filter by Form window on your screen should be similar to Figure 3-2.

The Filter by Form Window

Figure 3-2

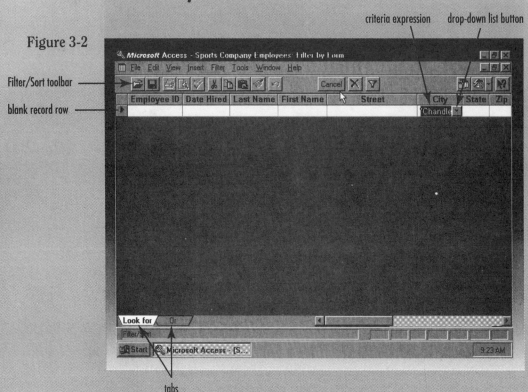

criteria expression

drop-down list button

Filter/Sort toolbar

blank record row

tabs

The Filter by Form window displays a blank version of the current datasheet with empty fields in which you specify the criteria. This window automatically displays a Filter/Sort toolbar that contains the standard buttons as well as buttons that are specific to the Filter by Form window. These buttons are identified below.

Close Filter

Clear Grid

Apply Filter

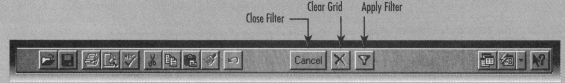

> Refer to Concept 7: Expressions in Lab 2 ro review this concept.

The window also includes two tabs, Look For and Or, where you enter the filter criterion. The criteria are entered in the blank field space of the record row as an expression. A **criteria expression** specifies the criteria for the filter to use. You can either type values or choose values from a drop-down list in the desired field to create the criteria expression.

Currently, the City field displays the criterion you last specified using Filter by Selection as the criteria expression. Notice that the field displays a drop-down list button. Each field will display a drop-down button when the field is selected. Clicking the button displays a list of values that are available in that field from which you can select to help you enter the criteria expression.

Since the City field already contains the correct criterion, you do not need to enter a different criterion. Next, you need to add the second criterion to the filter to include all records with a City field value of Mesa.

To instruct the filter to locate records meeting multiple criteria, you use the AND or OR operators.

Concept 2: AND and OR Operators

The AND and OR operators are used to specify multiple conditions that must be met for the records to display in the filter datasheet. The AND operator narrows the search, because a record must meet both conditions to be included. The OR operator broadens the search, because any record meeting either condition is included in the output.

The AND operator is assumed when you enter criteria in multiple fields. Within a field, typing the word "AND" between criteria in the same field establishes the AND condition. For example, in the book table you could enter "King" in the author name field, then you could enter "Horror" in the category field to display records where the author's name is King and the category is Horror.

The OR operator is established by entering the criterion in the Or tab, or by typing "OR" between criteria in the same field. For example, you could type "King" in the author name field, select the Or tab, then enter "Horror" in the category field. This filter would display those records where the author's name is King or where the category is Horror.

In this filter you will use an OR operator so that records meeting either city criterion will be included in the output. To include the city as an OR criterion, you enter the criterion in the Or tab.

> A value must be entered in the Look For tab before the Or tab is available.

Click: **Or tab**

The Or tab is opened and a new blank row is displayed. You will enter the expression specifying the criteria by selecting the criteria from the City drop-down list.

Click: ▣ **(in the City field)**

> You could also have entered the expression "Chandler" or "Mesa" in the City field of the Look For tab.

The list of all cities used in the table is displayed. To specify the criterion,

Choose: **Mesa**

Your screen should be similar to Figure 3-3.

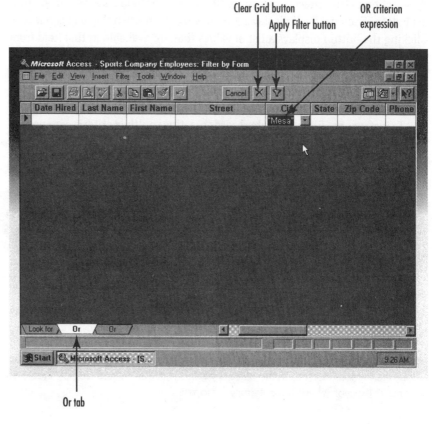

Figure 3-3

Clear Grid button
Apply Filter button
OR criterion expression

Or tab

<table>
<tr><td>▣ is a toggle button that applies and removes a filter.</td></tr>
</table>

The selected criterion is displayed in the City field. It is surrounded by quotes, as required of all text entries used in an expression. Then to apply the filter,

<table>
<tr><td>The menu equivalent is Filter/Apply Filter/Sort.</td></tr>
</table>

Click: ▽ **Apply filter**

The filtered datasheet displays the records for all employees who live in the city of Chandler or Mesa.

The manager's second request is to locate the employee whose last name begins with the letter "C."

<table>
<tr><td>You do not need to remove a filter before applying another.</td></tr>
</table>

Click: 🔲 **Filter by Form**

This filter requires that you enter an expression in the Last Name field. To clear all existing expressions from the Filter Form window,

<table>
<tr><td>The menu equivalent is Edit/Clear Filter.</td></tr>
</table>

Click: ✕ **Clear Grid**

Move to: **Last Name field**

To specify the criteria to find this employee, you will use a wildcard character in the expression.

Concept 3: Wildcard Characters

Wildcard characters are placeholders that represent any series of characters or any single character. They specify a value you want to find when you either know only part of the value or want to find all values that begin with a certain letter or match a specific pattern.

The six wildcard characters are described below.

Character	Use	Example
*	Matches any number of characters.	SMIT* locates SMITT, SMITH, SMITHERS. *ING locates all occurrences of values ending in "ing."
?	Matches any single character.	SMIT? locates SMITT and SMITH, but not SMITHERS. B?T locates BET, BIT, BUT, or BAT, but not BEAT.
[]	Matches any single character within the brackets.	B[IU]T locates BIT and BUT, but not BET or BAT.
!	Matches any character not in the brackets.	B[!IU]T locates BET and BAT, but does not locate BIT or BUT.
-	Matches any one of a range of characters that you specify.	[A-H]EAT locates BEAT, FEAT, and HEAT, but does not locate MEAT, NEAT, or SEAT.
#	Matches any single numeric character.	1#3 locates 153 or 163, but not 1453 or 19653.

The expression C* will find any series of characters that follows the letter C. The letter can be entered in either upper- or lowercase, because Access is not case sensitive.

Type: c*
Press: ⏎Enter

Your screen should be similar to Figure 3-4.

Figure 3-4

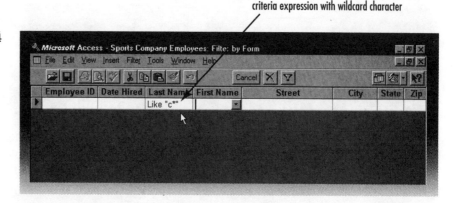

criteria expression with wildcard character

Access automatically converts the entry you typed to "Like 'c*'." Access gives you flexibility in the way you enter expressions, but it will display any typed expressions using the correct rules or syntax for the expression. In this case Access added the LIKE operator to the expression and enclosed the expression in double quotation marks. If you do not include an operator when using wildcard characters, Access automatically enters the appropriate operator for you.

Click: **Apply Filter**

The filtered datasheet displays the records for all employees (five) whose last names begin with the letter C. Now the manager can determine which employee sent the memo.

The manager has the needed information, so you can redisplay all records in the table and continue working.

Click:  **Remove Filter**

Close the Sports Company Employees table (save your changes).

The filter criteria you last specified are saved with the table, and the results can be redisplayed simply by applying the filter.

Creating a Query

Your next request for information is to provide a list of all employees and their hire dates. Although you could use a filter to get the information, a filter displays the entire record. You want the list to display only the employees' names and hire dates. To create this list, you need to use a query.

Concept 4: Queries

A **query** is a question you ask of the data contained in your database. You use queries to view data in different ways, to analyze data, and even to change existing data. Since queries are based on tables, you can also use a query as the source for forms and reports.

The five types of queries are described in the table below.

Select query	Description
Select query	Retrieves the specific data you request from one or more tables, then displays the data in a query datasheet in the order you specify. This is the most common type of query.
Crosstab query	Summarizes large amounts of data in an easy-to-read, row-and-column format.
Parameter query	Displays a dialog box prompting you for information, such as criteria for locating data. For example, a parameter query might request the beginning date and ending date, then display all records matching dates between the two specified values.
Action query	Makes changes to many records in one operation. There are four types of action queries: a make-table query creates a new table from selected data in one or more tables; an update query makes update changes to records, such as when you need to raise salaries of all sales staff by 7%; an append query adds records from one or more tables to the end of other tables; and a delete query deletes records from a table or tables.
SQL query	Created using SQL (Structured Query Language), an advanced programming language used in Access.

The result or answer to the query is displayed in a **query datasheet**. A query datasheet looks and behaves like a table datasheet, but is actually a dynamic view of data from the tables, selected and sorted as specified in the query. Since the query datasheet is dynamic, any changes you make to the data in a query datasheet will be made in the actual table as well.

All queries are created from the Queries tab.
Open the Queries tab.
To create the query,

Choose: New

The New Query dialog box on your screen should be similar to Figure 3-5.

Figure 3-5

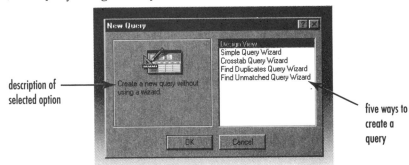

description of selected option

five ways to create a query

The New Query dialog box contains five options for creating queries. You can create a query from scratch in Query Design view or by using one of the four Query Wizards. The table below explains the type of query each of the four wizards creates.

Query Wizard	Type of Query Created
Simple Query Wizard	Select query
Crosstab Query Wizard	Crosstab query
Find Duplicates Query Wizard	Locates all records that contain duplicate values in one or more fields in the specified tables
Find Unmatched Query Wizard	Locates records in one table that do not have records in another. For example, you could locate all employees in one table who have no hours worked in another table.

To create a select query using the Simple Query Wizard,

Select: **Simple Query Wizard**
Choose: <kbd>OK</kbd>

In the first Simple Query Wizard window (shown in Figure 3-6), you specify the table and the fields from the table that will give you the desired query result. You need a list of employees and hire dates. That information is obtained from the Sports Company Employees table. From the Table/Queries drop-down list box,

Select: **Table: Sports Company Employees**

Then, to specify the three fields for the query, from the Available Fields list box,

Select: **Date Hired**
Click: <kbd>></kbd> **Add**

The Selected Fields list box displays the selected field name.

    In the same manner, add the Last Name and First Name fields to the Selected Fields list.

The dialog box on your screen should be similar to Figure 3-6.

Figure 3-6

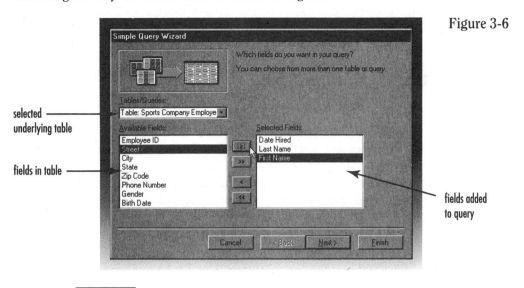

selected —
underlying table

fields in table —

fields added
to query

Choose: Next >

In the second Simple Query Wizard window, you are asked for a title.
Replace the suggested title in the text box with "Hire Date."

Choose: Finish

After a few moments, the query result is displayed in Query Datasheet view.
Your screen should be similar to Figure 3-7.

Figure 3-7

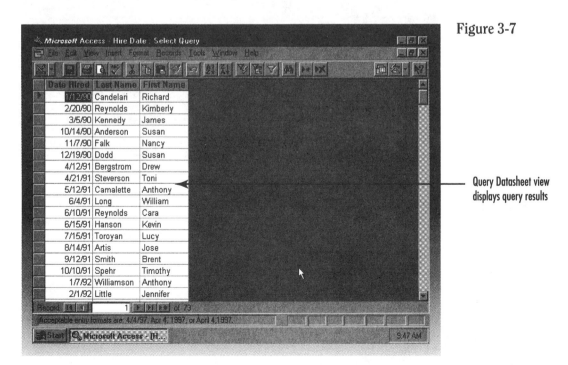

Query Datasheet view
displays query results

The query datasheet displays only the three specified fields for all records in the table. Query Datasheet view includes the same menus and toolbar buttons as in Table Datasheet view. This is because the same operations can be performed in both views.

Moving Columns

The order of the fields in the query datasheet reflects the order they were placed in the Selected Fields list. However, the Regional Manager wants the list of names to be organized with the first name before the last name. You can change the display order of the fields by moving the columns. To reorder columns, first select the column you want to move and then drag the selection to its new location. You want to move the First Name column to the left of the Last Name column.

> Reminder: Click on the First Name column heading when the mouse pointer is a .

Select the First Name column.

The entire column should be highlighted.

Click and hold the mouse button on the First Name column heading.

The mouse pointer is a 🔏, indicating you can drag to move the selection.

> The keyboard equivalent is [Ctrl] + [F8] to turn on Move mode. Then press [←] or [→] to move the column in the desired direction, then press [Esc].

Drag the First Name column one column to the left until a thick black line is displayed between the Date Hired and Last Name columns. Release the mouse button.

Clear the selection.

Your screen should be similar to Figure 3-8.

First Name column moved to new location

Figure 3-8

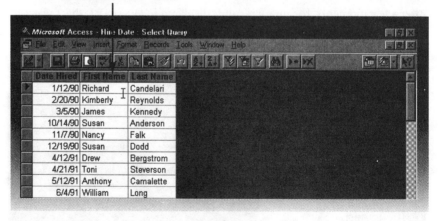

> You can move fields in Table Datasheet view in the same manner.

The selected column has moved one column to the left. Now the query datasheet is displayed in the order requested by the Regional Manager. Changing the column order in the query datasheet does not affect the field order in the table, which is controlled by the table design.

Querying Using Comparison Operators

The Regional Manager would like to recognize the employees who have worked with The Sports Company for at least five years. To help the manager locate these employees, you can modify the Hire Date query to create a list of all employees who were hired before January of 1992.

The query datasheet is based on settings that were entered in the Query Design window by the Wizard. To see the Query Design view,

Click:  **Design View**

> The menu equivalent is <u>V</u>iew/Query <u>D</u>esign.

Your screen should be similar to Figure 3-9.

The Query Design Window

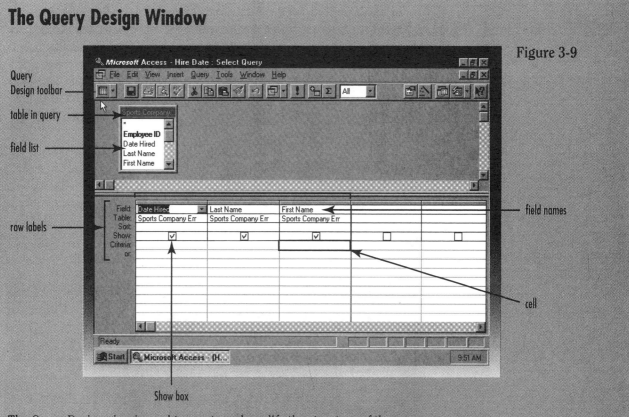

Figure 3-9

The Query Design view is used to create and modify the structure of the query. This view automatically displays a Query Design toolbar that contains the standard buttons as well as buttons that are specific to the Query Design view window. These buttons are identified below.

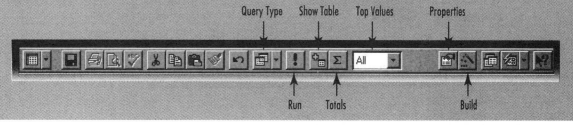

DATABASE

The Query Design window is divided into two areas. The upper area displays a list box of all the fields in the selected table. This is called the **field list**.

The lower portion of the window displays the **design grid**, where the settings that are used to define the query are displayed. Each column in the grid holds the information about each field to be included in the query datasheet. The design grid currently displays the Date Hired, Last Name, and First Name fields. Each row label identifies the type of information that can be entered. The intersection of the column and row creates a **cell**. This is where you enter expressions to obtain the query results you need.

Notice the boxes, called Show boxes, in the Show row. The Show box is checked for each field. This indicates that the query result will display the field column.

In the Criteria row of the Date Hired column, you need to enter a criteria expression to locate only those records where the date hired is prior to January 1992. To specify the criterion, you will enter an expression that contains a comparison operator. A **comparison operator** is used to compare two values. The comparison operators are = (equal to) <> (not equal to), < (less than), > (greater than), <= (less than or equal to), and >= (greater than or equal to). You will use the < comparison operator to locate all records with a date less than 1/1/92.

To specify the criterion,

Move to:	**Date Hired Criteria cell**
Type:	**<1/1/92**
Press:	⏎Enter

Your screen should be similar to Figure 3-10.

Run button

Figure 3-10

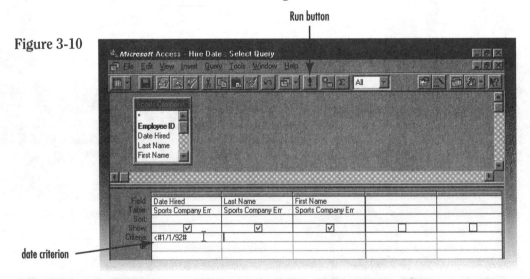

date criterion

The expression appears in the cell as <#1/1/92#. Access adds # signs around the date to identify the values in the expression as a date.

To display the query results, you run the query.

Click: **Run**

The menu equivalent is **Query/Run**. You can also click ▦ Datasheet View to run the query and display the query datasheet.

The query datasheet displays only those records meeting the date criterion. The record number indicator of the query datasheet shows that 16 employees were hired before January, 1992. Notice that the fields are again in the order they appear in in the Design grid.

Move the First Name column before the Last Name column.

Print a copy of the query datasheet for the Regional Manager.

Click 🖨 or use **File/Print** if you need to specify printer settings.

Specifying Multiple Criteria in a Query

Because many of the requests you get for information ask you to locate records using more than one criterion, you decide to try creating queries using multiple criteria. As in a filter, the AND and OR operators are used to specify several criteria in a query.

Switch to the Query Design view.

First you will query the table to find all employees who have a date hired <1/1/92 *and* have a first name that starts with S. When you enter criteria in separate fields on the same row of the grid, an AND operation is established.

To create this query, enter **s*** in the First Name Criteria cell.

Your screen should be similar to Figure 3-11.

Figure 3-11

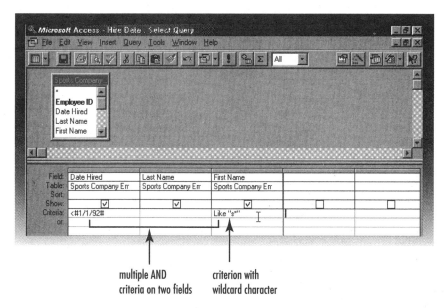

multiple AND criteria on two fields

criterion with wildcard character

Run the query.

The query datasheet shows that two employees were hired before January, 1992 and have a first name that starts with S.

Next you want to see how many employees have a hire date prior to 1/1/92 *or* have a first name that starts with S. When you enter criteria in separate fields on separate rows, an OR operation is established.

> You can use Cut and Paste to move the criterion.

Switch to the Query Design window. To create the OR operation, remove the Like "s*" criterion from the Criteria cell of the First Name column and enter it in the "or" cell of the First Name column.

Your screen should be similar to Figure 3-12.

Figure 3-12

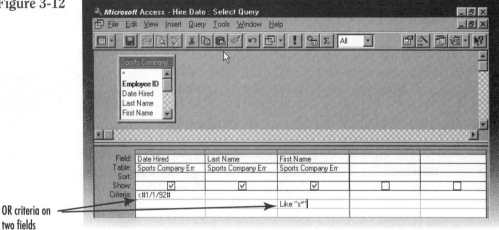

OR criteria on two fields

Run the query.

The query datasheet displays all records that meet either criterion.

> To clear cell contents, highlight the entry and press Delete.

Switch to Query Design view. Clear the criteria from the Date Hired Criteria cell and the First Name "or" cell.

You can also specify multiple criteria in a single field by using the AND and OR operators. The AND condition is established by typing the AND operator in the cell as part of the expression. An OR condition in a single field is established by entering the second criterion in the "or" row cell of the same field. To see how this works, you will find out how many employees have a hire date between 1/1/92 and 12/31/93.

> You can also specify the OR operator in a single field in the same manner.

To create this query, enter >=1/1/92 and <=12/31/93 in the Criteria cell of the Date Hired column.

Your screen should be similar to Figure 3-13.

> If an expression is entered incorrectly, an information box is displayed indicating the source of the error.

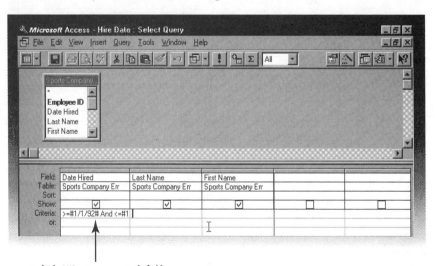

Figure 3-13

multiple AND criteria on a single field

Run the query.

Sixteen records were located in which the hire date met the specified criteria.

Close the Query Datasheet window. Save the changes to the query.

The Database window is displayed, and the query name is displayed in the Queries object list.

Note: If you are ending your session now, exit Access. When you begin Part 2, open the Sports Company Personnel Records database file.

Part 2

Querying Two Tables

The Regional Manager looked at the list of employees hired before January 1992 and suggested that the query would be more helpful if it included the employee's department. Unfortunately the Sports Company Employees table does not contain this information. This information, however, is available in another table named Employees by Department and Position.

From the Tables tab, open the Employees by Department and Position table.

Your screen should be similar to Figure 3-14.

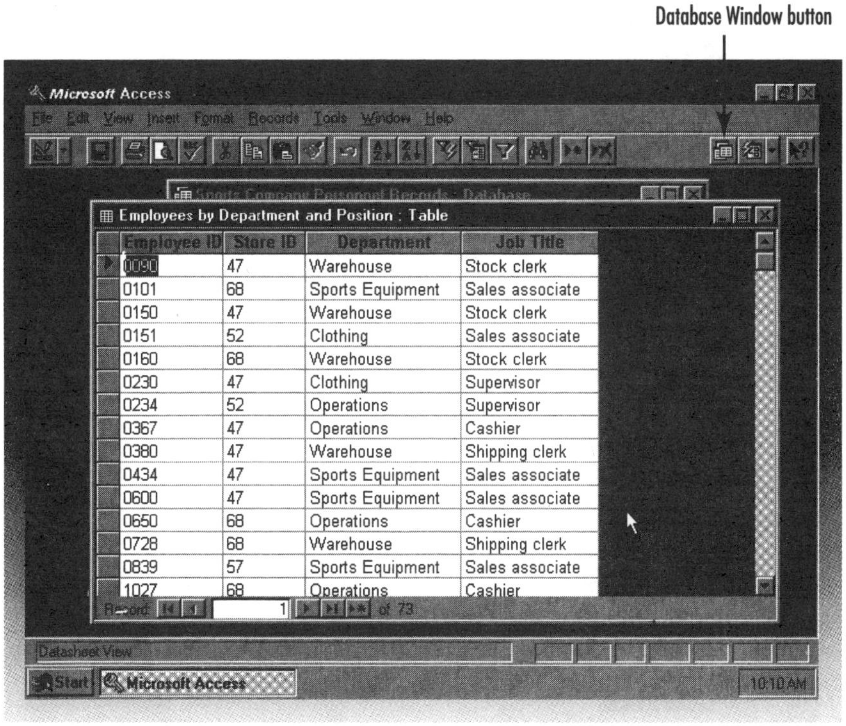

Database Window button

Figure 3-14

The Employees by Department and Position table contains four fields of data: Employee ID, Store ID, Department, and Job Title. To display the information the Regional Manager wants, you need to create a query using information from this table and from the Sports Company Employee table. A query that uses more than one table is called a **multitable query**.

To switch back to the Database window,

The menu equivalent is **W**indow/**1** Sports Company Personnel Records:Database.

You can also click on any visible part of a window to switch to that window.

Click:  **Database Window**

This time you will create the query from scratch.
Open the Queries tab.

Choose: **New/Design View/OK**

The Show Table dialog box on your screen should be similar to Figure 3-15.

Figure 3-15

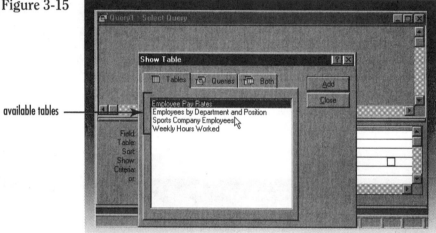

available tables

The Query Design window is open and the Show Table dialog box is displayed. It is used to add tables to the query design. The three tabs—Tables, Queries, and Both—contain the names of the existing tables and queries that can be used as the information source for the query. You need to add the Sports Company Employees and the Employees by Department and Position tables to the query design.

If necessary, open the Tables tab.

Select: **Sports Company Employees**
Choose: Add

The field list for the table is added to the query design. To add the second table,

You can also double-click the table name to add it to the query design.

Select: **Employees by Department and Position**
Choose: Add

A second field list for the Employees by Department and Position table is displayed next to the Sports Company Employees field list.

Close the Show Table dialog box. If necessary, maximize the Query Design window.

Your screen should be similar to Figure 3-16.

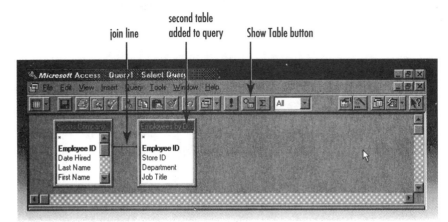

second table
join line | added to query | Show Table button

Figure 3-16

The single line between the two field lists indicates that the two tables have been temporarily joined.

Concept 5: Joins and Relationships

You can bring information from different tables in your database together if you **join** the tables. You join tables by defining a **relationship** between the tables. A relationship is made between tables usually through at least one common field. The common fields must be of the same data type, but can have different field names. When you add multiple tables to a query, Access automatically joins tables based on the common fields. This default join tells the query to check for matching values in the joined fields. When matches are found, the matching data is added to the query datasheet as a single record.

There are three types of joins: one-to-many, many-to-many, and one-to-one. The default, also called an **inner join**, is a **one-to-many relationship**. This is the most common type of join. In a one-to-many relationship, a record in table A can have many matching records in table B, but a record in table B has no more than one matching record in table A. For example, if your database has an Employee table and a Weekly Pay table, the two tables would most likely be joined on a common Employee Number or Social Security field. The Employee table would have many matches in the Weekly Pay table (one for each payday), but each individual record in the Weekly Pay table would have only one match in the Employee table (only one employee would get one specific check number).

A **many-to-many relationship** is one in which a record in table A can have many matching records in table B, and a record in table B can have many matching records in table A. A many-to-many relationship is only possible if there is also a third table in the relationship, known as a **junction table**, that serves as a bridge between the two tables.

A **one-to-one relationship** is one in which table A has only one matching record in table B, and table B has only one matching record in table A.

The diagram below shows that when the Employee ID fields of the two tables are joined, a query can be created using data from both tables to provide the requested information.

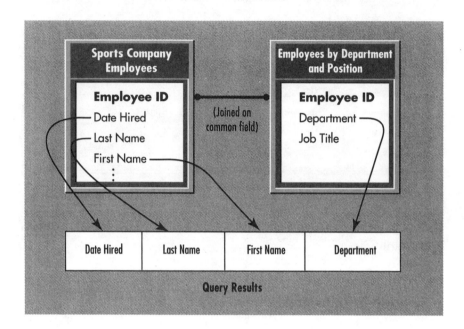

The type of relationship created using these two tables is a one-to-one relationship. This is because each record in the first table has one matching record in the second table.

Next you need to add the fields to the grid that you want to use in the query. There are five ways to add fields to the design grid:

■ Drag the field name from the field list to the grid. You can add several fields at once by pressing ⇧Shift and clicking to select adjacent fields, or by pressing Ctrl and clicking to select nonadjacent fields.

■ Double-click on the field name.

■ Select the cell drop-down arrow in the grid, then choose the field name.

■ Double-click the field list title bar to select all fields.

■ Click and hold on the first item, *, in the field list and drag to the field row to add all fields to the grid. Using * will automatically include any new fields that may later be added to the table and exclude deleted fields.

Add the Date Hired, Last Name, First Name, and Department fields, in that order, to the design grid.

Your screen should be similar to Figure 3-17.

Figure 3-17

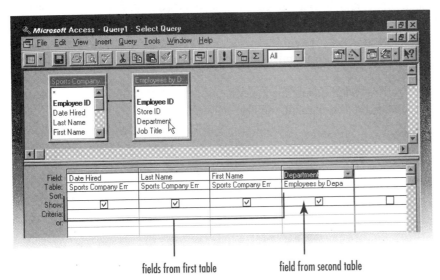

fields from first table   field from second table

The field names are added to the grid in the first blank column Field cell from left to right. The checkmarks in the Show boxes indicate that all the fields will be displayed in the query datasheet.

To specify the date hired criterion, enter the expression <1/1/92 in the Date Hired Criteria cell.

Run the query.

Your screen should be similar to Figure 3-18.

query results

Figure 3-18

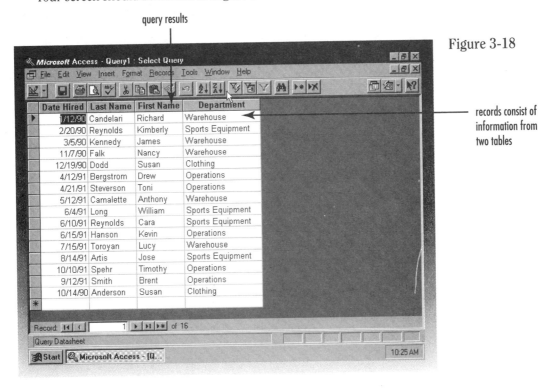

records consist of information from two tables

The query datasheet displays the same 16 records as in the original query, and in addition displays the Department field. Each record consists of information from both tables. Both tables must contain matching records in order for a record to appear in the query's result.

Change the column order to Department, Last Name, First Name, and Date Hired.

You also want to sort the query datasheet by Department and Last Name.

Select the Department and Last Name columns.

Click: ![icon] **Sort Ascending**

Clear the highlight.

Your screen should be similar to Figure 3-19.

fields in new order

Figure 3-19

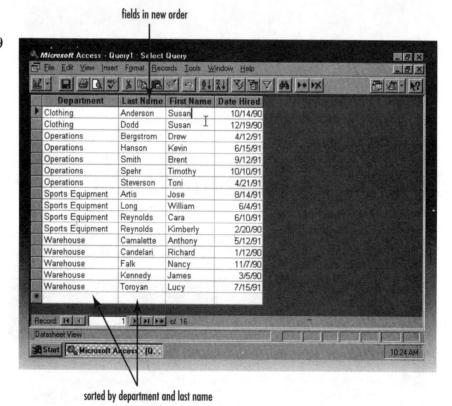

sorted by department and last name

The query datasheet displays the records in alphabetical order by department and last name in the specified column order.

Saving a Query

You would like to save this query for the Regional Manager. You can save a query as an object, then you can run the query whenever needed. To do this,

Choose: **File/Save As/Export**

If necessary, select "Within the current database as."
    To enter a new name for the query,

Type: **Pre 1992 Hire Date**
Choose: OK

You now have two named queries in the database: Hire Date and Pre 1992 Hire Date.

Querying Three Tables

Next the Regional Manager would like you to create some queries that will help in the analysis of the employee payroll information. The payroll information is in a table named Employee Pay Rates. This table contains the Employee ID and hourly pay rate.
    You will create a query that will locate all employees hired after 11/15/93 and who work in the Clothing department. The Regional Manager would like the query to also display the employees' hourly rates. To create this query, you can modify the existing query by adding the Employee Pay Rates table to the query design.
    Return to the Query Design.
    To add another table,

Click: **Show Table**

The menu equivalent is **Query/Show Table.**

Add the Employee Pay Rates table to the Query Design window.
    Access automatically links the Employee ID field of the Employee Pay Rates table to the Employees by Department and Position table.
    Close the Show Table dialog box.
    Add the Hourly Rate field to the design grid.
    Next you need to set up the criteria to display the requested information.
    Replace the existing criterion in the Data Hired Criteria cell with >11/15/93.
    Enter "clothing" as the criterion in the Department Criteria cell.
    Finally, you also want the query datasheet to display the records in alphabetical order by last name. Another way to set the sort order is to specify the sort direction in the Sort cell of the grid.
    Move to the Sort cell of the Last Name field.
    A drop-down list button appears.
    Open the drop-down list.

Select: **Ascending**

Your screen should be similar to Figure 3-20.

Figure 3-20

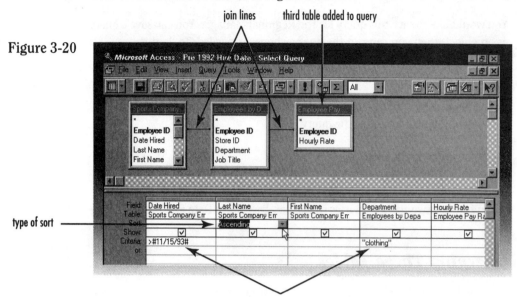

Run the query.

The query datasheet should be similar to Figure 3-21.

Figure 3-21

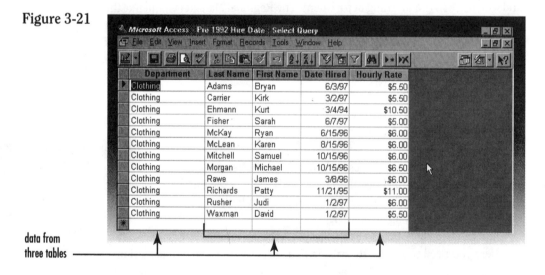

The query result shows, in alphabetical order by last name, the employees who were hired after 11/15/93 and work in the Clothing department. It also displays their hourly rate of pay. Notice that the currency format you used in the table is also displayed in the query's result.

The Regional Manager has also requested another list, sorted by Department, of all employees who earn less than $5.50 per hour.

To modify the query to display this information, return to Query Design view.

Since you no longer need the Date Hired field, you will remove it from the design grid. To remove a column, you must first select the column by clicking on the thin gray **column selector bar** just above the field name in the grid when the mouse pointer is ↓. To remove the Date Hired field,

Click: **the Date Hired selector bar**
Press: ⌐Delete⌐

Clear the criterion from the Department field.

Enter the expression <5.50 in the Hourly Rate Criteria cell.

Set the Department sort order to Ascending, and set the Last Name sort order to not sorted.

Your screen should be similar to Figure 3-22.

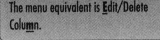

The menu equivalent is <u>E</u>dit/Delete Colu<u>m</u>n.

Deleting a column from the design grid does not change the underlying table.

Figure 3-22

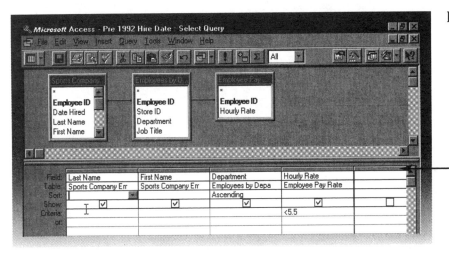

column selector bar

Run the query.

The query datasheet shows that 10 employees earn less than $5.50.

Creating a Calculated Field

The Regional Manager reviewed the list of employees and has decided it is time to give these employees a raise. You have been asked to create a query that will calculate a 5 percent increase for these employees.

Return to the Query Design window.

When creating queries you are not limited to just the fields in the database tables. You can also create fields based on information contained in other fields used in the query. This type of field is called a calculated field.

Concept 6: Calculated Field

A **calculated field** displays the result of a calculation in a query. You can perform a variety of calculations in queries. For example, you can calculate the sum of all inventory, the average salary for a department, or the highest sales figures among all sales personnel in the company.

You can create your own calculation or use one of Access's seven predefined calculations shown below.

Predefined Calculation	What It Calculates
Sum	Totals values in a field for all records
Average	Averages values in a field for all records
Count	Counts number of values, excluding empty cells, in a field for all records
Minimum	Finds lowest value in a field for all records
Maximum	Finds highest value in a field for all records
Standard Deviation	A measure of the dispersion of a frequency distribution
Variance	Square of the standard deviation

To create a calculated field, you enter an expression in the design grid that instructs Access to perform a calculation using the current field values. Then the calculated result is displayed in the calculated field column of the datasheet.

To create a calculated field, in the Field row of a blank column you enter the expression to perform the calculation.

Move to the Field row of a blank column.

You will need to enter a custom calculation to calculate the new pay rate for the records in the query. The first part of the expression is used to name the new calculated field. To name the field that will display the new hourly rate,

Type: **New Rate:**

The second part of the expression does the actual calculation. In this case, to calculate the raise, the expression will multiply the value in the Hourly Rate field by 1.05 to calculate the 5 percent increase for each employee. To complete the expression,

Field names are enclosed in square brackets in an expression.

If you made an entry error, a message box will appear advising you of the error. Clear the box and correct the expression.

Press: Spacebar
Type: **[Hourly Rate]*1.05**
Press: ←Enter

Before running the query, you would like to change the new field's properties so it will display the calculated values as currency with two decimal places.

Right-click: **New Rate column**

From the shortcut menu,

Choose: Properties

The Field Properties dialog box for the selected field is displayed. To specify a display format for values in the field,

Select: Format

From the Format drop-down list box,

Select: Currency

The Field Properties dialog box on your screen should be similar to Figure 3-23.

Figure 3-23

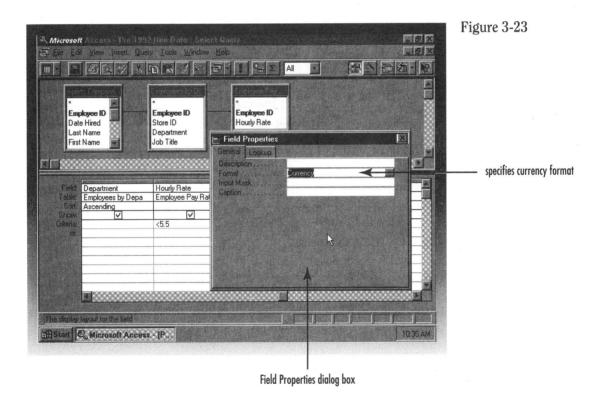

specifies currency format

Field Properties dialog box

Close the Field Properties dialog box and run the query.

Your screen should be similar to Figure 3-24.

calculated field results
displayed in currency format

Figure 3-24

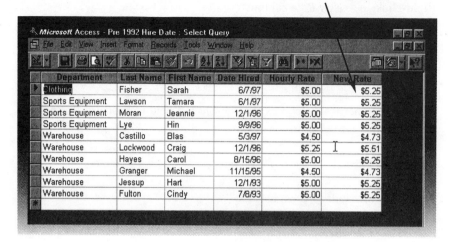

The query datasheet displays the 10 employees and shows their new pay rates in the last column. The New Rate column of values appears in the currency format you selected. This list will help the Regional Manager decide on raises for the employees.

You would like to save this query in case the Regional Manager wants to try different percent increases.

Save the query as Pay Rate Increase.

Finally, the Regional Manager has asked you to figure out what the average hourly rate is for all employees. Access can automatically make this calculation for you.

Switch to Query Design view.

The only field you want on the grid when calculating a total value is the field on which the calculation will be made. To quickly clear the design grid,

Choose: Edit/Clear Grid

Add the Hourly Rate field back to the grid.

To calculate the average hourly rate, you need to display the Total row in the Design grid. The ∑ Totals button toggles between hiding and displaying the row in the grid. The row is hidden by default.

The menu equivalent is **View/Totals**.

Click: Totals

Your screen should be similar to Figure 3-25.

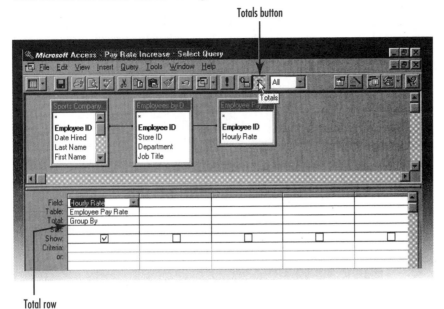

Figure 3-25

The Total row is displayed as the third row in the design grid. Every field in the grid must have a setting entered in the Total row. By default Access enters "Group By" as the setting. This setting is used to group data in the query. You need to change the setting to calculate the average of the Hourly Rate field.

Move to: Total cell of the Hourly Rate column

To specify the type of calculation, from the Total drop-down list,

Select: Avg

Run the query.
    Your screen should be similar to Figure 3-26.

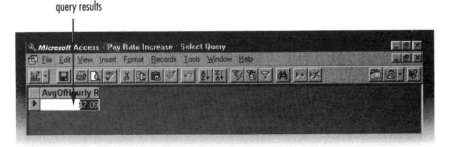

Figure 3-26

When summary calculations are performed, the query result displays one record with a totaled value. In this case Access calculates $7.09 as the average rate of pay. You can now send this information along with the printout to the Regional Manager.

Querying Four Tables

Click 🔢 to hide the Total row.

The last query the Regional Manager requested will display the weekly gross pay for all employees sorted by department. To calculate the weekly gross pay, you will need to use the Weekly Hours Worked table, which contains the employee numbers along with the hours worked in the past weeks.

Switch to the Query Design window. Clear the grid. Hide the Total row. Add the Weekly Hours Worked table to the Query Design.

This field list displays the fields Employee ID, Week Ending, and Hours. The table has been joined to the Employee Pay Rates table on the common field. Notice that Employee ID in this field list is not bold. When a field is bold, it indicates that it is a primary key field. Employee ID in this table is not a primary key field because there are multiple entries with the same numbers.

Add the Last Name, First Name, Department, and Week Ending fields to the design grid in that order. Sort the Department field in ascending order.

To calculate the gross pay, in the Field cell of a blank column,

Type: **Gross Pay: [Hourly Rate]*[Hours]**
Press: ⏎Enter

Set the Format property for the calculated field to display as currency.

You only need the gross pay calculated for the week ending 10/17/97.

Click on the Show box to clear the checkbox.

Enter the expression =10/17/97 into the Week Ending Criteria cell. Clear the Show box for the Week Ending field so the date will not display in the query datasheet.

Your screen should be similar to Figure 3-27.

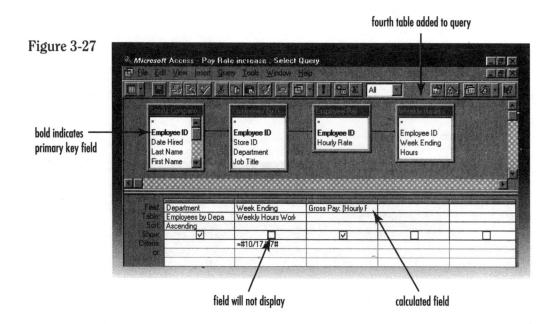

fourth table added to query

Figure 3-27

bold indicates primary key field

field will not display

calculated field

Run the query.

Your screen should be similar to Figure 3-28.

Figure 3-28

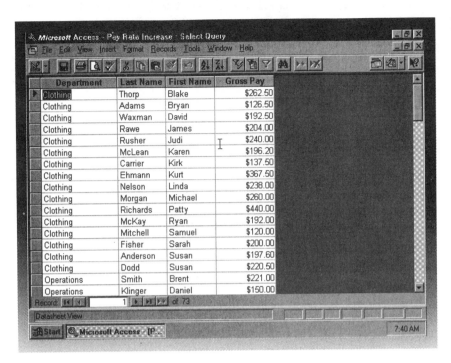

The query datasheet displays the gross pay for each employee sorted by department for the week ending 10/17/97.

Print a copy of the query datasheet for the Regional Manager.

Save this query as Gross Pay for 10/17/97. Close the Query Datasheet window. Close the Employees by Department and Position table.

Creating a Multiple-Table Form

You have been using several tables of employee information that need to be updated each time information changes in an existing record. The form you created to use with the Sports Company Employees table can only update the records in that table. You want to create a form that will update the Sports Company Employees, Employee Pay Rates, and Employees by Department and Position tables. The first thing you must do is create a query that will combine all the information you need.

If necessary, open the Queries tab.

Choose: New/Design View/OK

Add the Sports Company Employees, Employees by Department and Position, and Employee Pay Rates tables to the Query Design window. Close the Show Table dialog box.

You are now ready to add the fields to the query that you want to display in the new form.

From the Sports Company Employees table field list, add the following fields to the design grid in the order indicated (this will be the tab order on the form):

First Name
Last Name
Street
City
State
Zip Code
Phone Number
Gender
Birth Date
Employee ID
Date Hired

> The fields continue to be added to the grid even though they are not all visible onscreen. Use the scroll bar to move to the other fields.

From the Employees by Department and Position table, add the following fields to the query design grid:

Store ID
Department
Job Title

From the Employee Pay Rates table, add the Hourly Rate field to the design grid. Your screen should be similar to Figure 3-29.

Figure 3-29

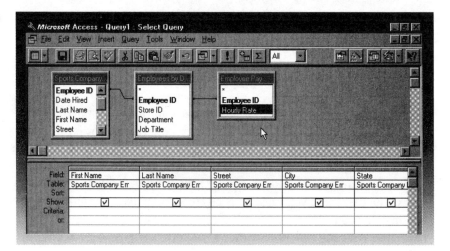

Save the query as Comprehensive Employee Query, then close the Query Design window.

You are now ready to create the new form based on the Comprehensive Employee Query you just created.

To create the form, open the Forms tab.

Choose: <u>N</u>ew/Form Wizard

Although you can create a form from scratch using Design view, it is much easier to create the form using a Wizard and then modify it in Form Design view.

From the list box called Choose the Table or Query Where the Object's Data Comes From,

Select: Comprehensive Employee Query
Choose:

To add all fields from the query to the form in the order in which you added them to the query design grid,

Select:
Choose:

The default columnar layout is acceptable for this form.

Choose:

This text will use Flax.

Select a style of your choice.

Choose:

Enter the form title "Employee Update Form."

Choose:

After a few moments, the Form window displays the form in the selected style and layout. Next you want to modify the layout of the Form.

Click: [icon] Design

If necessary, maximize the window. Rearrange the controls and enter the form title and headings as in Figure 3-30 on the next page. In addition, use the following features to improve the appearance of the form:

- ■   Set the font size of all controls to 10.
- ■   Size the controls as appropriate.
- ■   Set the title font to 20 and add color.
- ■   Set the Personal Data and Company Data font size to 12 and add color.
- ■   Adjust the spacing and alignment of controls.

Next you want to add transparent rectangles around the controls in the Personal Data and Company Data sections of the form.

To do this, use ▣ Rectangle and drag to create a box as you did to select multiple controls. Then use ◼ Back Color to set the object background to transparent and ◼ Border Color to add color to the border.

When you are done, view the form in Form view.

Your screen should be similar to Figure 3-30.

Figure 3-30

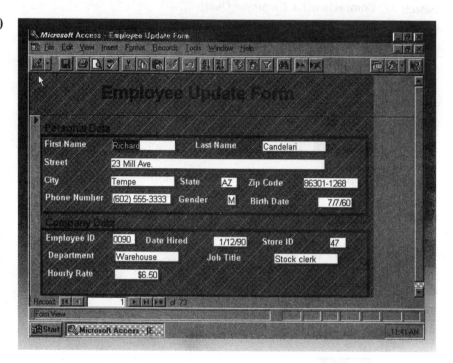

Use the Find Records command to quickly display the record containing your information.

To see how quickly the form can be used to update all three files, you will make several changes in the data.

Change the zip code to 85000-0000, the store ID number to 68, and your hourly rate to 9.75.

Print the form with your record information displayed. Close the form, saving your layout changes.

To verify that the changes were made to the tables, open each of the tables, locate your record, and note the changes.

As you can see, using a single customized form to update records in all three tables simultaneously is a great time-saving feature.

Close the open tables, saving any changes. Exit Access, responding Yes to any prompt to save.

LAB REVIEW

■ ■ ■ ■ ■ ■ ■ ■ ■ ■ ▪

Key Terms

action query (DB123)	join (DB133)
calculated field (DB140)	junction table (DB133)
cell (DB128)	many-to-many relationship (DB133)
column selector bar (DB139)	multitable query (DB132)
comparison operator (DB128)	one-to-many relationship (DB133)
criteria (DB116)	one-to-one relationship (DB133)
criteria expression (DB118)	parameter query (DB123)
crosstab query (DB123)	query (DB123)
design grid (DB128)	query datasheet (DB123)
field list (DB128)	relationship (DB133)
filter (DB116)	select query (DB123)
Filter by Form (DB117)	SQL query (DB123)
Filter by Selection (DB116)	wildcard character (DB121)
inner join (DB133)	

Command Summary

Command	Shortcut	Toolbar	Action
Edit/Delete Colu**m**n	Delete		Removes selected column from design grid
Edit/Cle**a**r Grid			Clears all fields from design grid
Edit/Cle**a**r Filter		▨	Clears all expressions in filter form
View/Query **D**esign		▨	Displays Query Design view
View/Data**s**heet		▨	Displays Query Datasheet view
View/**T**otals		Σ	Displays Total row in design grid
Records/**F**ilter/Filter by **S**election		▨	Displays only records that contain a specific value
Records/**F**ilter/**F**ilter by Form		▨	Displays blank datasheet for entering values to be displayed
Filte**r**/Appl**y** Filter/Sort		▨	Applies filter to table
Query/**R**un		▨	Displays query results in Query Datasheet view
Query/Show T**a**ble		▨	Displays Show Table dialog box
Window/**1** <name>:Database		▨	Displays Database window

DATABASE

Matching

1.   _____ **a.** intersection of a column and row

2. query   _____ **b.** output of a query

3. multitable query   _____ **c.** temporary restriction placed on displayed data to isolate specific records

4. criteria   _____ **d.** window used to design queries

5. [icon]   _____ **e.** symbols used to represent unknown characters in expressions

6. filter   _____ **f.** runs a query and displays query datasheet

7. design grid   _____ **g.** used to ask questions about database tables

8. wildcard operator   _____ **h.** query that uses data from more than one table

9. query datasheet   _____ **i.** set of limiting conditions

10. cell   _____ **j.** accesses Filter By Form feature

Fill-In Questions

1. A(n) _____ is used to isolate and display a specific group of records.

2. The _____ operator narrows the search for records that meet both conditions.

3. Placeholders called _____ are used to specify a value when you want to find all values that begin with a specific character.

4. _____ are used to view data in different ways.

5. A(n) _____ retrieves specific data from one or more tables and displays the results in a query datasheet.

6. The _____ of the query window is where the fields to be displayed in the query datasheet are placed.

7. Tables are joined by defining a(n) _____ between the tables.

8. A(n) _____ relationship is only possible if there is a junction table between the two tables.

9. A(n) _____ can be used to total all the values in a field.

10. In expressions field names are enclosed in _____ .

Discussion Questions

1. Discuss what filters are and how they can be used in a database. When would it be appropriate to use a filter?

2. Discuss the differences between the AND and OR filter conditions.

3. Describe the six wildcard characters that are available in Access. Give an example of each.

4. Discuss what a query can do and some advantages of using queries.

5. Discuss the three types of relationships. Give an example of how an inner join could be created in a database.

Hands-On Practice Exercises

■ ■ ■ ■ ■ ■ ■ ■ ■ ■ ▪

Step by Step

Rating System		
☆	Easy
☆☆	Moderate
☆☆☆	Difficult

☆

1. This problem is a continuation of Practice Exercise 4 in Lab 2. Debbie from Desert Rescue Cleaning Service wants you to help her use her database to make management decisions concerning her growing business. She needs to be able to compare rates by square feet among all of her clients, wants to identify her largest clients, and wants you to create a query that she can refer back to as her business grows to track total square feet cleaned and total income.

a. Open the Desert Rescue Cleaning Service database that you used in Lab 2. Filter the Clients table to display only those clients with 10,000 square feet or more. Print the filtered datasheet. Remove the filter.

b. Next, help Debbie create a new query based on the Clients table. Add the Company, Square Feet, and Rate fields to the design grid. Run the query, then print the query datasheet.

c. Debbie is pleased with the data you were able to extract for her. Now she wants to know which clients have at least 10,000 square feet of space. Return to Query Design view, then add the expression >=10000 in the Square Ft Criteria cell. Run the query, then print the query datasheet.

d. Debbie now wants a query, which she plans to use repeatedly, that will give her a summary of the size of her jobs and her expected income. Return to Query Design view, remove the criterion in the Square Ft column, then remove the Company field. Display the Total row in the design grid. Display the Total drop-down list and replace Group By with Sum in both fields in the grid. Run the query, then print the query datasheet. Save the query as Square Feet and Rates Totals.

☆☆

2. This problem is a continuation of Practice Exercise 3 in Lab 2. Eddie Fitzpatrick of TechnoBabble Electronics has been having some trouble getting his cousin Teddy to help him with his database, so he wants you to come help him make a few changes. While you are updating his records, Eddie also wants you to help him print a list of inventory supplied by his favorite supplier. Eddie is also working with his local bank to secure a small business loan and wants you to help him find the total value of each item in inventory.

a. Open the TechnoBabble Electronics database and the

Inventory table that you used in Lab 2. Use the Find button to locate item #7195, a personal computer. Change the quantity from 8 to 7. Filter the table to display only those records where the number on hand is less than 5. Print the filtered datasheet. Remove the filter. Close the Inventory table.

b. Open the TechnoBabble Electronics Inventory List form and add the following new records to the inventory:

TechnoBabble Electronics Inventory List

Item #: 5396
Description: Calculator, Desktop
Shelf: L-10   # On Hand: 10
Purchase Price: $24.60

Confidential
Supplier: BTO
Status: STOCK   Cost: 15.00

TechnoBabble Electronics Inventory List

Item #: 5837
Description: Projector, Computer Display
Shelf: P-17   # On Hand: 2
Purchase Price: $1123.25

Confidential
Supplier: BTO
Status: SPECORDER   Cost: $797.15

---

c. Now that you have helped Eddie update his records, you can help him find the list of inventory items from his favorite supplier, Business Technology Originators, with the supplier code BTO. Close the form, create a new query based on the Inventory table, then add the Item #, Description, and Supplier fields to the design grid. In the Supplier Criteria cell, enter the expression =BTO, then turn off the checkmark in the Show box so the Supplier field is not displayed in the query datasheet. Run the query. Print the query datasheet, then return to Query Design view.

d. Now you can help Eddie get the inventory totals for his bank loan officer. You will need to know the number on hand of each item and the item's cost to TechnoBabble to calculate the total value of each item. Delete the Supplier column from the design grid, then add the # On Hand and Cost fields to the grid. To create a calculated field, click in the Field cell of the next blank column and enter the expression Total Value: [Cost]*[# On Hand]. Set the format of the calculated field to currency. Run the query, then print the query datasheet.

e. So that Eddie can track the total value of his inventory as he buys and sells items, save the query as Inventory Value.

3. This problem is a continuation of Practice Exercise 2 in Lab 2. Michelle at Food for Thought has been updating her database, and has added a table that tracks billing by client number. Michelle recently spoke with Debbie at Desert Rescue Cleaning Service about the queries you helped Debbie create. Michelle needs the same kind of analysis of her own clients and wants you to help her find clients who had at least one party that cost more than $1000 during 1995.

a. Open Updated Catering Records, the database that contains Michelle's updated records for Food for Thought. Create a new query based on the Billing table, then add the Customer #, Amount, and Invoice Date fields to the design grid. To indicate invoices of more than $1000 for 1995, enter >1000 in the Criteria cell of the Amount column and >=1/1/95 AND <=12/31/95 in the Invoice Date column. Run the query.

b. Michelle realizes that the query datasheet is not really useful without the customer names. Return to Query Design view and add the Customers table to the Query window. Add the Company field to the design grid, then run the query.

c. Michelle now has the information she needs in the query datasheet, but would prefer that the company name be displayed between the Customer # and Amount columns. Move the Company column to the new location, then print the query datasheet and close the Query window without saving the query.

d. You are about to leave when Michelle remembers

that she got a good buy on beans and wants to find out which customers like baked beans. Use a filter to display only those customers who prefer baked beans. Print the filtered datasheet.

e. Michelle has all the information she needs, so remove the filter and close the table.

On Your Own

4. This problem is a continuation of Practice Exercise 1 in Lab 2. James O'Dell needs to gather data about his store inventory. He wants to gather information about a series of item numbers that he fears may be overstocked. In addition, he would like to see the value of each item in stock.

Open the Valley of the Sun Office Supplies database that you used in Lab 2, then create a new query to display all records where the item numbers begin with either a 2 or a 3. Include appropriate fields in the query. Run the query and print the query datasheet.

James wants more detailed information about the items you located in the first query. He wants to know which items begin with either a 2 or a 3 and have more than 40 items on hand. Run the query and print the query datasheet.

James has almost all the information he needs, but he would like to see dollar amounts for each item. Calculate the total value of each item in the query datasheet. Run the new query and print the query datasheet.

Save the query as Overstocked Items and close query window.

5. This problem is a continuation of Practice Exercise 5 in Lab 2. Now that you are on staff at the Go West Dude Ranch, Michael wants you to add some capabilities to his payroll records. You have already created a new table, called Time Card, that tracks weekly hours worked. Next you will add a field to the Staff Records table to track salaries. You will also create a form for the new table you created. Finally, you will create queries for figuring the weekly paychecks for each employee.

Open the Dude Ranch Payroll database with the updated records, then add the Pay Rate field to the Staff

Records table. Format the field to display as currency.

Enter the following pay rates for each employee in the Staff Records table:

Employee #	Pay Rate
015	$12.50
131	6.75
139	8.25
216	4.75
275	4.75

Due to a data processing error, your personal information was lost. Reenter your data, including a pay rate for yourself and an employee #.

Your updated database includes a Time Card table that tracks weekly hours worked by each employee. Create a columnar form based on the Time Card table and name the form Weekly Time Card. Use the new Weekly Time Card form to enter data for the current week:

Employee #	Hours Worked
015	40
131	38
139	27.25
216	40
275	20
Your #	Your Hours

Now you need to create a new query that will figure paychecks for all employees. Create a multitable query to display the pay rate and total hours worked for each employee during the current week. You will also need to calculate the gross pay for each employee. Format the gross pay field to currency. Print the query datasheet, then save the query as Weekly Paychecks.

6. This problem is a continuation of Practice Exercise 6 in Lab 2.

Open the My Contacts database and create a query to display company name, contact, and phone number for all records. Print the query datasheet.

Open the form you created in Lab 2. Change the form colors and fonts to make it easier to read and more attractive. Print one record in the revised form. Save any changes to your form.

Create at least two other queries of the data in your table that you can use to analyze the data. Print the query results.

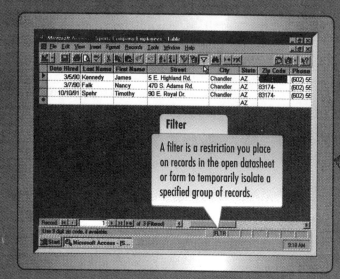

Filter

A filter is a restriction you place on records in the open datasheet or form to temporarily isolate a specified group of records.

Concepts

Filter

AND and OR Operators
Wildcard Characters

Queries

Joins and Relationships

Calculated Field

Queries

A query is a question you ask of a database that allows you to view data in different ways, to analyze data, and even to change existing data.

AND and OR Operators

The AND and OR operators are used to specify multiple conditions that must be met for the records to display in the query datasheet.

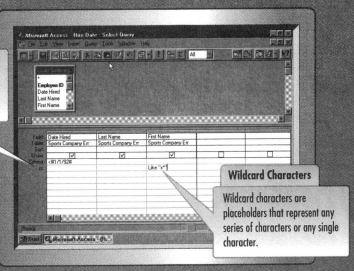

Wildcard Characters

Wildcard characters are placeholders that represent any series of characters or any single character.

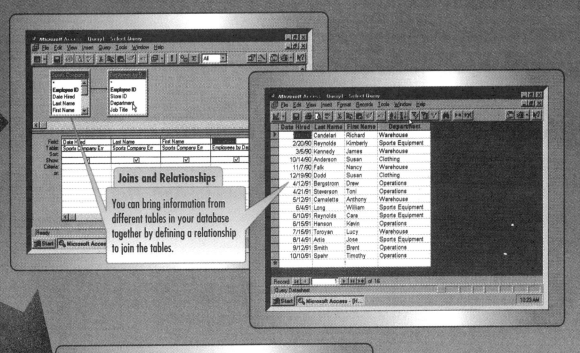

Joins and Relationships

You can bring information from different tables in your database together by defining a relationship to join the tables.

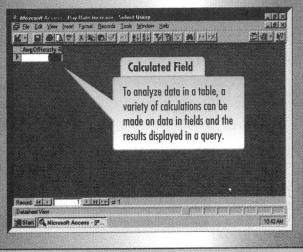

Calculated Field

To analyze data in a table, a variety of calculations can be made on data in fields and the results displayed in a query.

DB155

Creating and Modifying Reports

You have used Access to store information in tables, create forms, and analyze data through filters and queries. You have also provided others with the information they requested by printing the datasheets or forms.

The printed output is a simple report that is acceptable for many informal uses. There are many times, however, when you will want to display the results with a more professional appearance that is suitable for a formal report or presentation. In this lab you will learn how to create customized, professional reports from the data in tables or the results of queries. These reports group and summarize the data in an organized and attractive manner.

DB156

The following concepts will be introduced in this lab:

1. Reports	Reports are the printed output you generate from tables or queries.
2. Grouping Records	Records in a report can be grouped into categories to allow you to better analyze the data.
3. Group Calculations	If a report contains groups, you can perform calculations on the grouped data, such as a group total, an average, a minimum value, and a maximum value.
4. Layout Preview	Layout Preview displays a sample of the report as it will appear when printed.

CASE STUDY

The Regional Manager is impressed with your ability to use Access to quickly locate and analyze the data in the employee tables. You have used the program to automate the daily updates and changes that occur to the employee tables and to quickly find answers to many different types of queries. The last major task you need to do is to create weekly and monthly employee status reports.

Part 1

Using the AutoReport Wizard

Load Access for Windows 95. Put your data disk in drive A (or the appropriate drive for your system).

The Regional Manager would like a report that displays the employees' names and addresses ordered by name. You have already created and printed several simple reports using the Print command on the File menu. This time, however, you want to create a custom report of this information.

Concept 1: Reports

In Access, **reports** are the printed output you generate from tables or queries. It might be a simple listing of all the fields in a table, or it might be a list of selected fields based on a query. Access also includes a custom report feature that allows you to create professional-appearing reports. The custom report is a document that includes text formats, styles, and layouts that enhance the display of information. In addition, you can group data in reports to achieve specific results. You can then display summary information, such as totals, by group to allow the reader to further analyze the data. Creating a custom report displays the information from your database in a more attractive and meaningful format.

You will create the address list report using the data in the Sports Company Employees table in the Sports Company Personnel Records database.

Open the Sports Company Personnel Records database file.

Reports are created from the Reports tab of the Database window.

Open the Reports tab.

Use the Sports Company Personnel Records database from the end of Lab 3.

The menu equivalent is **I**nsert/**R**eport.

Choose: New

The New Report dialog box on your screen should be similar to Figure 4-1.

Figure 4-1

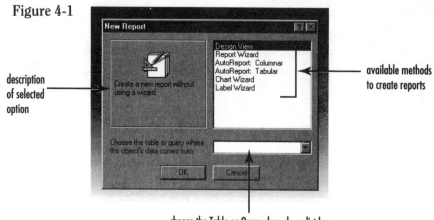

description of selected option

available methods to create reports

choose the Table or Query drop-down list box

The dialog box presents six ways to create a report. You can create a report from scratch in Design view, or by using the Report Wizard or one of the AutoReport Wizards. The Report Wizard lets you choose the fields to include in the report and it helps you quickly format and lay out the new report. The AutoReport Wizard creates a report that displays all fields and records from the underlying table or query in a predesigned report layout and style.

You decide to create a columnar report using the AutoReport Wizard.

Select: **AutoReport: Columnar**

To specify the table or query to be used to create the report, open the Choose the Table or Query drop-down list.

The list displays the names of objects in the database file on which a report could be based.

Select: **Sports Company Employees**

This is all the information you supply when using an AutoReport Wizard.

Choose: OK

The report takes a short time to prepare. The AutoReport Wizard creates a report using all the fields in the selected table or query. In addition, it uses a predefined report style and layout. When complete, the report is displayed in the Print Preview window.

To see more of the report, maximize the window.

Your screen should be similar to Figure 4-2.

Zoom Control button

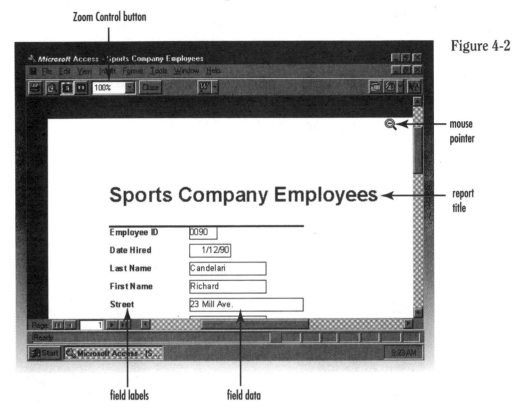

Figure 4-2

mouse pointer

report title

field labels   field data

The Print Preview window displays the report as it will appear when printed. Your report may be displayed with a different style. When creating an AutoReport, Access remembers the last autoformat report style used to create a report, then applies that same style to the new report. If the Autoformat command has not been used, the report will use the basic style, called Win95. You will learn how to change styles later in this lab.

The AutoReport Wizard displays each field on a separate line in a single column for each record. The fields are in the order they appear in the table. The report style shown in Figure 4-2 uses the table name as the report title and includes the use of text colors, typefaces and sizes, and horizontal lines and boxes.

Zooming the Window

Only the upper part of the first page of the report is visible in the window. To see more of the report in the window at one time, you can decrease the onscreen character size by specifying a smaller magnification percentage using the Zoom command. The default magnification percentage of 100% is displayed in the Zoom Control toolbar button. This setting shows the characters the same size as

> The Zoom feature is available in all Print Preview windows.

they will be when printed. You can increase the character size up to two times normal display (200%) or reduce it to 10%.

Open the [100%] Zoom Control drop-down list.

> The menu equivalent is **V**iew/**Z**oom/ 50%.

Choose: 50%

The text is reduced in size by half, allowing you to view more of the page in the window. You can now see three sides of the page.

You can also adjust the magnification to display the whole page in the window using the Fit option.

Open the [50%] Zoom Control drop-down list.

> The menu equivalent is **V**iew/**Z**oom/**F**it to Window.

Choose: Fit

Your screen should be similar to Figure 4-3.

Figure 4-3

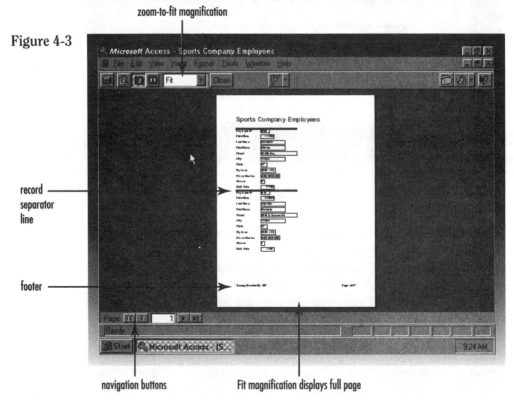

zoom-to-fit magnification

record separator line

footer

navigation buttons   Fit magnification displays full page

> Just as in Table, Form, and Datasheet views, you can use the navigation keys and navigation buttons to move through the pages of the report.

Now the entire page is visible, but most of the text is too small to read. However, you can now see the entire page layout. The report title appears at the top of the page, and each field of information is displayed on a separate line in a single column for each record. Each record is separated from the next by a horizontal line. The current date and page number appear at the bottom of the page in the footer. The first two records from the Sports Company Employees table are displayed on the first page of the report.

Display the second page of the report.

The second page of the report contains the third and fourth records in the table. You can also view multiple report pages at the same time in Print Preview. To view two pages,

Click: ⊞⊞ **Two Pages**

Your screen should be similar to Figure 4-4.

The <u>V</u>iew/Pages command can be used to display up to 12 pages of a report in the window.

Figure 4-4

Zoom button   One Page button   Two Pages button

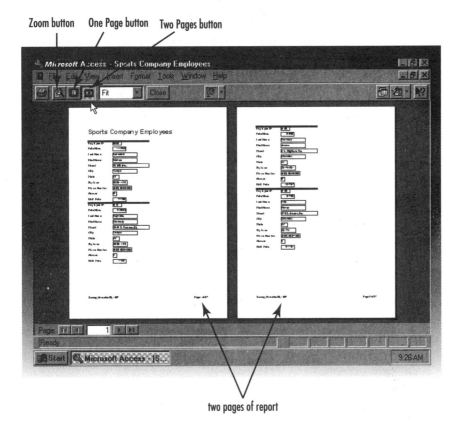

two pages of report

The first two pages of the report are displayed. To return the display to a single page,

Click: ⊟ **One Page**

Notice that the mouse pointer is a ⊕ when it is positioned on the page. This indicates that you can you can switch between the last magnification level you set and the Fit magnification by clicking on the report. The location of the pointer on the report when you click indicates the area of the report that will appear in the window.

    With the mouse pointer as ⊕, click on the first line in the report.
    The page is displayed again at 50% magnification.

You can also click ⊕ Zoom in the toolbar to zoom in and out.

DATABASE

After looking over the type of report created by the AutoReport Wizard, you decide the layout is inappropriate for your report because only two records are printed per page, making the report larger than 50 pages. In addition, you do not want the report to include all the fields from the table. To close the report file without saving it,

Choose: File/Close/No

Using the Report Wizard

You want the report to display the field contents for each record on a line rather than in a column. You also want to display the employee name and address information only. The Report Wizard will create this type of report. From the Reports tab,

Choose: New/Report Wizard/OK

The Report Wizard consists of a series of dialog boxes, much like the Form Wizard. In the first dialog box (see Figure 4-5) you specify the table or query to be used in the report and select the fields.

To specify the table, open the Tables/Queries drop-down list.

Select: Table: Sports Company Employees

The Available Fields list box displays all fields from the selected table. The Regional Manager wants the address list to include only the name and address information for each employee.

Add the fields to the Selected Fields list in the following order:

First Name
Last Name
Street
City
State
Zip Code

The Report Wizard dialog box on your screen should be similar to Figure 4-5.

underlying table or query

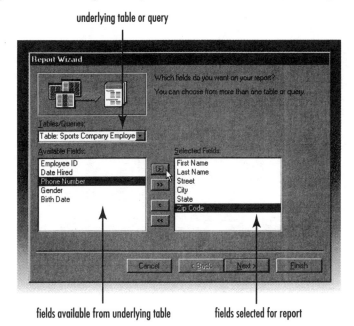

Figure 4-5

fields available from underlying table   fields selected for report

Five fields are still in the Available Fields list. You do not have to include all the fields in the table on a report. To move to the next Report Wizard dialog box,

Choose:

This dialog box asks you to specify how to group the report. The manager does not want the report grouped by any category. To move to the next dialog box,

> You will learn about grouping later in this lab.

Choose:

The next dialog box (see Figure 4-6 on the next page) is used to specify a sort order for the records. A report can be sorted on up to four fields. The manager would like the report sorted by last and first name. The Last Name field is specified first.

Open the number 1 drop-down list.

Select: Last Name

The default order of ascending is appropriate.
Next you will specify First Name as the second field to sort on.
Open the number 2 drop-down list.

> Clicking 🔢 toggles between ascending and descending sort order.

Select: First Name

The dialog box on your screen should be similar to Figure 4-6.

Figure 4-6

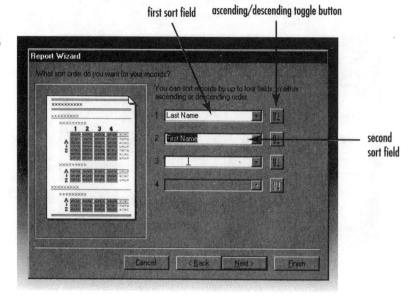

The report will be sorted in ascending order by last name and by first name within same last names.

Choose: Next >

The next dialog box is used to change the report layout and orientation. The default report settings create a tabular layout using portrait orientation. In addition, the option to adjust the field width so all fields fit on one page is selected. Because this report is very wide, the only change you will make is to change the orientation to landscape.

Select: **Landscape**

Choose: Next >

In this dialog box you select a style for the report.
Select each style to preview the style options.
You believe the Bold style is most appropriate for this report.

Select: **Bold**

To move to the next dialog box,

Choose: Next >

The last Report Wizard dialog box is used to add a title to the report. To replace the table name with a more descriptive report title,

Type: **Employee Address Report**

The title will also be used as the report object name when the report is created. The defaults for the other options in this dialog box are acceptable.

Choose: Finish

The program takes a minute to generate the report, during which time Report Design view is briefly displayed. In a few moments, the completed report with the data from the underlying table is displayed in the Print Preview window.

Set the Preview window magnification to Fit to view the entire report page. Your screen should be similar to Figure 4-7.

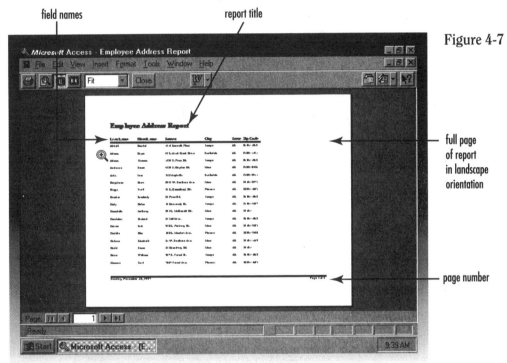

Figure 4-7

The Print Preview window displays the first page of the report in landscape orientation using the selected Bold report style. The report title reflects the title you specified using the Wizard. The names of the selected fields appear on a single line and easily fit across the page with the orientation set to landscape. Each record is listed on a separate row below the field names.

The page number in the footer indicates the report is a total of four pages. To view all four pages,

Choose: View/Pages/4

The layout of all four pages is displayed in the Print Preview window.

Return the display to one page and set the magnification to 100%.

Notice that the Last Name field is the first field, even though you selected it as the second field. This is because the sort order field overrides the selected field order.

Move to the page of the report that contains your name.
To print the page containing your record,

Choose: File/Print

If necessary, select the appropriate printer for your system.
To specify the page to print,

Select: Pages

Type the page number containing your record in the From and To text boxes.

Choose: ⬛ OK

Close the Employee Address Report file.

The Database window is displayed again, and the report object name is listed in the Reports object list. The Report Wizard automatically saves the report using the report title as the object name.

Creating a Report Based on a Query

The next report you want to create will display the employees' gross pay grouped by store and department. You have sketched out the report to look like the one shown below.

Gross Pay Report for xx/xx/xx

Store ID: XX
   Department: XXXXXXXX

Employee ID	Last Name	First Name	Gross Pay
XXXXXXXX	XXXXXXX	XXXXX	$XXXX.XX
XXXXXXXX	XXXXXXX	XXXXX	$XXXX.XX
Sum by Dept.			$XXXXX.XX
Avg by Dept.			$XXXXX.XX
Sum by Store			$XXXXX.XX
Avg by Store			$XXXXX.XX

To create this report, you will use the query you created in Lab 3 and saved as Gross Pay for 10/17/97. It is usually helpful to run the query first to remind you of the data that the query gathers.

Use the scrollbar to scroll the Preview window.

The page number is displayed in the page indicator box.

The ⬛ Print button prints the entire report.

If you create a report based on multiple tables, the relationship between tables must be established first using **T**ools/**R**elationships.

To run the query, from the Queries tab, open the Gross Pay for 10/17/97 query.

The query datasheet displays the Department, Last Name, First Name, and Gross Pay fields. In addition, you need the report to display the Employee ID and the Store ID fields. To include these fields in the report, you need to add them to the query design grid.

Switch to Query Design view. Add the Employee ID and Store ID fields to the design grid. Run the query.

To improve the organization of the query result, arrange the field columns so Store ID is the second column and Employee ID is the third column. Clear the highlight.

Your screen should be similar to Figure 4-8.

Figure 4-8

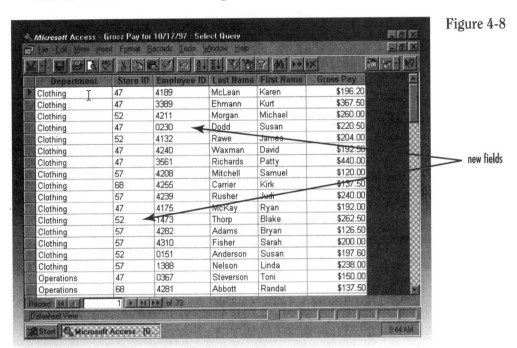

new fields

Close the query and save it using the same name.

Now you are ready to create a report using the data from the query. You can also create a new object from any object tab in the Database window.

Open the 🔲 New Object drop-down list.

Subject: **New Report**

The New Report dialog box is displayed. The name of the selected query in the Queries tab of the Database window is displayed in the drop-down list text box.

Choose: **Report Wizard**

Choose: ▨ OK ▨

The Available Fields list box displays the fields that are included in the design grid in the Gross Pay for 10/17/97 query. To add all the fields to the selected fields list,

Click: `>>`

Choose: `Next >`

In this dialog box you need to select the fields on which you want to group the report.

Concept 2: Grouping Records

Records in a report can be **grouped** by categories to allow you to better analyze the data. It is often helpful to group records and calculate totals for the entire group. For example, it might be useful for a store manager to group payroll records by department. Then, rather than getting a long list of pay for individual employees, the manager could get a report showing total payroll for each department. A mail order company might group orders by date of purchase, then by item number to see detailed sales information.

In Access you can create a report that will automatically group records based on fields you choose to group by. You can group by up to 10 fields in any one report.

> The Priority buttons can be used to change the grouping order of priority.

Groups should be created based on priority from the largest to smallest. To group the report by store number and then by department within store number,

Select: Store ID
Click: `>`
Select: Department
Click: `>`

The dialog box on your screen should be similar to Figure 4-9.

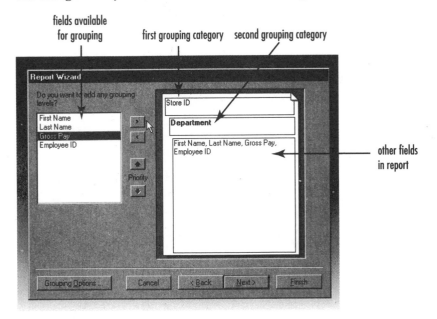

fields available
for grouping

first grouping category   second grouping category

other fields
in report

Figure 4-9

Choose: Next >

In this dialog box you specify a sort order for the data grouped within each field. You would like the report sorted by last name, then by first name.

Select Last Name as the first field to sort on and First Name as the second field to sort on.

You also want to summarize your data by displaying a total and average for each department. To do this,

Select:  Summary Options ...

The Summary Options dialog box on your screen should be similar to Figure 4-10.

Figure 4-10

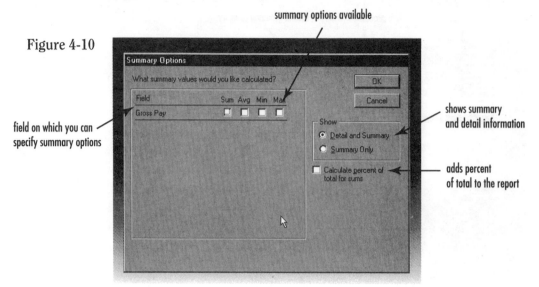

summary options available

field on which you can specify summary options

shows summary and detail information

adds percent of total to the report

Concept 3: Group Calculations

If you group data in your report, you can perform one or more of the following calculations on values: Sum (adds all values by group), Avg (calculates the average value for the group), Min (calculates the lowest value for the group), and Max (calculates the highest value for the group).

You can select multiple calculations to complete different analyses of the data. For example, a mail order company might calculate the sum of different products sold on each day of the month and the average sale for each day. You can also calculate the percent of total for the sums. For example, the mail order company might want to know what percentage of total sales were made on a specific product for June 15.

You can further customize the report to display both detailed information and the summary information, or just the summary information while hiding the details about the individual items.

To calculate a sum and average for the gross pay by department and store,

Click:	Sum
Click:	Avg
Choose:	OK
Choose:	Next >

The dialog box on your screen should be similar to Figure 4-11.

available layouts

Figure 4-11

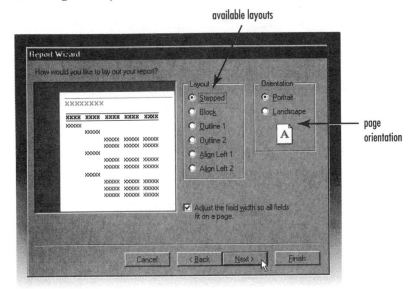

page
orientation

In this dialog box you are asked to select from six different layout options for a grouped report.

Select each layout option and look at the sample previews.

To use the Outline 1 layout option,

Select: Outline 1

You decide that the Portrait orientation is acceptable because there are fewer fields of information in this report than in the previous one. To display the next dialog box and select the report style,

Choose: Next >

Select: Casual

Choose: Next >

In the last dialog box, edit the report title to be "Gross Pay Report for 10/17/97."

You have completed the report using Report Wizard.

Choose: Finish

After a few moments, the report is displayed in the Print Preview window.

Set the magnification to 75%.

Your screen should be similar to Figure 4-12.

Figure 4-12

first grouping category

second grouping category

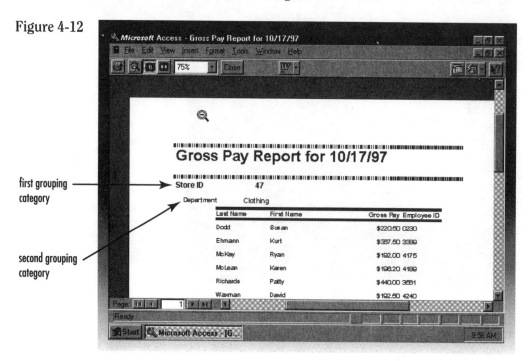

The data in the report is grouped by store and department, and the records are alphabetized by last name within groups. The information for store 47 is the first store group, and the Clothing department is the department group within the store group.

Scroll the report to see the summary data at the bottom of the clothing group.

In addition, each department group displays a count of employees and the sum and average values below the Gross Pay data column.

Display page 2 and, if necessary, scroll the report to see the information at the end of the store 47 group and the beginning of the store 52 group.

Your screen should be similar to Figure 4-13.

summary information for department

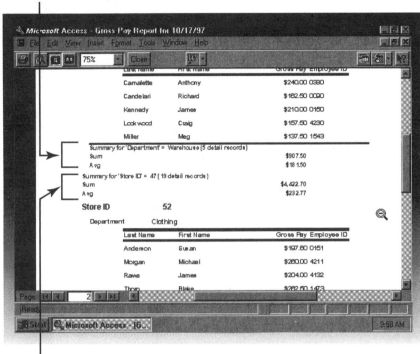

Figure 4-13

summary information for store

The summary information for store 47 appears above the Store 52 group head.
It includes a count value, and total and average gross pay values for the store.

    Display the top of the last page of the report.

    A grand total value for all stores appears at the end of the report.

    Display the top of page 1 again.

Note: If you are ending your session now, close the Report file and exit Access.
When you begin Part 2, open the Sports Company Personnel Records database
file. Then Preview the Gross Pay Report for 10/17/97.

Part 2

Modifying the Report Design

As you looked through the report, you saw several changes you wanted to make
to the report. The first change is to rearrange the order of the fields in the report
and to size the fields appropriately. In addition, you want to make the store
group head more noticeable, to change the display of the date in the footer to
exclude the day of the week, and to center the title over the report.

    To modify the appearance of the report,

Click:  Close Window

If you started at Part 2, choose **V**iew/
Report **D**esign.

DATABASE

The Report Design view window shown in Figure 4-14 is displayed. The Report Design view controls the layout of your report. As you can see, it is very similar to Form Design view. To customize the report design to meet your needs, you can add, delete, move, and size the controls and define different report features.

If necessary, move the Toolbox to the right border of the window.

Report Design View Window

Figure 4-14

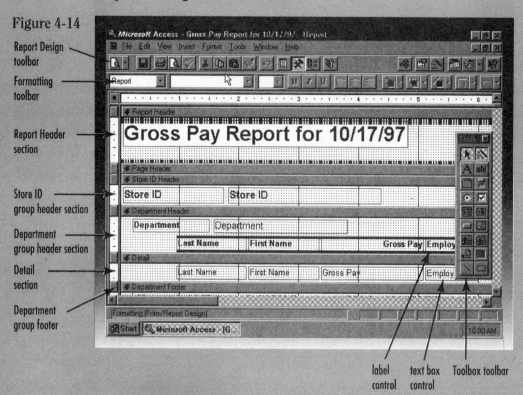

Report Design toolbar
Formatting toolbar
Report Header section
Store ID group header section
Department group header section
Detail section
Department group footer

label control   text box control   Toolbox toolbar

Like Form Design view, the Report Design view menu contains commands for working in the Report Design window. In addition, it also displays horizontal and vertical rulers, and three toolbars: Report Design, Formatting, and Toolbox.

The Formatting and Toolbox toolbars are the same as in Form view. The Report Design toolbar contains the standard buttons as well as buttons that are specific to the Report Design view window. These buttons are identified below.

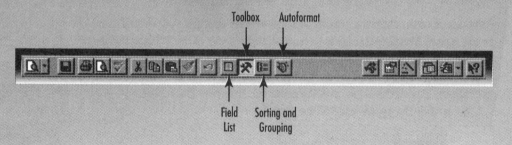

Toolbox   Autoformat

Field List   Sorting and Grouping

The Report Design view window consists of seven report sections, which break the report into distinct areas consisting of one or more lines. Above each section is the section name.

Report Header Contains information to be printed once at the beginning of the report. The report title is displayed in this area.

Page Header Contains information to be printed at the top of each page. In an ungrouped report, the column headings displaying the field names often are displayed in this area. The Page Header section is empty in the current report.

Group Header Contains information on groups. This report has two Group Headers: Store ID Header and Department Header. The information in the Group Headers is displayed each time there is a new group.

Detail Section Contains the records of the table. The field column widths are the same as the column widths set in table design.

Group Footers There is one Group Footer for each group. The Group Footers often contain formulas that instruct Access to display group totals. In this report, there are totals by Department and by Store ID in the Group Footers.

Page Footer Contains information to be printed at the bottom of each page, such as the date and page number.

Report Footer Contains information to be printed once at the end of the report. The current Report Footer includes a grand total for all employees.

Some of these sections may not be currently visible in the Report Design window.

Moving and Sizing Controls

The first change you will make is to reorganize the display order of the fields in the report. Notice that the Department header section displays the label control for each field column, while the Detail section contains the text box control. Report controls are selected and manipulated just like Form controls. However, unlike Form controls, the text and label controls are not attached. You will select both controls and move them simultaneously.

You can add fields to a report using **V**iew/Field List. Added field controls are inserted as compound controls. Use Cut and Paste to separate the controls to move them into separate report sections.

Click: Employee ID (in the Department Header section)

Hold down ⇧Shift.

You may need to scroll the window horizontally to see the Employee ID controls.

Click: Employee ID (in the Detail section)

Both controls are selected. Selected controls can be moved and sized just like Form controls.

Move the selected controls to the left of the Last Name controls.

Next you want to reduce the size of the Gross Pay field to better fit the data. Select the Gross Pay controls and size them appropriately.

In a similar manner, select the other related controls and move them to the locations shown in Figure 4-15.

When you are done, your screen should be similar to Figure 4-15.

Figure 4-15

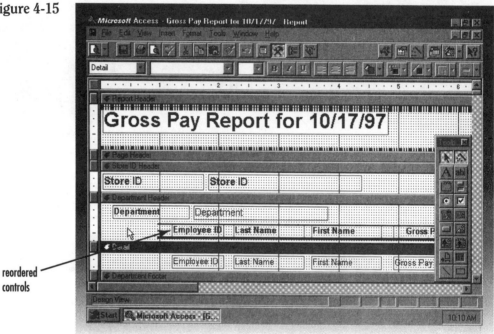

reordered controls

To see how this change has affected the report, you will preview the report using Layout Preview.

Concept 4: Layout Preview

There are two ways to view the report as it will appear when printed. You can use Print Preview to view the entire report page by page. Because this view displays all the data in the report, it takes longer to generate. This is the view you have seen whenever a new report is displayed, and is the view you used when previewing forms.

Another way to view the report is to use Layout Preview to take a quick look at the report. Layout Preview displays just a sample of the data in the report so you can quickly check the report's layout. Because it does not display all the data, it is much quicker to generate.

As a general rule, you should use Print Preview to view the entire report as it will print. Use Layout Preview for quick checks of design layout. When a report is large and you just need to check a layout change you have made, this is the preferred view.

Open the 🔳 View drop-down list.

Select: 🔍 Layout Preview

The menu equivalent is **V**iew/La**y**out Preview.

Your screen should be similar to Figure 4-16.

report in Layout Preview

Figure 4-16

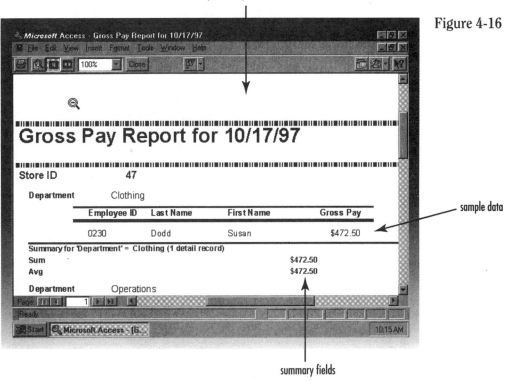

sample data

summary fields

The Layout Preview shows a few records in each group as a sample of the data. The change in the order of the fields improves the organization of the report. However, you notice that the summary fields for Gross Pay no longer align with the columns.

To return to Design view,

Click: Close   **Close Window**

You need to move the controls for the Gross Pay summary fields.

Scroll the window to see the Department and Store ID Footer sections. Adjust the size and placement of the four Gross Pay summary controls to align with the Gross Pay controls in the Detail section.

Align the right border of the controls.

Changing Control Properties

The next change you will make is to change how the date is displayed in the Page Footer.

Scroll the window to see the Page Footer section.

Notice that the date control in the Page Footer is =Now(). This is an expression that directs Access to enter the current date maintained on your computer into the report. Each control has property settings that affect how the control looks and acts. By default the property setting associated with the date control displays the date in the Long Date format. To change the date control properties,

Select the date control.

> The menu equivalent is **V**iew/**P**roperties, or Properties on the shortcut menu. You can also double-click a control to display its properties.

Click: **Properties**

The property sheet dialog box for the date control is displayed.

If necessary, open the Format tab to display the Format Properties.
Your screen should be similar to Figure 4-17.

Format Properties tab for selected control

Figure 4-17

date format

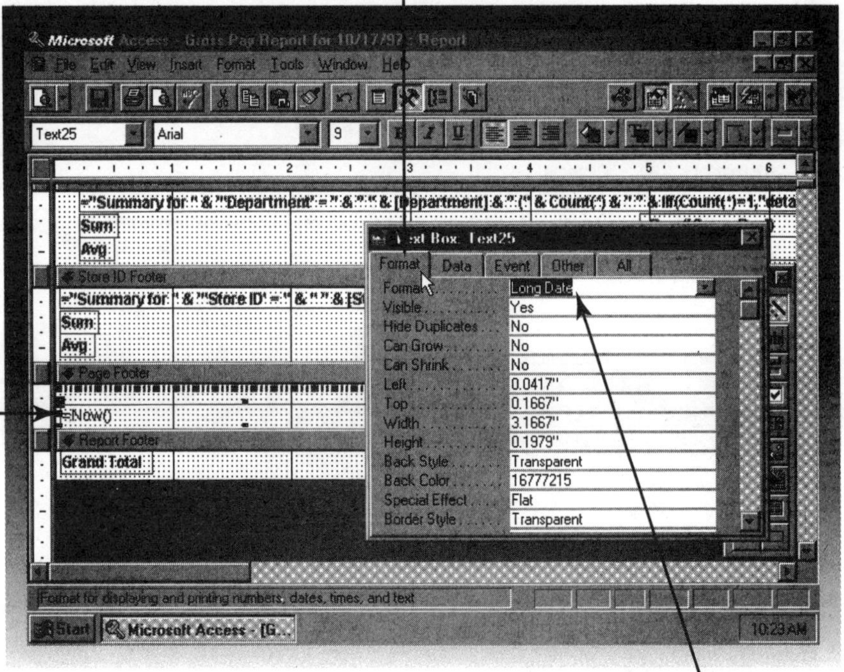

The Format tab lists the format properties associated with the selected control. The format properties contain the same options as in Table Design and vary with the data type of the field. The Format text box displays "Long Date." This is the setting that controls the date format.

Open the Format drop-down list.

The date format styles are listed. To display the date in the mm/dd/yy format,

Select: **Short Date**

Close the dialog box. Using Layout Preview, preview the changes you have made to the report. Scroll to the bottom of the page.

Your screen should be similar to Figure 4-18.

Figure 4-18

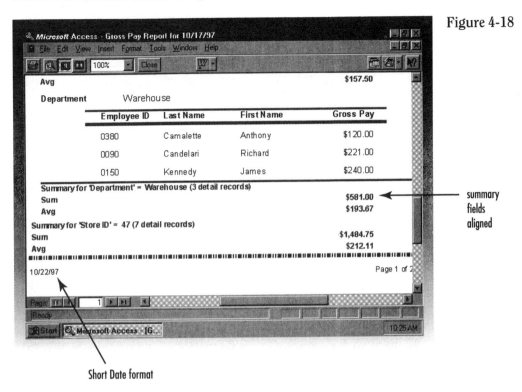

Short Date format

The Gross Pay summary fields are aligned with the Gross Pay column of data, and the date appears in the new Short Date format.

Return to Design view.

Adding Font, Color, and Line Enhancements

Next, to make the Store ID heading stand out more, you will change the text color and add a horizontal line above the controls to help visually separate report areas.

Select the Store ID label and text box controls in the Store ID Header section. Open the 🔳▾ Fore Color drop-down list. Select a color of your choice from the color palette.

The Store ID label in both controls appears in the selected color.

Above the Store ID control, you want to create a horizontal line.

Click: ◨ Line

Move to the space above the Store ID control and drag from the left margin to the 6.5-inch position on the ruler.

A thin horizontal line is created. You want the line to be thicker.

Open the ▣▾ Border Width drop-down list and select 3-pt.

A heavier line is drawn.

Use ▣▾ Border Color to change the color of the line to the same color as the Store ID.

> Do not extend the line beyond the 6.5" ruler position or the report width will be too wide to fit on a single page.

Your screen should be similar to Figure 4-19.

Figure 4-19

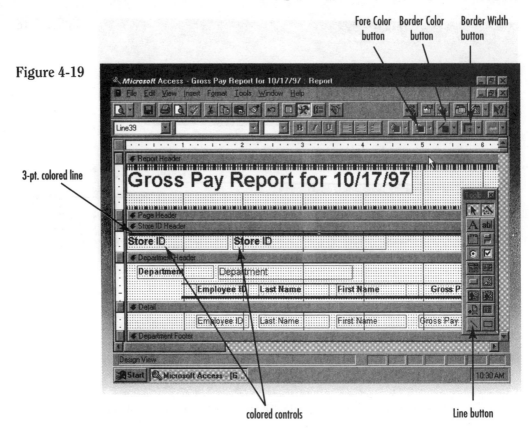

Finally, you also want to center the title over the report and change the background shading color of the Report Header control.

To center the title, select the report title control (in the Report Header section). Drag the title until the left border of the box aligns with the .5-inch ruler mark and the control is centered vertically in the Report Header section, as shown in Figure 4-20 on the next page.

Next you will add a background shading color to the title control in the Report Header section (the title control should still be selected).

Open the Back Color drop-down list box. Select a color of your choice from the color palette.

Your screen should be similar to Figure 4-20.

0.5-inch ruler mark   Back Color button

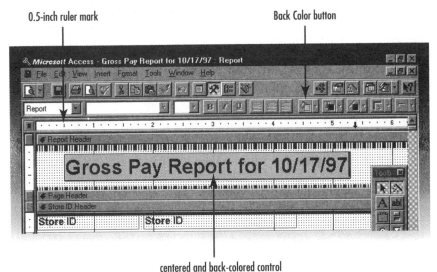

Figure 4-20

centered and back-colored control

You are now ready to view your report as it will look when you print it.

View the report using Print Preview.

The title appears centered and with the background color you selected. The Store ID appears in the color you selected and the colored horizontal line helps identify this group.

Change the display to view two pages.

Your screen should be similar to Figure 4-21.

formatted report in Print Preview

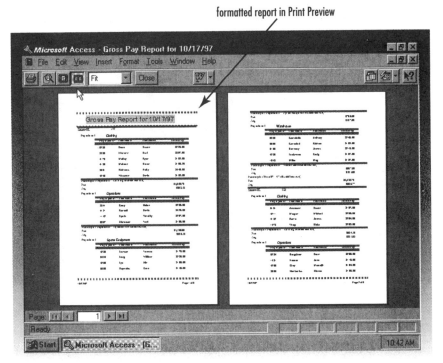

Figure 4-21

Now you can see that the changes you made to the Store ID section of the report make it much easier to locate the beginning of a new section.

Print the entire report. Close the report, saving any layout changes.

Open the Database window Reports tab.

The names of the two reports you have created are displayed in the Reports object list.

Creating Mailing Labels

Finally, you want to set up a report to print mailing labels for every employee in the Sports Company Employees table. A sample of a mailing label appears below:

> Susan Anderson
> 4389 S. Hayden Rd.
> Mesa, AZ 84101

The Report Wizard includes a Label Wizard that will create mailing labels. To use this feature, from the Reports tab,

Choose: N̲ew/Label Wizard

Open the Choose the Table or Query drop-down list.

Select: **Sports Company Employees**
Choose: **OK**

The Label Wizard dialog box on your screen should be similar to Figure 4-22.

Figure 4-22

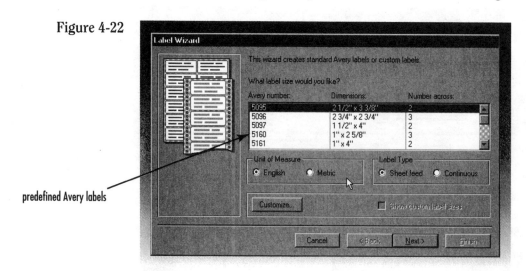

predefined Avery labels

In the first Label Wizard dialog box, you specify the type of label you want to create. You can either use a predefined label or create a custom label. The Sports

Company uses mailing labels made by Avery, number 5160. These labels appear three across the width of the paper.

To use this type of label, select Avery number 5160.

Choose: Next >

In this dialog box you specify the font and text color settings for the labels. The default font is Arial and the default font size is 8.

To change the font size, open the Font Size drop-down list.

> The font settings in this dialog box retain the previous settings chosen using the Label Wizard, so other settings may be displayed.

Select: 10

Choose: Next >

Just as with other reports, you select the fields from the table to include in the labels. Unlike other reports, however, as you select the fields, you also design the label layout in the Prototype Label box. You may type any additional text, such as punctuation or a holiday message, directly onto the prototype.

Add the First Name field to the Prototype Label box.

The dialog box on your screen should be similar to Figure 4-23.

Figure 4-23

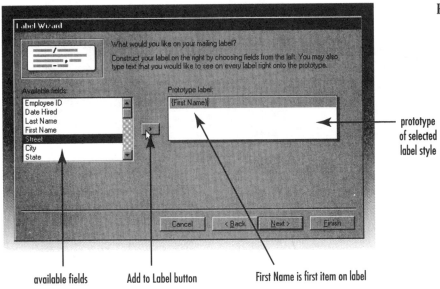

available fields   Add to Label button   First Name is first item on label   prototype of selected label style

The First Name field is displayed in the Prototype Label box. The last name will be on the same line as the first name, separated from the first name by a space. To enter a space to separate the first and last names,

Press: Spacebar

Add the Last Name field to the label prototype.

The next field, Street, will be the second line of the label. To create a new line,

Press: ←Enter

Add the Street field.

Press: ←Enter

To complete the rest of the label, add the City, State, and Zip Code fields to the prototype using the punctuation and spacing shown in Figure 4-24.

When you are done, the dialog box on your screen should be similar to Figure 4-24.

Figure 4-24

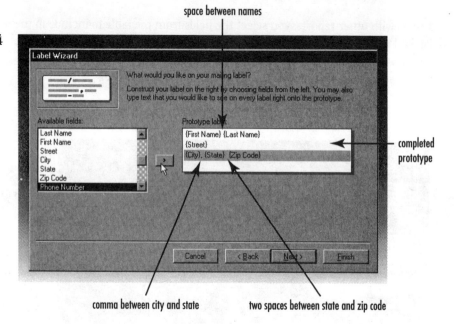

space between names

completed prototype

comma between city and state

two spaces between state and zip code

Choose: Next >

In the next dialog box you can specify a field on which to sort the labels. You want to take of advantage of postal discounts resulting from mailings that are sorted by zip code.

Add the Zip Code field to the Sort By list box.

Choose: Next >

To enter a name for the labels report file,

Type: **Employee Mailing Labels**

You have given Access all the information it needs to create the labels. The other setting in this window displays the labels onscreen as they will appear when printed.

Choose: Finish

Maximize the Print Preview window. Zoom the window to 75% to see all three columns of labels.

Your screen should be similar to Figure 4-25.

75% zoom

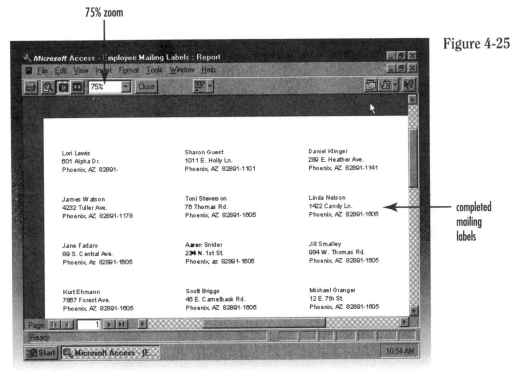

Figure 4-25

completed mailing labels

Three mailing labels appear across the width of the page. The placement of the labels on the page corresponds to the 5160 Avery labels you selected in the Labels Wizard. The labels are also sorted by zip code, from left to right across the rows, then down the page from top to bottom.

Print the page of labels that displays your name. Close the mailing labels report.

If you are ready, exit Access.

LAB REVIEW

■ ■ ■ ■ ■ ■ ■ ■ ▪ ▪ ▪

Key Terms

Detail Section   (DB175)
group   (DB168)
Group Footers   (DB175)
Group Header   (DB175)
Page Footer   (DB175)
Page Header   (DB175)
report   (DB157)
Report Footer   (DB175)
Report Header   (DB175)

Command Summary

Command	Toolbar	Action
View/Report/**D**esign		Displays report in Design view
View/La**y**out Preview		Displays report layout as it will appear when printed
View/**P**roperties		Displays properties for selected control
View/**Z**oom	`100%`	Changes magnification of Preview window
View/P**a**ges		Changes number of previewed pages
Insert/**R**eport		Creates new report

Matching

1. Summary Options   _____   a. creates a simple report using all fields in table
2. grouping   _____   b. displays a sample of how report will appear when printed
3. Page Footer section   _____   c. allow predefined calculations to be performed in grouped reports
4. Layout Preview   _____   d. displays entire page in Preview window
5. Report Footer section   _____   e. contains information that prints at top of first page of report
6. Detail section   _____   f. part of report that contains table data
7. AutoReport Wizard   _____   g. contains information that is printed at end of report
8. tabular style   _____   h. contains information that prints at bottom of each report page
9. Report Header section   _____   i. displays table fields as individual rows
10. View/Zoom/Fit to Window   _____   j. arranges data by major categories for clarity and ease of understanding

Fill-In Questions

1. Printed output generated from tables or queries is called a(n) _____.

2. The _____ creates a report that displays all the fields and records from the underlying table or query.

3. The _____ allows you to choose the fields to include in the report.

4. The _____ window displays the report on the screen as it will appear when it is printed.

5. You can display the whole page in the window by adjusting the magnification to _____.

6. Records _____ by categories allow better analysis of data.

7. Reports that are grouped can contain _____ fields.

8. The summary option that calculates the average value for a group is _____.

9. The _____ section of Report Design view contains information to be printed at the top of each page.

10. _____ and _____ can be added to the design of a report to enhance the report's appearance.

Discussion Questions

1. Discuss the advantages of creating reports.

2. Discuss how grouping records in a report makes the report more meaningful.

3. Discuss how queries can be used to create reports. What are the advantages of creating a report from a query?

4. Discuss how summary options can be used in a report. Give examples of the kinds of information that could benefit from summary data.

Hands-On Practice Exercises

Step by Step	Rating System	☆	Easy
		☆☆	Moderate
		☆☆☆	Difficult

☆

1. This problem is a continuation of Practice Exercise 4 in Lab 3. James O'Dell at Valley of the Sun Office Supplies is still worried about his inventory and his suppliers. He wants to print a report of all overstocked items so he can encourage his sales staff to push those items.

   a. To review James' query that locates the overstocked items, and to help him create a report based on the query, open the Valley of the Sun Office Supplies database you updated in Lab 3, then open the Queries tab and run the Overstocked Items query. Examine the data in the datasheet, then close the Query dynaset.

   b. To create James' new report, open the Reports tab, then create a tabular AutoReport based on the Overstocked Items query.

   c. Print the report, then close the Report window and save the report as Overstocked Items.

2. This problem is a continuation of Practice Exercise 3 in Lab 3. Michelle at Food for Thought Catering wants to know the sum of all the purchases made by each of her customers. She needs you to help her create a query to find the information and then a report to print it out.

   a. Open the Updated Catering Records database you updated in Lab 3. Create a new query and add the Billing and Customers tables to the design grid. Add the Company and the Amount fields to the grid, then save the query as Billing History. Run the query and review the data.

Michelle likes the data, but it does not explain exactly what she wanted to know. The query shows each invoice amount for every customer, but does not give a total of all invoices for every customer. You assure Michelle that you can best retrieve that information by creating a report that groups invoices by company then gives a sum for each company.

b. Close the query datasheet. Create a new report using the Report Wizard. Base the query on the Billing History query you just created, then add all fields in the query to the report.

c. Group the data by company and add a summary option to calculate the sum of the Amount field for each company. You think Michelle could also benefit from knowing what percentage of her business goes to each client, so check the Calculate Percent of Total for Sums box.

d. Select a layout, use portrait orientation, and choose an appropriate style. Name the report Income by Company, then preview the report.

e. As you look through the report, you notice that some company names do not display completely in the text box controls. Modify the report design by adjusting the text box controls and making changes to improve the report appearance, such as lines, text color, boxes, and font changes.

f. Preview, then print the report.

g. Close the Report window, saving any layout changes.

3. This is a continuation of Practice Exercise 5 in Lab 3. Michael at Go West Dude Ranch wants to know how he is spending his money. It seems to disappear quickly every time he does payroll. He also needs to know the total gross payroll per week so he can better budget his money. You assure Michael that you can get all the information he needs by creating a query and a report.

a. Open the Dude Ranch Payroll database you updated in Lab 3, then open the Weekly Paychecks query in Design view. You determine that this query will work well for the report you need, but you need to remove the criteria from the Pay Date column. Remove the criteria, save the query using the same name, and close the Query window.

b. Create a new report using the Report Wizard and base it on the Weekly Paychecks query you just updated. Add the Pay Date, Employee #, First Name, Last Name, and Gross Pay fields to the Selected Fields list box.

c. Group the report by Pay Date (Access will then group the Pay Date by month), then sort it by Pay Date (to divide the weeks within the months).

d. You decide that in addition to knowing the sum of his payroll, Michael might be better able to see how his money is being spent if he knows the average pay of his employees. Add Summary Options to calculate a sum and an average of the pay.

e. Select an appropriate layout, use landscape orientation so all the data will fit, and select a style. Name the report Payroll Summary, then preview the report.

f. Make any changes to adjust the size of controls, and improve the appearance of the report by adding such features as lines, color, and font changes. Then preview the report again. Print the report.

On Your Own

4. This problem is a continuation of Practice Exercise 1 in Lab 3. Debbie at Desert Rescue Cleaning Service wants to do some target marketing, sending flyers to all customers who have at least 10,000 square feet of space. She also wants to know what her average client in Arizona is like. She wants to determine this by examining the average rate and the average square feet of all her Arizona customers. Debbie calls you to help her out.

Open the Desert Rescue Cleaning Service database you updated in Lab 3, then create a new query, named Big Clients, that will select clients with at least 10,000 square feet of space.

After creating the query, you tell Debbie she can use it for many different reports. All she needs right now is mailing labels for those select few big clients. Create mailing labels for Debbie, then print the labels and save the report as Big Clients Labels.

To help Debbie with her other request, you need to create a new report based on the Clients table that will tell Debbie what the average rate and square footage are for all of her Arizona clients. (Hint: You should group the report by state, and format the square footage field to standard or fixed.) Make the report look attractive so Debbie can take the report to her next staff meeting. Name the report Average Arizona Clients, then print the report.

☆☆☆

5. This problem is a continuation of Practice Exercise 2 in Lab 3. Eddie at TechnoBabble needs his database updated again, and this time his cousin Teddy is on extended vacation in the Bahamas. Eddie calls you and wants your immediate attention. In between your other jobs and the work at the Dude Ranch, you rush over to help. Eddie needs a new table that lists his suppliers by code, name, and phone number, and he wants a form to use for data entry.

Using the TechnoBabble Electronics database you updated in Lab 3, create a table of suppliers to hold the information below and make the Supplier field the primary key field. Then create a form, Suppliers, to enter the information.

Supplier	Supplier Name	Phone Number
AMS	AMERICAN MEMORY SERVICE	(602) 555-7896
BOC	BALANCED OUTPUT COMPANY	(303) 555-3426
BTO	BETTER TECH OFFERINGS	(970) 555-8620
CCR	CRYSTAL CLEAR RADIOS	(619) 555-1762
CTC	CELLULAR TELEPHONE CO.	(202) 555-4139
HSC	HOME SECURITY CORP.	(602) 555-8760
LLM	LASER LIGHT MANAGEMENT	(602) 555-5700
MEE	MUSICAL ELECTRONIC ENGINEERING	(303) 555-1999

Now that the new information is in the database, Eddie wants to see a report showing the total value of both regular stock items and special order items that are currently on hand, grouped by supplier name and by status. Create a query, named Inventory Status, then a new report, named On Hand Inventory Status Report, to help Eddie find the data he needs. Print the report.

☆☆☆

6. This problem is a continuation of Practice Exercise 6 in Lab 3. Open the My Contacts database file you have been working on and last updated in Lab 3.

Create mailing labels for all the contacts in your table. Print the mailing labels.

Create a query and a report of your choice using the data in your database. Print the report.

Concept Summary

Creating and Modifying Reports
4

Reports

Reports are the printed output you generate from tables or queries.

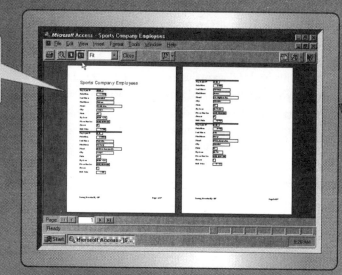

Group Calculations

If a report contains groups, you can perform calculations on the grouped data, such as a group total, an average, a minimum value, and a maximum value.

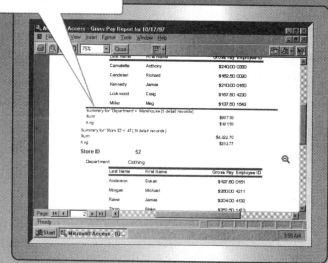

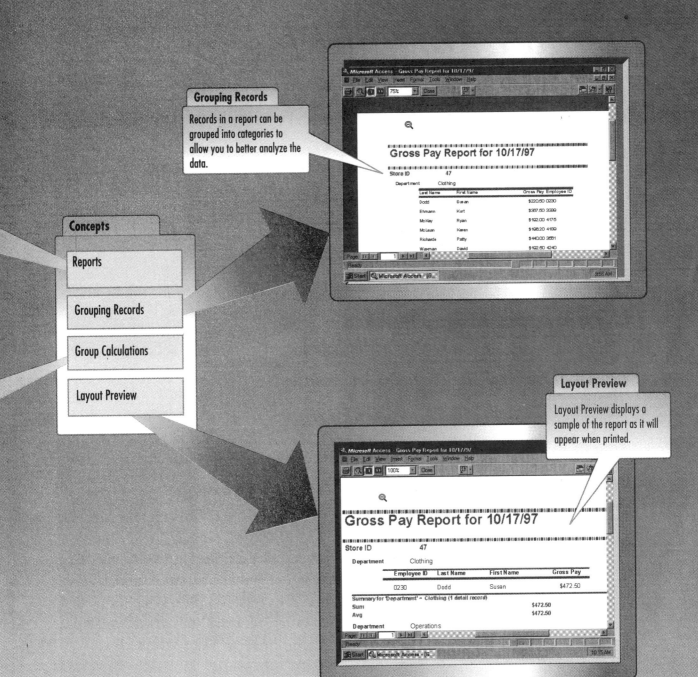

Concepts

Reports

Grouping Records

Group Calculations

Layout Preview

Grouping Records

Records in a report can be grouped into categories to allow you to better analyze the data.

Layout Preview

Layout Preview displays a sample of the report as it will appear when printed.

Sharing Information Between Applications

There are times you may want to include information created using Access in other applications. For example, you might want to include the results of a query in a memo. Or you might want to copy a table into a spreadsheet program where you can more easily perform mathematical analysis of the data. There may also be information from another application that you want to use in Access, such as data from another database file or spreadsheet.

L ike most other software applications, the files created using Access have their own unique format. Unfortunately, Access is not very amenable to sharing data between applications because of its unique format. However, it does provide a means for translating data into forms that can be used by other applications. It can also translate data from other applications into a format that can be used by Access.

Concept Overview

The following concepts will be introduced in this lab:

1. Importing and Exporting	Importing retrieves data that has been saved in another format into an Access table, and exporting saves data created using Access in another format.
2. Linked Object	Information can be pasted into another application document as a linked object that stores a graphic representation of the data in the destination document and creates a live link to the source document.

CASE STUDY

You have used Access to obtain information from the Employee database that was requested by the Regional Manager. Now you want to include the query results with a brief memo to the manager.

You have also been asked to create a letter to all employees, offering them a special employee credit card. You have created the letter and will perform a mail merge with data from the Sports Company Employees database to supply the inside address information for the letter.

Note: This lab assumes that you have completed Lab 3 of Access. You need the database file Sports Company Personnel Records that you saved at the end of Lab 3.

Part 1

Importing Access Data into a Word Document

Start the Access 7.0 program. Put your data disk in the appropriate drive for your system.

One of the first queries you created for the Regional Manager was a list of employees who were hired before 1/1/92.

Open the Sports Company Personnel Records database from your data disk. Open the Pre 1992 Hire Date query. If necessary, maximize the window.

Note: If a Parameters dialog box is displayed, choose ▭ OK ▭ to reset the sort order of the Department and Last Name fields in the query datasheet.

Your screen should be similar to Figure 5-1.

Figure 5-1

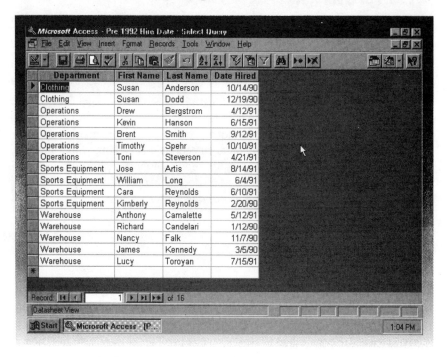

The 16 employees who were hired before January 1, 1992 are listed in the query datasheet. To copy the output from the query into a memo to the Regional Manager, you need to convert the query output to a file format that can be used in Word.

Access uses importing and exporting of data to assist in the data transfer between applications (see Concept 1). The Save As/Export command on the File menu is used to convert database objects into the different file formats that can be used in other applications. Alternatively, you can use drag and drop between the applications to copy the database object. Although drag and drop does not create a separate file, it converts the object into a rich text format that is accepted by Word. This is the file format you would most likely select of the three text file formats.

Refer to the Drag and Drop section of the Windows 95 Review for information on this feature.

Concept 1: Importing and Exporting

Importing retrieves data that has been saved in another format into an Access table, and **exporting** saves data created using Access in another format. There are many different types of file formats. Access will import and export data in the following formats.

Text files (.ASC, .TXT, .CSV, .TAB)—These include delimited text and fixed-width text.

Delimited text is a file containing values separated by commas, tabs, semicolons, or other characters, as in the following examples:

1/12/89 0:00:00,"Candelari","Richard"
2/20/89 0:00:00,"Reynolds","Kimberly"
3/5/89 0:00:00,"Kennedy","James"

Fixed-width text is a file containing values arranged so that each field has a certain width, as in the examples below:

1/12/89 0:00:00   Candelari   Richard
2/20/89 0:00:00   Reynolds   Kimberly
3/5/89 0:00:00   Kennedy   James

Rich text format—a file format that retains all the format settings such as font, alignment, and number formatting for column heads and data as shown below.

Date Hired	Last Name	First Name
1/12/89	Candelari	Richard
2/20/89	Reynolds	Kimberly
3/5/89	Kennedy	James

- Excel versions 3, 4, 5, 7 (.XLS)
- Lotus 1-2-3 releases 2.2–5.0 (.WKS, .WK1, .WK3)
- Paradox releases 3.0–5.0 (.PDX)
- FoxPro versions 2, 2.5, 2.6, 3.0 (.DBF)
- dBase III, IV, and V (.DBF)
- SQL Database

Access can import files saved in any of these formats and converts the information into an Access table. Access files that are exported to any of these formats can be read and used by any programs that use these formats.

DATABASE

To use drag and drop, both applications must be open and visible in the window. The memo to the regional manager has already been created using Word 7.0.

Load Word 7.0 for Windows 95. Open the document Query Results. Your screen should be similar to Figure 5-2.

Figure 5-2

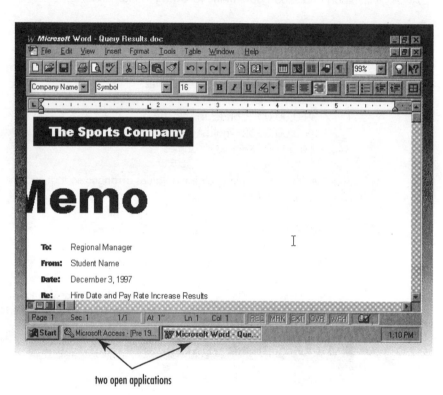

two open applications

This document contains the text of the memo to the manager.

Replace "Student Name" in the memo header with your name. Scroll the memo to read the memo text.

The memo consists of three paragraphs. It also includes blank space between paragraphs where you will enter the information from Access related to the topic discussed in the paragraph.

To display both applications at the same time on the desktop, tile the two open applications vertically in the window.

Now you are ready to use the drag and drop feature to copy and paste the query results.

Switch to the Access application window and use Edit/Select All Records to select the query datasheet table. Drag the selected table to the space below the first paragraph of the memo in the document.

> Refer to the Arranging Windows section of the Windows 95 Review for information on this feature.

> The mouse pointer is a 🔍 when you can drag the selection.

> You can also copy the query datasheet to the Clipboard and then paste it into the document.

Your screen should be similar to Figure 5-3.

Figure 5-3

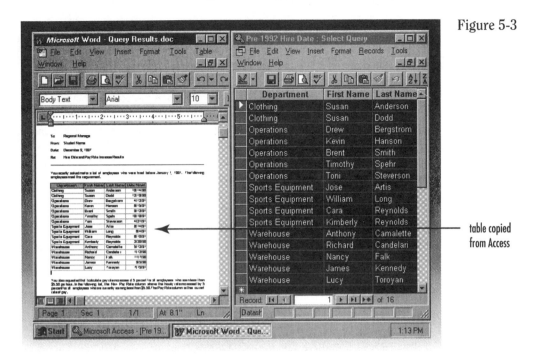

table copied from Access

The table is copied into the memo document. It appears as a formatted table, having retained the format settings that it had in Access. The table can now be manipulated like any other Word table.

Undo the vertical window tile. Switch to Word and scroll the memo to view the table. Move to the bottom of the table. Create a page break below the table.

> Press Ctrl + ←Enter to create a manual page break.

Linking an Access Table

The second query result you want to include in the memo calculated the pay rate increase for all employees who were earning less than $5.50 an hour. This query result will be displayed below the second paragraph of the memo. You saved this query as Pay Rate Increase.

Move to below the second paragraph of the memo (located on the second page).

As you consider the memo, you are concerned that the manager may ask you to modify the query to provide a different analysis of the pay rate increase. In anticipation of this possibility, you decide to link the query object to the memo. Then, if this request is made, the memo will automatically be updated when you modify the query.

Concept 2: Linked Object

You can also paste information into another application as a **linked object**. When an object is linked, the data is stored in the **source document** (the document it was created in). A graphic representation of the data is displayed in the **destination document** (the document in which the object is inserted). A connection to the information in the source document is established by the creation of an **object field code**. This code contains references to the location of the source document and to the object within the source document that is linked to the destination document. When changes are made in the source document that affect the linked object, the changes are automatically reflected in the destination document when it is opened. This is called a **live link**.

When you create links the date and time on your machine should be accurate. This is because the program refers to the date of the source file to determine whether updates are needed when you open the destination document.

To create a link to the query from within Word, you use the Database command on the Insert menu or the  button on the Database toolbar.

Display the Database toolbar.

The Database toolbar buttons are identified below.

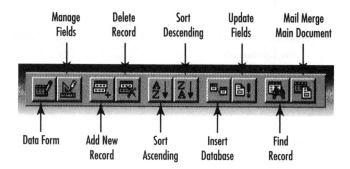

Click:  **Insert Database**

Your screen should be similar to Figure 5-4.

Database toolbar   Insert Database dialog box

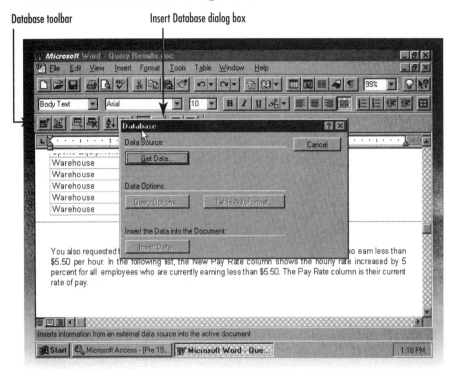

Figure 5-4

The Database dialog box appears. First you need to specify the database file to be inserted into the memo.

Select: **G̲et Data**

If necessary, select the drive containing your data disk from the Look In drop-down list.

The only files that are listed are Word document files, because the selected file type in the Files of Type drop-down list box is Word Document.

To display Microsoft Access file types, select MS Access Database [*.mdb] from the Files of Type drop-down list. Open the file Sports Company Personnel Records.mdb.

In the Microsoft Access dialog box, you select the table or query you want to insert in the Word document.

Open the Queries tab and select Pay Rate Increase.

Choose:  OK

The Database dialog box is displayed again. The Query Options button allows you to modify the query settings. Since you want it to appear as it is, you do not need to use this option. The AutoFormat button lets you select a format to apply to the table. If you do not select a format style, the datasheet is copied into the document as an unformatted table.

> You could also apply a format to the table after it is inserted into the document.

Select: T̲able AutoFormat...

> This text uses the Columns 1 AutoFormat style.

Select a style of your choice.

Choose: [OK]

Finally, to insert the data into the document,

Choose: **Insert Data**

From the Insert Data dialog box, to specify that all records are included in the inserted table, the All option is used. If necessary,

Select: **All**

Then, to insert the data as a field so the data can be updated whenever the source changes,

Select: **Insert Data as Field**
Choose: [OK]

The link to the database file and to the query object is established.
After a few moments your screen should be similar to Figure 5-5.

> If necessary, scroll the window to see the entire table.

Figure 5-5

Insert Database button

linked Access table

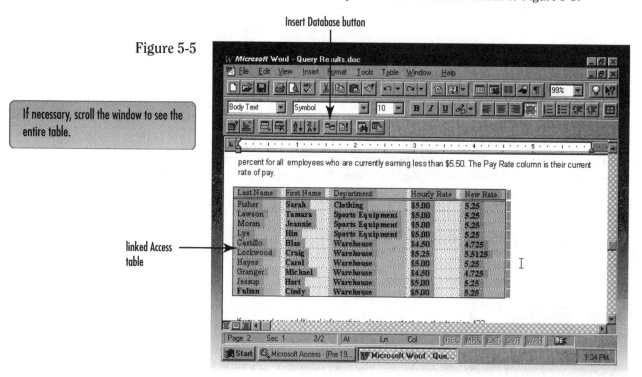

The table is inserted into the document in the selected format style. The table lists the 10 employees who earn less than $5.50 and their new rates of pay.

If necessary, insert a blank line between the paragraph and the table.

You dropped off a copy of the memo to the manager, and after a short time, you receive a call asking you to include employees who are earning $5.50 and to increase the pay rate percentage from 5 percent to 7.5 percent. To make these changes, you need to modify the query design.

Switch to Access. Close the Pre 1992 query. Open the Pay Rate Increase query in Design view.

Change the Hourly Rate criterion to <=5.50. Change the New Rate formula to calculate the increase at 7.5 percent. Run the query.

The query datasheet now lists 22 employees who earn $5.50 or less, and also lists their new pay rate based on a 7.5 percent increase.

Save the query using the same name.

Switch to Word.

The Word table has not changed to reflect the changes made in the source file. To update data in the fields,

Click: **Update Fields**

Your screen should be similar to Figure 5-6.

> The currency format set in query design for the calculated field is not copied to the Word document.

> If you were opening the Word document, the changes would be automatically updated.

> You can also press `F9` or choose Update Fields on the Shortcut menu. The object must be selected when you update it.

Update Fields button

Figure 5-6

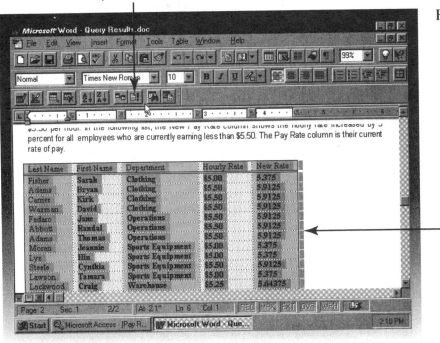

updated Access query in Word document

The table is redrawn to include the new records and now reflects the data in the revised query.

Update the memo text in the paragraph above the table to reflect the change in data shown in the table.

Save the memo using the filename Revised Query Results. Print the document. Close the Database toolbar. Exit Word.

Exporting Access Data to Excel

Next you want to copy the Gross Pay for 10/17/97 query datasheet to an Excel workbook so that you can perform additional mathematical analysis on the data.

Close the Pay Rate Increase query.

The Database window should be displayed. Rather than opening the query, you can simply select the query object name from the Queries tab and save it in an Excel file format.

Select (highlight) the Gross Pay for 10/17/97 query object name.

Choose: **File/Save As/Export**

The option To an External File or Database is selected. Since this is what you want to do,

Choose: OK

From the Save Query In dialog box, you specify the name and location of the new file. In addition, you must select the type of file you want it saved as.

If necessary, select the drive containing your data disk as the location to save the file.

Next you need to change the type of file to an Excel 7.0 file type.

Open the Save as Type drop-down list box and select Microsoft Excel 5-7.

The dialog box on your screen should be similar to Figure 5-7.

Figure 5-7

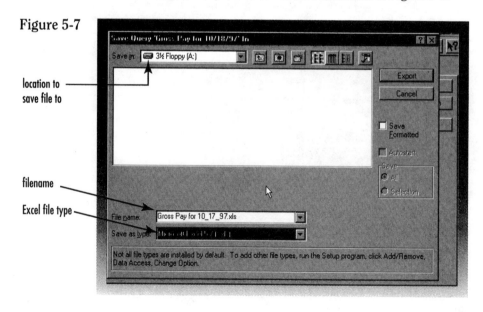

location to save file to

filename

Excel file type

The File Name text box displays the query name as the filename. Notice that the filename also displays the .XLS file extension of the selected file type.

You also want the saved file to include the formatting. This will preserve the fonts and field widths set in the query. To do this,

Select: **Save Formatted**

In addition, you can automatically open the Excel application and have the exported file opened in a new worksheet by using the AutoStart option.

Select: **AutoStart**
Choose: **Export**

The database query is saved to a file in an Excel file format, and Excel is loaded.

Your screen should be similar to Figure 5-8.

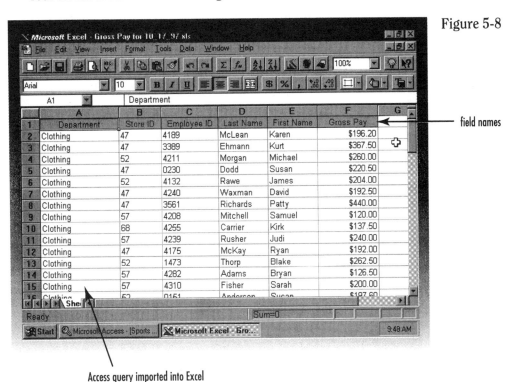

Figure 5-8

field names

Access query imported into Excel

The new workbook file is open with the information from the query displayed in it. The field names are placed in the first row of the spreadsheet, and the data begins in row 2. The column heads and column widths are formatted as they appeared in the query datasheet. Now the data can be manipulated using Excel commands and features. For example, it would be easy to calculate total and average values by departments.

Display a grand total of the Gross Pay column in cell F75.

The changes you have made to the worksheet do not affect the Access table from which the data was obtained.

Print the worksheet. Save the worksheet using the same filename. Exit Excel.

> Click Σ to sum the Gross Pay column.

Part 2

Creating a Mail Merge Using Word and Access

Note: It is helpful if you have completed the Merge section of Lab 4 of Word. If you have not, read the information in that section to become familiar with the procedure before completing the following section.

The Sports Company has also decided to send all its employees a Sports Company credit card. The body of the letter to accompany the credit cards has already been created and saved as Employee Credit Card Letter on your data disk. You want the letter to display each employee's name and address information as an inside address and to include the first name in the salutation.

This data is maintained in the Sports Company Employee table of the Sports Company Employee database. To include this information for each employee in the letter, you will perform a mail merge between Word and Access.

First you will need to create a query to include all fields needed in the inside address.

Create a query named Employee Address using the Sports Company Employees table that will display each employee's first name, last name, street, city, state, and zip code (in that order).

To help in sorting the mail, you would also like the merged letters in sorted order by zip code.

Set the sort order of the Zip Code field to ascending.

Finally, you want to test the merge with a small amount of records. You will limit the scope of the query to employees in the city of Chandler.

Enter Chandler in the City criteria field.

Then, to include your record in the query output, in the "or" row of the grid, enter your first and last name in the appropriate criteria fields.

Your screen should be similar to Figure 5-9.

Figure 5-9

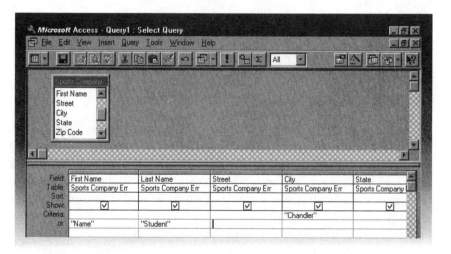

Run the Query.

The query result should display four records.

If the output does not display three records with a city of Chandler in addition to your record, fix the query grid criteria to achieve the correct results.

Save the query as Employee Address. Close the Query window. From the Database window, select the Employee Address query object.

The Mail Merge feature is used to insert field data from an Access table into a Word document. Performing a mail merge between Access and Word is part of the automated Office Links feature. The ⊞ Office Links drop-down list button includes three choices:

Merge It	Starts the Mail Merge Wizard that merges Access data with a Word document
Publish It with MS Word	Outputs to an .RTF file format, loads Word, and opens the file in a new document window
Analyze It with MS Excel	Outputs the object to an Excel file format, loads Excel, and opens the file in a new workbook

> ⊞ Merge It is the default Office Links button.

To perform a Mail Merge using the selected query object,

Click: ⊞ **Merge It**

> The menu equivalent is Tools/OfficeLinks/Merge It.

The Mail Merge Wizard dialog box is displayed. The default selection to link the data to an existing Word document is correct.

> You can also begin a mail merge from within Word.

Choose: OK

The Select Microsoft Word Document dialog box appears next.

If necessary, select the drive containing your data disk as the location.

Select: Employee Credit Card Letter document file
Choose: Open

If necessary, maximize the window.

Your screen should be similar to Figure 5-10.

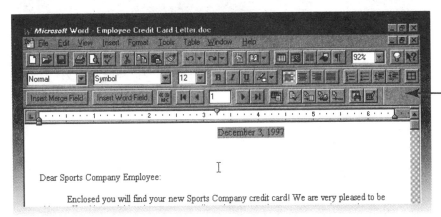

Figure 5-10

Mail Merge toolbar

Word is loaded, and the Employee Credit Card Letter document is opened. In addition, the Mail Merge toolbar is displayed. Next you need to enter the merge fields in the letter to create the inside address.

Move to the line above the salutation (Ln 4).

The first merge field you will specify will display each employee's first name in the inside address. To insert the first merge field code,

Choose: Insert Merge Field

From the drop-down list of field names,

Select: First_Name

Your screen should be similar to Figure 5-11.

Figure 5-11

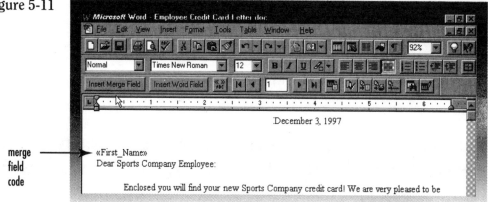

merge
field
code

The Last Name merge field will be entered next on the same line. To insert a space following the merge field code,

Press: Spacebar

Continue to select the field names to add the merge fields to the letter until your screen is similar to Figure 5-12.

Figure 5-12

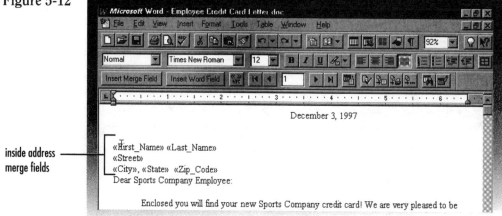

inside address
merge fields

Insert two blank lines above the salutation.

The last change you need to make to the document is to insert each employee's first name in place of "Sports Company Employee" in the salutation.

Replace the text "Sports Company Employee" with the First Name merge field.

You are now ready to merge the addresses from Access into the Word document. To do this,

Click:  **Merge to New Document**

The menu equivalent is Tools/Mail Merge/Merge/Merge.

Your screen should be similar to Figure 5-13.

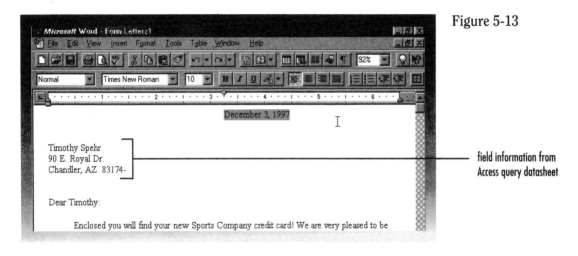

Figure 5-13

field information from Access query datasheet

After a few seconds, Word displays the first personalized letter. The field information from the first record in the query replaces the appropriate merge field codes. The merge fields create a link to the Access database and query. Whenever needed, you can reopen the Word document to print a batch of letters using the current data in the Access table.

Scroll the file to view the other letters. Print the letter displaying your information only. Close the merge document without saving it. Save the merge form letter document as Employee Credit Card Letter Merge. Close the document window.

Exit Word and Access.

LAB REVIEW

■ ■ ■ ■ ■ ■ ■ ■ ■ ■ ■

Key Terms

destination document   (DB198)
export   (DB195)
import   (DB195)
linked object   (DB198)
live link   (DB198)
object field code   (DB198)
source document   (DB198)

Command Summary

Command	Button	Action
Word		
Insert/Database		Inserts a database table or query into Word
Access		
Tools/OfficeLinks/Merge It	🅰️	Starts the Word Mail Merge

Fill-In Questions

1. Data that is _____ has been saved in another format into an Access table.

2. _____ saves data created using Access in another format.

3. Text that is _____ contains values separated by commas.

4. When an object is _____, the data is stored in the source document.

5. When a document has a(n) _____, changes are automatically reflected in the destination document.

Discussion Questions

1. Discuss the difference between importing and exporting data. Give examples of how each could be used.

2. Discuss the types of formats in which Access can save data. What feature is used to save data in a different format?

3. Discuss the differences between fixed-width and delimited text. Give examples of how data would be displayed with each type.

4. Discuss how an object can be linked from Access to another application. Discuss how a live link works.

Hands-On Practice Exercises

Step by Step

Rating System	
☆	Easy
☆☆	Moderate
☆☆☆	Difficult

1. This problem is a continuation of Practice Exercise 4 in Lab 3. James O'Dell, the manager of the Valley of the Sun Office Supply company, has asked you for an inventory report on all supplies whose cost is over $3.00 and quantity is more than 50.

    a. Open the Valley of the Sun Office Supply database and create a query that displays the item number, item name, and price of all products that have a quantity on hand greater than 50 and are priced over $3.00.

    b. Save the query as Stock with Quantities over 50.

    c. Open Word and enter the following text.

> **TO:**   **James Green**
>
> **FROM:**   [your name]
>
> **DATE:**   [current date]
>
> **Below is the information you requested on inventory.**

    d. Copy the query results into the Word document.

    e. Save the memo as Stock On Hand. Print the document.

2. To complete this problem, you will use the Sports Company Personnel Records database. The Sports Company wants to invite all employees who have worked for the company since before 1992 to a special recognition luncheon. You have been asked to write invitations to these employees.

    a. Open the Sports Company Personnel Records database file and select the Pre 1992 Hire Date query object.

    b. Load Word and create the following memo.

> **To:**   **Sports Company Employee**
>
> **From:**   [your name]
>
> **Date:**   [current date]
>
> **You are cordially invited to a luncheon in honor of all employees who have worked for The Sports Company since before 1992. The luncheon will be held at the Corporate Center on May 25. Please RSVP to your department manager by May 20.**

    c. Save the memo as Employee Luncheon.

    d. Merge the first and last names of the employees from the query in place of the "Sports Company Employee" text in the memo.

    e. Print one of the merged letters. Do not save the merged document. Resave the memo.

3. This problem is a continuation of Practice Exercise 5 in Lab 3. The Dude Ranch Payroll Service Company has recently introduced several new services. You have been asked to write a letter to all Phoenix customers announcing the new services.

    a. Open the database and create a query that contains the name and address information of all customers whose city is Phoenix.

b. Open Word and create the following letter:

[current date]

Dear Customer:

   The Dude Ranch Payroll Company is offering several new services described in the enclosed brochure. In appreciation for your business and as an incentive to try one of our new services, enclosed you will find a voucher for a 5 percent discount on the cost of our new services.

We hope to hear from you soon.

Sincerely,

[your name]

c. Save the letter as Dude Ranch New Services.

d. Enter merge fields in appropriate locations in the Word document. Merge the addresses from the Access query into the Word document. Print one letter from the merged document.

e. Do not save the merged document.

On Your Own

4. Debbie of Desert Rescue Cleaning Service would like you to create a letter to be sent to all her customers. Use the Desert Rescue Cleaning Service database for the names and addresses to be included in the letter. The letter should thank the customers for their loyalty and offer them a 10% discount for recommending another customer to Desert Rescue Cleaning Service. Merge the addresses from the database into the letter you create. Save and print the letters.

5. Using the Sports Company Personnel Records database, export the Pay Rate Increase query to Excel. In Excel, calculate the average Hourly Rate and New Rate by department and for all employees. Add a worksheet title. Include your name and the current date in a subtitle. Print the worksheet.

Sharing Information Between Applications

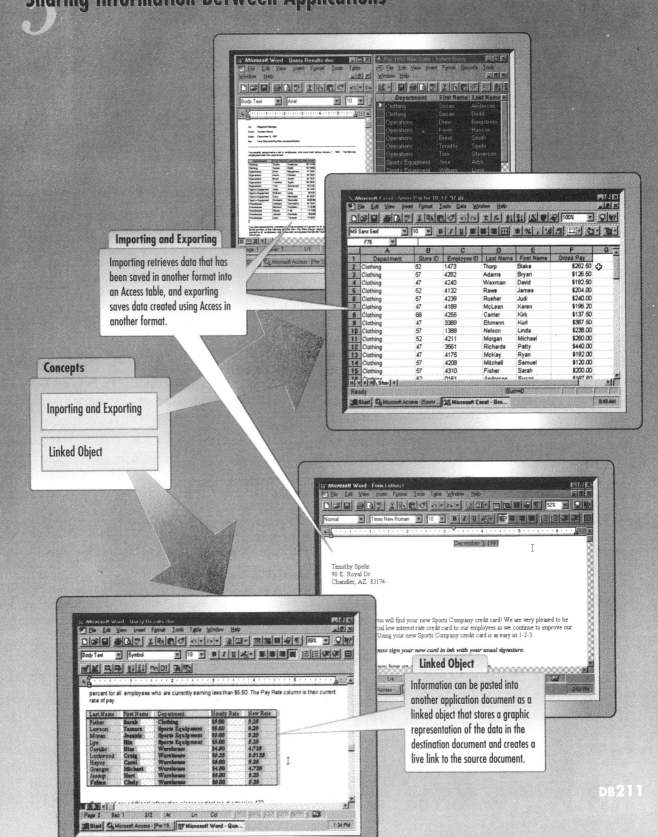

Importing and Exporting

Importing retrieves data that has been saved in another format into an Access table, and exporting saves data created using Access in another format.

Concepts

Inporting and Exporting

Linked Object

Linked Object

Information can be pasted into another application document as a linked object that stores a graphic representation of the data in the destination document and creates a live link to the source document.

Case Project

This project is designed to reinforce your knowledge of the database features used in the Access labs. You will also be expected to use the Help facility to learn more about advanced features available in Access.

Marianne Virgili is the Director of the Glenwood Springs Chamber Resort Association. The Director has asked you to create a database file of the Chamber members.

Part I

In this section you will create the tables that will make up your database.

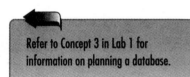

Refer to Concept 3 in Lab 1 for information on planning a database.

a. On paper, design a table to hold information about the Chamber members. The table should include a membership number, the business name, address (including street, city, state, and zip code), a telephone number, and contact name.

b. On paper, design a table to hold the types of businesses that belong to the Chamber Resort Association. This table should include the membership number, type of business, and the number of employees the business employs. (*Hint:* Companies employ a single number of employees, for example, "1" or "50", not "1 to 50".)

c. On paper, design a table to hold the dues payments for the Chamber members. This table should include the membership number, date the payment is due, and the amount of the payment. The amount of payment is based on the number of employees the company employs. The companies are divided into three categories: small (1 to 20 employees), medium (21 to 60 employees), and large (61 or more employees). Small companies' dues are $200, medium are $300, and large are $500.

d. In Access create a database to hold the three tables.

e. From your paper designs, create the three tables. Add descriptions to fields that do not have field names that fully describe how the data should be entered. Change the field widths and properties as necessary. Create key fields. Save the tables using appropriate names.

f. Create a customized form for each of the tables.

g. Use the customized forms to enter 25 members into the tables. (Add yourself as one of the company names.) Be sure to enter the same membership number for each individual member so the records can be joined in queries and reports. Also remember that the number of employees determines the payment amount due.

Part II

You will use the tables you created in Part I to create queries on the data.

a. Create a query that shows the membership number, member name, and the city. Sort the query by city.

b. Print the query datasheet.

c. Create a query that shows the types of businesses that belong to the Chamber Resort Association, along with the name, membership number, and number of employees they employ.

d. Sort the query by type of business and membership number.

e. Save the query as Member Type.

f. Print the query datasheet.

g. Create a query to display the members that employ more than 50 employees. Display any fields you feel would be appropriate in a report that contains this data.

h. Print the query datasheet.

Part III

In this section you will create reports from the data in your tables.

a. Create a customized report that shows the due date for all members whose dues are due from the current date to two months from now. Include any fields you feel would be appropriate for this report. Use groups if necessary and add an appropriate title.

b. Print the report.

c. Open the saved query Member Type. Create a customized report from the query. Group the report by type of business.

d. Print the report.

e. Create a customized report that groups the companies by categories (small, medium, and large). Total the dues payments for each group and display the percentage for each group. Include the members' names and any other fields that you feel are appropriate.

f. Print the report.

Glossary of Key Terms

Action query: Query used to make changes to multiple records in one operation.

Answer Wizard: Part of the Access Help feature that determines what type of help is needed based on questions typed into the Help screen.

AutoReport Wizard: Creates a report, either tabular or columnar, based on a table or query, and adds all fields to the report.

Best Fit: A feature that automatically adjusts column width to fit the longest entry.

Calculated field: Field based on information contained in multiple fields of the database, or the results of an expression rather than actual data.

Cell: The space created by the intersection of a vertical column and a horizontal row.

Column selector bar: In Query Design view, the thin gray bar just above the field name in the grid.

Column width: The number of characters that are displayed in a column.

Columnar form: A form layout that displays information in columns with labels (field names) down the left side of the form and text boxes in an adjacent column.

Comparison operator: A symbol used in expressions that allows you to make comparisons. The > (greater than) and < (less than) symbols are examples of comparison operators.

Compound control: Two related controls, such as a text box control and its associated label control.

Control: In Form and Report Design views, information such as text boxes that tell Access where to place data and text.

Criteria expression: An expression that will select only the records that meet certain limiting criteria.

Crosstab query: Summarizes large amounts of data in an easy-to-read, row-and-column format.

Current record: The record, containing the insertion point, that will be affected by the next action.

Database: An organized collection of related information.

Datasheet form: A form layout that is similar to a table datasheet, in that information is displayed in rows and columns.

Datasheet view: Window that displays a table, form, or query in row-and-column format.

Data type: Attribute for a field that determines what type of data it can contain.

Design grid: The lower part of the Query Design window, which displays settings that are used to define the query.

Design view: Used to create new database objects and modify the design of existing objects.

Destination document: The document in which a linked object is inserted.

Detail section: Section of Form and Report Design that contains the records of the table.

Edit mode: In Datasheet view, when an insertion point is displayed.

Export: To save data created using Access in another format.

Expression: Description of acceptable values in a validity check, which can contain any combination of the following elements: operators, identifiers, and values.

Field: A single category of data in a table, the values of which appear in a column of a datasheet.

Field list: A small window that lists all fields in an underlying table.

Field name: Label used to identify the data stored in a field.

Field property: An attribute of a field that affects its appearance or behavior.

Field selector: A small gray box or bar in datasheets and queries that can be clicked to select the entire column. The field selector usually contains the field names.

Field size: Field property that limits a text data type to a certain size or limits numeric data to values within a specific range.

Filter: A restriction placed on records in an open form or datasheet to temporarily isolate a subset of records.

Filter by Form: This feature provides a blank version of the current form or datasheet. Values are typed into the blank form or selected from a pull-down list. Records are filtered based on the values entered into the blank form.

Filter by Selection: A type of filter that displays only records containing a specific value.

Font: The typeface, size, and style of printed characters.

Form: A database object used primarily for data entry and making changes to existing records.

Form Datasheet view: Row-and-column layout of the fields and data in the form.

Form Design view: Used to create or modify a form.

Form Footer: Displays information such as instructions, notes, or grand totals. A form footer appears at the end of the last page of a form.

Form Header: Displays information such as a title, instructions, or graphics. The form header appears at the top of the screen or, if printed, on the first page.

Form Preview: Displays the form as it will appear when printed.

Form view: Used to enter, edit, and view data. Form view is easier to work with than Datasheet view.

Formatting toolbar: In Form and Report Design views, contains buttons used to customize the appearance of the form or report.

Group: A way of organizing data on a common attribute. When data is grouped, calculations can be performed on all data in each group.

Group Footer: Section of Report Design that contains group totals.

Group Header: Section of Report Design that contains information on the groups.

Identifier: A part of an expression that refers to the value of a field, control, or property.

Import: To retrieve data that has been saved in another format into an Access table.

Inner join: The most common type of join between tables.

Input mask: Used in fields and text boxes to format data and provide control over what values can be entered into a field.

Join: Creates a relationship between tables by linking common fields in multiple tables.

Junction table: The third table in a many-to-many relationship, the one that serves as a bridge between tables.

Label: Descriptive titles, instructions, or notes found on a form or report.

Landscape: Printing orientation that prints a report across the length of the page.

Layout Preview: A fast way to check layout of a report using only a sampling of the data.

Linked object: An object that is pasted into another application. The data is stored in the source document, and a graphic representation of the data is displayed in the destination document.

Literal character: A value such as a number, string, or date that Access evaluates exactly as entered.

Live link: When the source document is edited, the changes are automatically reflected in the destination document.

Many-to-many relationship: Records in both tables can have many matching records in the other table.

Mask character: A character used in an input mask.

Monospaced: Describes a font in which the width of each character takes up the same amount of space.

Multitable query: A query that uses more than one table.

Navigation buttons: Used to move through records in Datasheet and Form views. Also available in the Print Preview window.

Navigation mode: In Datasheet view, when the entire field is highlighted.

Object: A table, form, or report that can be selected and manipulated as a unit.

Object field code: Points to the location of the source document.

Object tab: In the Database window, used to select the type of object.

One-to-many relationship: Records in one table can have many matching records in a second table but the second table can only have one match in the first table.

One-to-one relationship: Records in both tables only have one matching record.

Operator: A symbol or word used to make a comparison.

Orientation: The direction the paper prints, either landscape or portrait.

Page Footer: Section of Report Design that contains information to be printed at the bottom of each page.

Page Header: Section of Report Design that contains information to be printed at the top of each page. The column headings displaying the field names are displayed in this area.

Parameter query: Query that prompts for a criterion before locating the data.

Pitch: A measurement of the width of characters.

Point: A measurement of the height of characters. One point equals approximately 1/72 inch.

Portrait: Printing orientation that prints the report across the width of a page.

Primary key: One or more fields in a table that uniquely identify a record.

Print Preview: Displays the entire report page by page as it will appear when printed.

Proportional: Describes a font in which some letters, such as m or w, take up more space than other letters, such as i or t.

Query: Used to view data in different ways, to analyze data, and to change data.

Query datasheet: Where the result or answer to a query is displayed.

Record: A row of a table, consisting of a group of related fields.

Record number indicator: A small box that displays the current record number in the lower left corner of most views. The record number indicator is surrounded by the navigation buttons.

Record selector column: Displayed to the left of the first column; it can be used to select an entire record in Datasheet view.

Relational: Database in which a relationship is created by having a common field in the tables. The common field lets you extract and combine data from multiple tables.

Relationship: A link made between tables, usually through at least one common field.

Report: Printed output generated from queries or tables.

Report Footer: Section of Report Design that contains information to be printed once at the end of the report.

Report Header: Section of Report Design that contains information to be printed once at the beginning of the report. By default, the report title and date are displayed in this area.

Scalable: A font that can be printed in almost any type size, depending on the capabilities of the printer.

Select query: Retrieves data you request and displays it in a query datasheet in the order you specify.

Selection handles: Boxes that surround a selected object.

Sort: A temporary record order in the Datasheet that reorders records in a table.

Source document: The document in which a linked object is created.

SQL query: Query created using Structured Query Language.

Startup window: The initial Access window.

Summary options: Options for performing summary calculations on groups of data in a grouped report. Includes sum, average, minimum, and maximum.

Switchboard: Startup window that makes it easier to move from one task to another in a database.

Tab order: The order in which Access moves through a form or table when the Tab key is pressed.

Table: Consists of vertical columns and horizontal rows of information about a particular category of things.

Tabular form: A form layout in row-and-column format with records in rows and fields in columns.

Template: Includes predefined settings for creating databases.

Text box: Used on a form or report to display data from a table or query.

Toolbox: Set of tools used to place controls on a form or report.

Typeface: The appearance and shape of characters, such as Times Roman and Courier.

Type size: The height or width of characters.

Type style: The special attributes assigned to characters, such as bold, italic, or underline.

Undo: A feature used to cancel your last action.

Validation text: Text that is displayed when a validation rule is violated.

Validity check: Process of checking to see whether data meets certain criteria.

Value: A part of an expression that is a number, date, or character.

Wildcard characters: Placeholders for other characters when using Find and Replace, queries, filters, and expressions.

Command Summary

Command	Shortcut	Toolbar	Action
File/New Database	Ctrl + N	🗋	Opens a new database
File/Open Database	Ctrl + O	📂	Opens an existing database
File/Close	Ctrl + W	▦	Closes open window
File/Save	Ctrl + S	🖫	Saves the open object
File/Page Setup			Displays Page Setup dialog box
File/Print Preview		🔍	Displays file as it will appear when printed
File/Print	Ctrl + P	🖨	Prints contents of file
File/Exit	Alt + F4	✕	Exits Access from current window
Edit/Undo Current Field/Record	Esc	↶	Cancels last action
Edit/Cut	Ctrl + X, Delete	✂	Deletes selected record
Edit/Select Record	⇧Shift + Spacebar		Selects current record
Edit/Select All	Ctrl + A		Selects all controls in Form and Report Design view
Edit/Find	Ctrl + F	🔎	Locates specified data
Edit/Replace	Ctrl + H		Locates and replaces specified data
Edit/Delete Column	Delete		Removes selected column from design grid
Edit/Delete Row		⇥	Deletes selected field from table in Design view
Edit/Primary Key		🔑	Defines a field as a primary key field
Edit/Clear Grid			Clears all fields from design grid
Edit/Clear Filter		✕	Clears all expressions in filter form
View/Query Design		▨	Displays Query Design view
View/Datasheet		▦	Displays table data in Datasheet view

Command	Shortcut	Toolbar	Action
View/Zoom		100%	Changes magnification of Preview window
View/Pages			Changes number of previewed pages
View/Properties			Displays properties for selected control
View/Form Design			Switches to Form Design view
View/Totals		Σ	Displays Total row in design grid
Insert/Database			Inserts a database table or query
Insert/Field			Inserts a new field in table in Design view
Insert/Report			Creates a new report
Filter/Apply Filter/Sort			Applies filter to table
Query/Run			Displays query results in Query Datasheet view
Query/Show Table			Displays Show Table dialog box and adds a table to Query window
Format/Column Width			Changes width of Datasheet columns
Format/Hide Columns			Hides selected columns in Datasheet view
Format/Unhide Columns			Redisplays hidden columns
Format/Align/Left			Aligns selected controls to left
Format/Size/To Fit			Sizes selected controls to fit data in control
Format/Vertical Spacing/Make Equal			Equalizes vertical space between selected multiple controls
Records/Filter/Filter by Form			Activates Filter by Form feature
Records/Filter/Filter by Selection			Activates Filter by Selection feature
Records/Sort/Ascending			Reorders records in ascending alphabetical order
Records/Apply Filter/Sort			Applies the open filter to the data and displays the dynaset
Records/Remove Filter/Sort			Removes sort order or filter and redisplays original records and order
Records/Data Entry			Modifies Datasheet by hiding existing records and entering Data Entry mode
Tools/OfficeLinks/Merge It			Starts a Word Mail Merge
Window/1 <Name>: Database			Displays another database window
Help/Answer Wizard			Displays Help feature

Windows 95 Review

The following is an alphabetical arrangement of the most common Windows 95 features. The features are described in general. Wherever applicable, a How To section discusses how to perform the task.

Arranging Windows: There are two ways to arrange windows: cascade and tile.

Cascade	Layers open windows, displaying the active window fully and only the title bars of all other open windows behind it.
Tile	Resizes each open window and arranges the windows vertically or horizontally on the desktop

Cascading windows is useful if you want to work primarily in one window but you want to see the title of other open windows. Tiling is most useful when you want to work in several applications simultaneously, because it allows you to quickly see the contents of all open windows and move between them. However, the more windows that are open, the smaller the space available to display the tiled window contents.

The commands to tile windows on the Windows 95 desktop are displayed in the taskbar shortcut menu. In most Windows 95 applications, the commands are found in the Window menu.

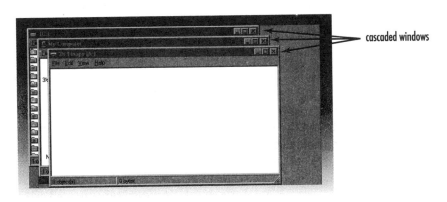

cascaded windows

three vertically tiled windows

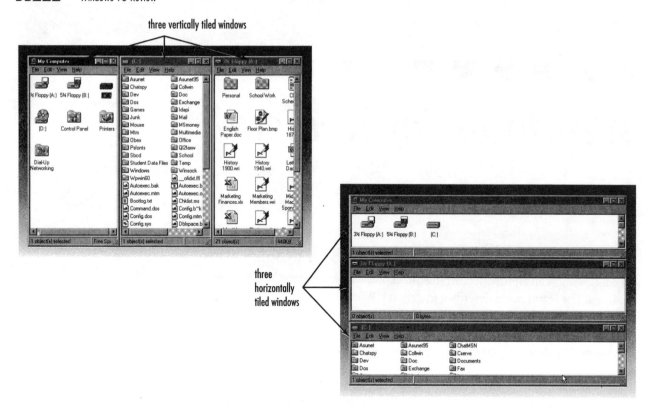

three horizontally tiled windows

Cut, Copy, and Paste: All Windows applications include features that allow you to remove (cut), duplicate (copy) and insert (paste) information from one location to another. The location that contains the information you want to cut or copy is called the source. Then the command to cut or copy the selection is used, and the selection is stored in a temporary storage area in your computer's memory called the Clipboard. Finally, you select the location, called the destination, where you want to insert a copy of the information stored in the Clipboard and use the Paste command.

How To: The commands to perform these tasks are found in the Edit menu. The toolbar equivalents are ✂ Cut, 📋 Copy, 📋 Paste, and the keyboard shortcuts are Ctrl + X to Cut, Ctrl + C to Copy and Ctrl + V to Paste. The information must be selected before it is copied or cut.

Desktop: The Windows 95 screen is called a desktop. It displays icons that represent various tools and features. Like your own desk at home, you can add and remove items from the desktop, rearrange items, or you can get rid of them by throwing them away in the "trash." You can also open items and, much like a drawer in your desk, find other tools or materials you have stored. You can place these items on the desktop or take items off the desktop and place them in the "drawer." Just like your own desk, your most frequently used items should be on the desktop so you can quickly begin work, while those items that you use less frequently should be put away for easy access as needed.

Dialog Box: A dialog box is how Windows programs provide and request information from you in order to complete a task. All dialog boxes have a title bar at the top of the box that displays a name identifying the contents of the dialog box. Inside the dialog box are areas to select or specify the needed information and command buttons.

How To: Select an item in a dialog box by clicking on the item, by pressing [Alt] and the underlined letter, or by tabbing to the item. Type information in a text box. Select (highlight) an item in a list box. Click on option buttons and check boxes to turn on/off the item.

Tab dialog box: Many dialog boxes include tabs that open to display options related to the feature in the tab. The tab names appear across the top of the dialog box and indicate the different categories of tabs. The tab name of the active tab is displayed in bold. The options displayed in the open tab are the available options for the feature.

How To: To select and open a tab in a tab dialog box, click on it with the mouse or move to the tab using [Ctrl] + [Tab↹] to select the tab to the right or [Ctrl] + [⇧Shift] + [Tab↹] to select the tab to the left.

Dialog Box features: The features shown in the table below are found in dialog boxes. However, not all features are found in every dialog box.

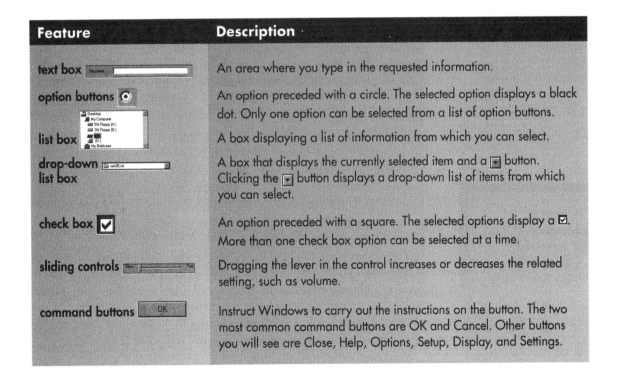

Feature	Description
text box	An area where you type in the requested information.
option buttons	An option preceded with a circle. The selected option displays a black dot. Only one option can be selected from a list of option buttons.
list box	A box displaying a list of information from which you can select.
drop-down list box	A box that displays the currently selected item and a ▼ button. Clicking the ▼ button displays a drop-down list of items from which you can select.
check box	An option preceded with a square. The selected options display a ☑. More than one check box option can be selected at a time.
sliding controls	Dragging the lever in the control increases or decreases the related setting, such as volume.
command buttons	Instruct Windows to carry out the instructions on the button. The two most common command buttons are OK and Cancel. Other buttons you will see are Close, Help, Options, Setup, Display, and Settings.

Drag and Drop: Common to all Windows applications is the ability to copy or move selections by dragging and dropping. This feature is most convenient for copying or moving short distances or when the place you want to drag and drop to is visible onscreen. Using drag and drop does not copy to the Clipboard.

How To: First select the item to be copied or moved. Then point to the selection and drag. A drag-and-drop insertion point $+$ appears while dragging to show where the selection will be pasted. When you release the mouse button, the selection is copied or moved to the new location. To copy, hold down Ctrl while dragging. The mouse pointer displays a + when you copy.

Editing: Making changes to or correcting existing entries is called editing. Editing is commonly performed in all applications as well as within text boxes used in dialog boxes or Wizards.

How To: Generally, editing is performed by moving the insertion point to the location of the error, deleting the text that needs to be modified, and retyping the entry correctly. Two frequently used keys to delete entries are the Backspace key (removes characters to the left of the insertion point) and the Delete key (removes characters to the right of the insertion point). You can also select the text to be removed and replace it with existing text as you type.

Files and Folders: The information your computer uses is stored in files. The instructions used to run a program are stored in program files. For example, the word processing program on your computer consists of many files that contain the program statements required to use the program. The information you create while using a program is stored in data files. For example, if you write a letter to a friend using the word processing program, the contents of the letter are stored as a data file.

In addition, you can create folders and subfolders in which you store files that are related. Storing related files in folders keeps the disk organized and makes it much easier to locate files. Both files and folders are identified by names that are descriptive of the contents of the file or folder.

The organization of folders, subfolders, and files on your disk is called a hierarchy or tree. The top-level folder of the disk is the main or root folder. This folder is created when the disk is formatted. All folders are branches from the main folder. Subfolders are branches under a folder. Files can be stored in the root folder, a folder, or a subfolder. The figure in (left) is a graphical representation of folders and subfolders.

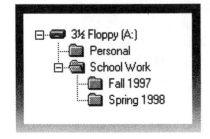

Help: The Windows Help facility is a quick way to find out information about commands or features. The Help menu is always the last menu in the menu bar and always contains a Help Topics command. This command opens the Help Topics tab dialog box. The three tabs, Contents, Index, and Find, provide different methods of getting help information. The Find tab allows you to select a word from a list that you need help on and then locates and displays all topics containing the word. The Contents tab displays broad Help categories preceded with book icons. Clicking on the book opens the book and displays additional books or specific Help topics. Topics are preceded with a ? icon, and when selected open the related Help window. The Index tab area allows you to select a topic from a list that you need help on. Windows Help can also display brief screen tips.

How To: Select Help Topics from the Help menu to open the Help dialog box. Clicking ▣ What's this? in a dialog box and then clicking on the area in the box that you want Help information on displays a Screen Tip for the item. Clicking the ▣ button in the toolbar displays Help Screen Tips on toolbar buttons, commands, or other items on the screen.

Insertion Point: The insertion point appears in a text entry area to show your location within the text. It appears as a vertical blinking bar.

How To: The insertion point is moved using the directional keys or by clicking in the text at the location you want the insertion point to appear. The mouse pointer appears as an I-beam when positioned in text, to make it easy to indicate where to move the insertion point.

Menus: A menu is one of many methods you can use to tell the program what you want it to do.

Start menu: The Start menu is a special Windows 95 menu that is used to access and begin all activities you want to perform on the computer.

How To: Click the Start button on the taskbar to open the Start menu.

Menus bars: Most menus are displayed in the menu bar immediately below the title bar of the window. When opened, a menu displays a list of commands, called a drop-down menu. Horizontal lines within many menus divide the commands into related groups.

How To: Most menu bar menus can be opened simply by clicking on the menu name. Using the keyboard, you need to press [Alt] or [F10] and type the underlined letter of the menu name. To clear a menu without making a selection, click anywhere outside the menu or press [Esc].

Shortcut menus: Other menus, called Shortcut menus, pop up when you right-click on an item. They contain commands related to the object you were pointing to when you right-clicked.

How To: Right-click an item to display its Shortcut menu.

Selecting and Choosing commands: Once a menu is open, you can select and choose commands from the menu. Selecting indicates a command is "ready" to be used. Choosing a command performs the action associated with the command.

How To: You select a command by moving the highlight bar, called the selection cursor, to the command. Simply pointing to the command moves the selection cursor to it. (You can also move the selection cursor with the directional keys on your keyboard if it is more convenient.) You choose the selected command by clicking on it, or by typing the underlined command letter, or by pressing ⌐Enter⌐. When the command is chosen, the associated action is performed.

Menu features: The features shown in the tables below are found on menus. However, not all features are found on every menu.

Feature	Description
ellipses (...)	Indicates that a dialog box will be displayed for you to specify additional information needed to carry out the command.
▶	Indicates a submenu of commands will be displayed.
dimmed command	Indicates that the command is not available for selection until certain other conditions are met.
shortcut key	A key or key combination that can be used to execute a command without using the menu.
checkmark (✔)	Indicates a toggle type command. Selecting it turns the feature on and off. The checkmark indicates the feature is on.
Bullet (•)	Indicates that the commands in that group are mutually exclusive: only one can be selected. The bullet indicates the currently selected feature.

A mouse

Mouse: The mouse is a hand-held hardware device that is attached to your computer. It controls an arrow ▹ called the mouse pointer that appears on your screen. The pointer movement is controlled by the rubber-coated ball on the bottom of the mouse. This ball must move within its socket in order for the pointer to move on the screen. The ball's movement is translated into signals that tell the computer how to move the onscreen pointer. Some computers use a track ball to move the mouse pointer. The direction the ball moves controls the direction the pointer moves.

The mouse pointer changes shape on the screen depending on what it is pointing to. Some of the most common shapes are shown in the table on the next page (right).

How To: Moving the mouse across your desktop moves the pointer in the direction you are moving the mouse. The mouse is held in the palm of your hand with your fingers resting on the buttons. If you pick up the mouse and move it to another location on your work surface, the pointer will not move on the screen.

On top of the mouse are two buttons. You use these buttons to choose items on the screen. The mouse actions and descriptions are shown in the next table.

Action	Description
Point	Move the mouse so the mouse pointer is positioned on the item you want to use.
Click	Quickly press and release the left mouse button.
Double-click	Quickly press and release the mouse button twice.
Drag	Move the mouse while holding down a mouse button.
Right-click	Quickly press and release the right mouse button.

Pointer Shape	Meaning
	Select
	Horizontal Resize
	Vertical Resize
	Diagonal Resize
	Move
	Help Select
	Unavailable
	Wait
	Text Select

Moving Windows: When open, windows may appear in different locations on your desktop. Sometimes the location of the window is inconvenient. Moving a window simply displays the window at another location on the desktop. It does not change the size of the window.

How To: A window is moved by clicking on the title bar and dragging an outline of the window to the new location on the desktop.

Naming Files: To save your work as a file on the disk, you must assign it a filename. The filename should be descriptive of the contents of the file. Windows 95 applications allow you to use long filenames of up to 255 characters. A filename can contain the letters A to Z, the numbers 0 to 9, spaces, and any of the following special characters: underscore (_), caret (^), dollar sign ($), tilde (~), exclamation point (!), number sign (#), percent sign (%), ampersand (&), hyphen (-), braces ({}), parentheses (), "at" sign (@), apostrophe ('), and the grave accent (`). Filenames cannot contain commas, backslashes, periods or any the following characters: \ / : * ? " < > |.

In addition to a filename, a filename extension can be added. A filename extension is up to three characters and is separated from the filename by a period. Generally a filename extension is used to identify the type of file. It is not always necessary to enter a filename extension, because most application programs automatically add an identifying filename extension to any files created using the program. For example, Word 7.0 files have a filename extension of .doc. The parts of a file name are shown below:

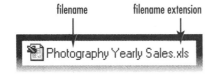

filename   filename extension

DATABASE

Properties: Properties are the settings associated with objects and files.

> **How To:** An object's properties can be viewed using the View/Properties command or the Shortcut menu. A file's properties are viewed and changed using the File/Properties command. The Properties command is also commonly located on the Shortcut menu. The Property sheet displays the property settings.

Saving Files: While using any application, the document you are creating is stored in your computer's temporary memory as you work. It is lost if you do not save your work to a file on a disk. The file is a permanent copy of your document that is named and can be accessed at a later time. Although many programs create automatic backup files if your work is accidentally interrupted, it is still a good idea to save your work frequently.

> **How To:** Two commands on the File menu of all Windows programs can be used to save a file: Save and Save As. The Save command saves a document using the same path and filename by replacing the contents of the existing disk file with the changes you have made. The Save As command allows you to select the path and provide a different filename. This command lets you save both an original version of a document and a revised document as two separate files. When you save a file for the first time, either command can be used.

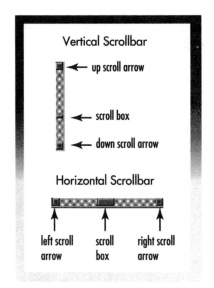

Vertical Scrollbar

←— up scroll arrow

←— scroll box

←— down scroll arrow

Horizontal Scrollbar

left scroll arrow   scroll box   right scroll arrow

Scroll Bar: Whenever there is more information than can be displayed in a window or list box, a scroll bar is displayed. It is used with a mouse to bring additional lines of information into view. The vertical scroll bar is used to move vertically, and the horizontal scroll bar moves horizontally in the space. All scroll bars have scroll arrows and a scroll box. The location of the scroll box on the scroll bar shows your relative position within the area of available information. In many scroll bars, the size of the scroll box also indicates the relative amount of the information that is available. For example, a small box indicates that only a small amount of the total available information is displayed, whereas a large box indicates that almost all or a large portion of the total amount of available information is displayed.

> **How To:** Clicking the scroll arrows in the vertical scroll bar scrolls the information in the window line by line vertically in the direction of the arrows. Clicking the scroll arrows in the horizontal scroll bar moves the information in the window horizontally. Dragging the scroll box moves vertically or horizontally to a general location within the area. Clicking above or below the scroll box moves information by screenfuls within the window.

Selecting: When an item is selected, it is highlighted and will be affected by the next action that is performed.

How To: Clicking an item on the screen selects the item. The keyboard can also be used to select items. Generally, pressing Tab⇆ moves the highlight forward to the next item and ⇧Shift + Tab⇆ moves it backward.

Selecting Text: Selecting text expands the highlight to cover the area of text that will be affected by your next action. Selecting text is commonly used to modify existing entries in a dialog box and in most applications.

How To: There are many methods you can use to select an area of text. The most common method is to drag the mouse across the text. You can drag in any direction in the document to extend the highlight. You can drag diagonally across text to extend the highlight from the character the insertion point is on to the last character in the selection. You can also drag in the opposite direction to deselect text. Additionally, you can use the keyboard to select text by holding down ⇧Shift while pressing a directional key. Either method requires that you move the insertion point to the beginning or end of the area to be selected before you select it. You can also select the entire document using the Select All command on the Edit menu in all Windows 95 applications. Pressing Delete removes all selected text. Typing new text automatically replaces all selected text.

Sizing Windows: A window may appear on the desktop in different sizes, and sometimes the current size is too small or too large. A window can be changed to just about any size you want.

How To: Clicking the ▣ Maximize button enlarges a window to its largest possible size, and clicking the ▣ Minimize button reduces a window to a button. A window can be custom sized by pointing to the window border and dragging the border. Dragging inward decreases the size, and dragging outward increases the size. Dragging a corner increases or decreases the size of the two adjoining borders at the same time.

Status Bar: A status bar at the bottom of the window displays information about program settings you are using and the task being performed.

Toolbar: The toolbar is a bar of button icons displayed below the menu bar. Toolbar buttons replace menu selections for many of the most common commands. The icons graphically represent the feature that is activated when selected.

How To: Click on the button to activate the command. A Tooltip consisting of the button name and a brief description displayed in the status bar can be displayed for each toolbar button by pointing to the button.

DATABASE

Undo: Common to all Windows applications is the ability to undo the effects of last action or command. However, some actions you perform cannot be undone. If the Undo command is unavailable, it appears dimmed and you cannot cancel your last action. Some programs allow you to undo multiple actions, up to a certain limit.

How To: Choose the Undo command from the Edit menu. The keyboard shortcut is Ctrl + Z, and the toolbar button equivalent is ↶ Undo. If the Undo button displays a ▾, clicking it displays a drop-down list of the most recently performed actions that can be undone. Selecting from the list reverses the selected action as well as all subsequent actions.

Window: A window is a rectangular section of the screen that is dedicated to a specific activity or application. The window border outlines the window. All windows have the basic parts shown below:

Feature	Description
title bar	A bar located at the top of the window that displays the application name.
Control-menu box	An icon located on the left end of the title bar that when opened displays the Control menu. This menu consists of a list of commands that are used to move, size and otherwise control the window.
Minimize button ▭	Used to reduce a window to a button.
Maximize ▢	Used to enlarge a window to its maximum size.
Restore button ▤	Returns the window to its previous size.
Close button ☒	Used to exit the application running in the window and close the window.
menu bar	Displays a list of menus that can be used within the application displayed in the window.
scroll bar	Whenever the window cannot fully display the information, a scroll bar is displayed.

Windows 95: Windows 95 is an operating system program that controls all the parts of your computer. It uses a graphical user interface (GUI, pronounced "gooey") that displays pictures called icons representing the items you use. The icons are buttons that when "pushed" activate the item.

All Windows programs have a common user interface, which makes it easy to learn and use all types of programs that run under Windows. A common user interface means that programs have common features, such as menu commands and toolbars. For example, a command such as Save in a spreadsheet program is also found on the same menu (File), has the same toolbar button, and performs the same action as it does in a word processing program.

Index

Notes